T0338648

Cryptography
in the Information
Society

Highly Recommended Titles

Cryptology for Engineers: An Application-Oriented Mathematical Introduction
by Robert Schmied
ISBN: 978-981-120-804-1
ISBN: 978-0-00-098922-2 (pbk)

Cryptography
in the Information
Society

Boris Ryabko

Russian Academy of Sciences, Russia &
Novosibirsk State University, Russia

Andrey Fionov

Siberian State University of Telecommunications and
Information Sciences (SibSUTIS), Russia

 **World Scientific**

NEW JERSEY · LONDON · SINGAPORE · BEIJING · SHANGHAI · HONG KONG · TAIPEI · CHENNAI · TOKYO

Published by

World Scientific Publishing Co. Pte. Ltd.

5 Toh Tuck Link, Singapore 596224

USA office: 27 Warren Street, Suite 401-402, Hackensack, NJ 07601

UK office: 57 Shelton Street, Covent Garden, London WC2H 9HE

Library of Congress Control Number: 2020949542

British Library Cataloguing-in-Publication Data
A catalogue record for this book is available from the British Library.

CRYPTOGRAPHY IN THE INFORMATION SOCIETY

ISBN 978-981-122-615-1 (hardcover)
ISBN 978-981-122-616-8 (ebook for institutions)
ISBN 978-981-122-617-5 (ebook for individuals)

For any available supplementary material, please visit
https://www.worldscientific.com/worldscibooks/10.1142/11988#t=suppl

Desk Editor: Nur Izdihar Binte Ismail

Typeset by Stallion Press
Email: enquiries@stallionpress.com

Printed in Singapore

Preface

The aim of the authors was to provide a comprehensive introductory course on cryptography without resorting to complex mathematical constructions. All themes are conveyed in a form that only requires the knowledge of secondary school mathematics. The higher-algebraic terminology (rings, fields, etc.) is mostly not used since it may be foreign to the majority of the intended readers. Nevertheless, all mathematical results are strict and consistent. All methods are described in sufficient detail to enable their computer implementation. Justification for every method is always given, sometimes with reference to known results in number theory and other fields. When it is appropriate, algorithms written in pseudo-code are provided. Numerical examples are supplied for all methods.

Our experience in teaching students in Finland and Germany shows that there is a lack of such books. Of course, there are lots of books on cryptography in English. But many books are too comprehensive and too difficult to study. On the other hand, there are very easy books that just review cryptographic methods and techniques without elucidating how they "work". The authors believe they have found a golden mean between the two poles.

The book describes the main techniques and features of contemporary cryptography in such a way that key results are strictly proved. The topics covered include block ciphers, stream ciphers, public key encryption, digital signatures, cryptographic protocols, elliptic curve cryptography, theoretical security, blockchain and cryptocurrencies, issues of random numbers, and steganography. Preference is given to the methods that become (part of) cryptographic standards.

We assume that the primary readership will be academia — students and teachers in the field of information technology. There are chapters and sections that can be taught at the undergraduate, graduate and PhD levels. Typical courses may be titled as "Cryptography", "Data security", "Information security", etc. We also suggest that the book will be helpful for IT specialists from industry who wish to become qualified users of cryptographic algorithms, and those who are looking for an elementary course to start a career as a developer of cryptosystems.

We hope that the present book will help the reader not only understand the main problems and methods of contemporary cryptography but also appreciate the beauty and elegance of its ideas and results.

B. Ryabko
A. Fionov

Acknowledgments

The work is supported by the Russian Foundation for Basic Research under the grant no. 18-29-03005.

Contents

Chapter 1

Introduction

Let us begin the study of cryptography with the classic problem of transmitting secret messages from a sender A to a receiver B. Both the sender and the receiver may be persons, organizations, or various technical systems. Sometimes one speaks of A and B as of subscribers of some network, users of some computer system, or, more formally, abstract "parties" or "entities" participating in an information exchange. But it is often more convenient to identify the participants in such an exchange as humans and to use the names Alice and Bob instead of A and B.

It is assumed that messages are transmitted over an open communication channel which can potentially be accessed by a third party different from the sender and receiver. Such a situation arises in radio transmission (say, from a mobile phone) and is possible even in such "trusted" systems as wire telephones and telegraphs, as well as in ordinary mail. The Internet, as the leading channel of communication for people all over the world, is known to be extremely vulnerable to unauthorized access by third parties. In this environment, not only the copying of data, but also the deletion of data and the substitution of data with other data, is easily implemented.

It is generally assumed in cryptography that the person who sends and/or receives messages has an adversary or enemy E, who can be a competitor in business, a member of a criminal group, a foreign intelligence agent, or even an excessively jealous spouse, and that the adversary can read and analyze the messages transmitted. The adversary is often thought of as a person called Eve who has powerful computing facilities and is able to use cryptanalytic methods. Of course, Alice and Bob want their messages to be completely unclear to Eve, and, to achieve this, they use appropriate ciphers.

Before A transmits a message to B over an open communication channel, A encrypts (or enciphers) the message. In his turn, B, after having received the encrypted message (ciphertext), decrypts (or deciphers) it to recover the initial text (plaintext). It is important for the problem considered in this chapter that Alice and Bob can agree in advance about the cipher to be used (or rather about certain parameters thereof) *not via an open channel* but via a special "secure" channel which is inaccessible to Eve. Such a secure channel can be maintained with the aid of trusted messengers or couriers, or Alice and Bob can agree on the cipher during a private meeting, etc. It is necessary to take into account that, usually, maintaining the secure channel and transmitting messages over this channel is much more expensive compared with transmitting messages over an open unsecured channel, and (or) that the secure channel cannot be used at any time. For instance, courier post is far more expensive than the regular post. Courier post also transmits messages much slower than, say, electronic mail, and it might not be possible to use it at any hour and in any situation.

For something more concrete, consider the example of a cipher. Since the need for encryption began centuries ago, some ciphers are named after renowned historical persons. These ciphers are often used to introduce simple initial concepts and we shall follow that tradition. Let us start with a well-known cipher by Gaius Julius Caesar. In this cipher, each letter of a message is replaced by the letter which is 3 letters ahead of it in the alphabet. For instance, the letter A is replaced by D, the letter B by E, and so on. The last 3 letters X, Y, Z are replaced by A, B, C, respectively. Thus the word SEQUENCE transforms into VHTXHQFH under the Caesar cipher.

Other Roman Caesars have modified the cipher by using shifts of 4, 5, and sometimes more letters. We can describe such ciphers in a general way if we enumerate (encode) the letters by their ordinal numbers (from 0 to 25). Then the rule of encryption will be

$$c = (m + k) \bmod 26, \qquad (1.1)$$

where m and c are the ordinals of letters of plaintext and ciphertext, respectively, and k is an integer called the cipher key (in the Caesar cipher considered above, $k = 3$). (Here and after $a \bmod b$ denotes the remainder from the division of integer a by integer b, the remainder being taken from the set $\{0, 1, \ldots, b - 1\}$. For instance, $13 \bmod 5 = 3$.)

To decrypt the ciphertext one should apply an "inverse" algorithm

$$m = (c - k) \bmod 26. \qquad (1.2)$$

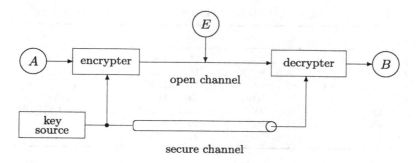

open channel

secure channel

Fig. 1.1   A classic secret communication system.

Let's imagine that the sender and receiver have agreed to use the cipher (1.1) but, to make the adversary's job more difficult, decide to occasionally change the cipher key. For that purpose, Alice somehow generates the number k and sends it to Bob over a secure channel, after which they communicate messages encrypted with that k. The key may be changed prior to each communication session or after transmitting a specified number of letters (say, every ten letters is enciphered using a different key) and so forth. In this situation, the key is said to be generated by a key source. A schematic view of the cryptosystem considered is shown in Fig. 1.1.

Proceed now to the discussion about the actions of the adversary who tries to recover the message and find the secret key, or, in other words, to break the cipher. Every attempt to break a cipher is called an *attack* to the cipher (or cryptosystem). It is generally assumed in cryptography that the adversary always has the ciphertext at her disposal and can learn everything about the encrypting algorithm used and the nature of data transmitted, but only does not know the secret key. These are Kerckhoffs's assumptions, named after the scientist who was the first to formulate the main requirements of ciphers [Kerckhoffs (1883)]. Sometimes these assumptions may seem "overcautious" but such "overcautiousness" is by no means superfluous if, say, you send an order to transfer one million dollars from one account to another.

In our example, Eve knows that the plaintext was encrypted according to (1.1), the message is in English, and the ciphertext is VHTXHQFH. But the key is unknown to her.

The most obvious method to recover plaintext from ciphertext is to search through all possible keys (this is a so-called *brute-force attack* or *exhaustive key search*). Thus Eve successively tries all possible keys

Table 1.1   Decrypting the word VHTXHQFH by exhaustive key search.

k	m	k	m	k	m	k	m
1	UGS	8	NZ	15	GS	22	ZL
2	TF	9	MYKOY	16	FRD	23	YK
3	SEQUENCE	10	LX	17	EQC	24	XJ
4	RD	11	KWI	18	DP	25	WIU
5	QC	12	JV	19	COAE	26	VHTXHQFH
6	PB	13	IU	20	BN		
7	OAM	14	HT	21	AMY		

$k = 1, 2, \ldots$, applying them to the decrypting algorithm and estimating the results of decryption. Let us also try to use this method. The results of decrypting the ciphertext VHTXHQFH according to (1.2) under various keys are shown in Table 1.1. In the majority of trials it was sufficient to decrypt only a few letters to reject the corresponding key due to the non-existence of a word in English that begins with these letters.

We can see from Table 1.1 that the key $k = 3$ was used and hence the message SEQUENCE was enciphered. Moreover, when checking for the other possible values of the key, it was not necessary to decrypt all 8 letters since the key might often be rejected after 2 or 3 initial letters have been decrypted. This example shows that the Caesar cipher is completely insecure: in order to break it, one needs to analyze several initial letters of the message, after which the key is disclosed unambiguously and, consequently, the whole message may be deciphered.

Why is the cipher which we have considered a weak one, and how might its security be increased? Consider another example. Suppose that Alice hid some important documents in a safe with a 5-digit combination lock. Now she would like to tell Bob the combination for opening the safe. She decides to use an analogue of the Caesar cipher adapted to the digits of the decimal number system:

$$c = (m + k) \bmod 10. \tag{1.3}$$

Suppose she has sent Bob the ciphertext 26047. Eve tries to decrypt it, as earlier, by searching through all possible keys. The results of her work are shown in Table 1.2.

We can see that all the variants are equivalent and Eve cannot decide on which combination is the correct one. Based on the ciphertext only, she is unable to find the secret key. Of course, before intercepting the encrypted message she had 10^5 possible lock combinations, and after that only 10.

Table 1.2 Decrypting the sequence 26047 by exhaustive key search.

k	m	k	m
1	15936	6	60481
2	04825	7	59370
3	93714	8	48269
4	82603	9	37158
5	71592	0	26047

But it is important to note that in this particular example we have only 10 possible values of the key. Under such a key (comprising only one decimal digit) Alice and Bob could not count on better security.

The message in our first example is a text in natural language (English). So it obeys numerous rules, the various letters and their combinations have different probabilities and, in particular, many combinations are forbidden (this property is referred to as redundancy of the text). And that is why the key was easily found and the message recovered, i.e. the redundancy had made it possible to break the cipher. In contrast, in our second example, all combinations of digits are admissible. The "language" of the combination lock does not possess any redundancy. Therefore even a simple cipher applied to messages in that language becomes unbreakable. In one of the classical works of cryptography [Shannon (1949)], a deep and elegant theory of secret key ciphers is constructed and, specifically, a "correct" measure of redundancy is suggested. We shall briefly touch upon these topics in Chap. 7, and in Chap. 8 some modern secret key ciphers will be described.

The attack to the cipher considered in the previous examples is said to be a *ciphertext-only attack*. But sometimes a so-called *known-plaintext attack* to the cipher may occur. This happens if Eve has at her disposal some plaintexts corresponding to previously transmitted ciphertexts. Eve tries to discover the secret key by examining the plaintext–ciphertext pairs. If she succeeds, she will be able able to decrypt all further messages from Alice to Bob.

One can imagine an even more "serious" attack, a so-called *chosen-plaintext attack*. In this attack, an adversary not only can access some plaintext–ciphertext pairs but is also able to create plaintexts on her own and encrypt them under the embedded key that she wants to discover. For instance, during World War II, Americans, having bribed the guards, stole the cipher-machine in the Japan Embassy for two days during a weekend and had an opportunity to input various plaintexts and to obtain their corresponding ciphertexts. They could not open the machine to directly determine the installed key because the damage would be detected and all the keys immediately changed (this and many other stories can be found in [Kahn (1967)]).

It may seem that the known- and chosen-plaintext attacks are rather artificial and hard to maintain. It is so to some extent. But the designers of modern cryptosystems strive to make them invulnerable even to those kinds of attacks and there are great achievements in this direction. It is customary to think that it is more reliable to use a cipher secure against chosen-plaintext attacks rather than to organizationally ensure the impossibility of such attacks. Extremely cautious people do both things.

So, we have become acquainted with the main characters of cryptography — Alice, Bob, and Eve — and with important notions of that science — a cipher, a key, an attack, open and secure channels. Note that an intriguing fact is connected with the last item: it is possible to construct secure cryptosystems without secure channel! In such cryptosystems Alice and Bob compute a secret key in such a way that Eve cannot reproduce the computation. This discovery was made in the seminal works [Diffie and Hellman (1976); Mercle (1979)] and has constituted a new epoch in modern cryptography. The main part of this book will be devoted to this kind of cryptosystem, referred to as *public-key* or *asymmetric-key* schemes.

Problems and Exercises

1.1 Find the keys of the Caesar ciphers if the following plaintext–ciphertext pairs are known:

(a) ORANGE – FIREXV
(b) APRICOT – XMOFZLQ

1.2 Decrypt the following messages encrypted with the Caesar cipher and an unknown key k, $0 < k < 26$:

(a) UNSJFUUQJ
(b) GUHAI

Chapter 2

Public Key Cryptosystems

2.1 Prehistory and Main Ideas

Let's consider three problems whose solutions will help us better understand the ideas and methods of public-key cryptography. All these problems are of great practical interest.

The first problem is storing passwords in a computer. We know that every user in a network has a confidential password. In order to log in to the network the user has to type in his/her login name (usually, publicly known) and password. The issue is the following: if the password is stored on a computer disk, then Eve can read it through perhaps, temporarily dismounting the disk. Therefore it is necessary to store passwords in such a way that they cannot be read (but can still be verified).

The second problem has occurred due to advent of radars and systems of air defense. When a plane crosses a border, the radar system asks for a password. If the password is valid then the plane is admitted, otherwise the flight is denied. The problem here is that the password has to be transmitted over a public open channel (air) and can therefore be overheard by the enemy. When an enemy plane is asked for a password, it can simply replay the intercepted one and get admittance.

The third problem is similar to the previous one. It arises in computer networks with remote access, e.g. in interactions between a bank and a client. In the beginning of a session the bank asks the client for the userid and password, but Eve can overhear the transmission since the communication line is public.

Nowadays all these problems are solved by applying cryptographic methods. The solution is based on the important notion of the one-way function.

Definition 2.1. Let there be a function

$$y = f(x) \tag{2.1}$$

defined on a finite set X $(x \in X)$, for which the inverse function exists

$$x = f^{-1}(y). \tag{2.2}$$

The function is said to be one-way if Eq. (2.1) is "easy" to compute for all x but for "essentially all" y the reverse computation (2.2) is "infeasible" (say, it requires 10^6–10^{10} years on a supercomputer).

This definition is certainly informal. A rigorous definition of a one-way function may be found in the literature (see, e.g. , [Menezes *et al.* (1996); Goldwasser and Bellare (2008)]) but for our purposes the one given above will suffice.

As an example of a one-way function, let us consider the following:

$$y = a^x \bmod p, \tag{2.3}$$

where p is a large prime number (i.e. an integer that is divisible only by 1 and itself) and a and x are positive integers (some restrictions will apply in the sequel). The inverse function is denoted as

$$x = \log_a y \bmod p \tag{2.4}$$

and is called the *discrete logarithm*.

To make the computation of (2.4) really infeasible on all modern computers one has to use numbers of length more than 512 bits. In practice, other one-way functions are also used, e.g. so-called *hash functions* (considered in Chapter 8) that operate with shorter numbers of length 128–160 bits.

First we show that the computation of (2.3), i.e. modular exponentiation, can be carried out fast. Begin with the example of the computation of $a^{16} \bmod p$. We can write

$$a^{16} \bmod p = (((a^2)^2)^2)^2 \bmod p,$$

i.e. the value of this function is obtained for 4 modular multiplications instead of 15 in the "naive" variant $a \times a \times \cdots \times a$. This is what the general algorithm is based upon.

To describe the algorithm we introduce the quantity $t = \lfloor \log_2 x \rfloor$, i.e. the integer part of $\log_2 x$ (in what follows all logarithms are binary, so we shall not indicate the base 2 henceforth). Compute the series of numbers

$$a, \quad a^2, \quad a^4, \quad a^8, \quad \ldots, \quad a^{2^t} \quad (\bmod\ p). \tag{2.5}$$

In (2.5) each number is obtained by squaring the preceding number modulo p. Write the exponent x in the binary system:

$$x = (x_t x_{t-1} \ldots x_1 x_0)_2.$$

Then the value $y = a^x \bmod p$ can be computed as

$$y = \prod_{i=0}^{t} a^{x_i \times 2^i} \bmod p \tag{2.6}$$

(all operations are modulo p).

Consider an example. Let us compute the value of $3^{74} \bmod 100$. We have $t = \lfloor \log 74 \rfloor = 6$. Compute the series of numbers (2.5):

$$
\begin{array}{ccccccc}
3 & 3^2 & 3^4 & 3^8 & 3^{16} & 3^{32} & 3^{64} \\
3 & 9 & 81 & 61 & 21 & 41 & 81.
\end{array} \tag{2.7}
$$

Write the exponent in the binary system:

$$74 = (1001010)_2$$

and compute by (2.6):

$$
\begin{array}{ccc}
3^{64} & 3^8 & 3^2 \\
\end{array}
$$
$$81 \times 1 \times 1 \times 61 \times 1 \times 9 \times 1 = 69. \tag{2.8}$$

As few as 8 multiplications were required (6 multiplications for the computation of (2.7) and 2 for that of (2.8)).

In the general case, we have the following:

Proposition 2.1. (complexity of exponentiation) *The number of multiplications required to compute* (2.3) *using the described method does not exceed* $2 \log x$.

Proof. To compute the series (2.5) t multiplications (squarings) are required, to compute y by (2.6) we need at most t multiplications (see the example on page 9). So the total number of multiplications does not exceed $2t$. Since $t = \lfloor \log x \rfloor \leq \log x$ the correctness of the proposition is obvious. $\qquad\qquad \Box$

Table 2.1   The number of multiplications required for computing direct and inverse functions.

The number of decimal digits in p	Computation of (2.3) ($2\log p$ multiplications)	Computation of (2.4) ($2\sqrt{p}$ multiplications)
12	$2 \times 40 = 80$	2×10^6
60	$2 \times 200 = 400$	2×10^{30}
90	$2 \times 300 = 600$	2×10^{45}

Remark 2.1. It will be shown later that in exponentiation modulo p, it makes sense to use only exponents $x < p$. So we can say that the number of multiplications required to compute (2.3) does not exceed $2\log p$.

It is important to note that as effective algorithms for computing the inverse function (2.4) are unknown, one of the methods, called the "baby-step giant-step" algorithm, will be described in detail in Sec. 3.2. This method requires on the order of $2\sqrt{p}$ operations. Let us show that under large p the function (2.3) is actually one-way if the "baby-step giant-step" algorithm is used. The results are given in Table 2.1.

We can see that if the length of the modulus is about 50–100 decimal digits then the direct function can be computed shortly but the inverse one is practically non-computable. Consider, for example, a supercomputer that multiplies two 90-digit numbers for 10^{-14} sec (for contemporary computers this is not achievable). To compute (2.3) such a computer will require

$$T_{\text{dir.}} = 600 \times 10^{-14} = 6 \times 10^{-12}\,\text{sec}$$

but to compute (2.4)

$$T_{\text{inv.}} = 10^{45} \times 10^{-14} = 10^{31}\,\text{sec},$$

i.e. more than 10^{22} years. We see that the computation of inverse functions is practically impossible if the length of the numbers is about 90 decimal digits and the use of parallel and distributed systems does not essentially affect the situation. In the example considered, we assumed that the inverse function was computed for $2\sqrt{p}$ operations. At the present time, "faster" methods for computing discrete logarithms are known but the pattern is the same: the number of required operations is far greater than $2\log p$. So, we can conclude that the function (2.3) is indeed one-way with only one reservation: nobody has strictly proved that the inverse function (2.4) cannot in principle be computed as fast as the direct function.

Now we shall use the one-way function (2.3) to solve all three problems stated at the beginning of the section, taking into account that any other one-way function may be used instead.

Begin with the concept of storing passwords in a computer. The solution to the problem is based on the idea that passwords are not stored at all! To log in to the computer the user types in his/her login name and password. Let, for instance, the login name be "fruit" and the password "apricot". The computer treats the word "apricot" as the binary record of the number x and computes (2.3), where a and p are two non-secret numbers, perhaps, publicly known. After that the computer creates and stores the pair (login name, y), where y is obtained from (2.3) under $x =$ password. Upon the user's login, after entering the pair ("fruit", "apricot"), the computer finds by (2.3) a new value y_{new} under $x =$ "apricot" and compares it with the y already stored in the memory. If y_{new} is the same as the y corresponding to the specified login name the user is admitted to the system. Otherwise, access is denied.

Eve might try to find x if she somehow learned y. However we have seen that even with 90-digit numbers it would require more than 10^{22} years. In that way, the presented scheme of storing passwords is reliable and used in many operating systems.

Let us discuss a solution to the second problem (a plane and air defense system). One can use the following method. Each "legitimate" plane is assigned a secret name (i.e. password) which is known only to the air defense system and to the pilot (or, more precisely, to the on-board computer). Let, for instance, one of the planes be assigned the secret name FALCON. Let the plane be approaching the border on January 1, 2019 at 12:45. Then the on-board computer constructs the word

$$\text{FALCON} \quad 19 \quad 01 \quad 01 \quad 12 \quad 45$$
$$(\text{name} \quad \text{year} \quad \text{month} \quad \text{day} \quad \text{hours} \quad \text{minutes}).$$

In other words, the on-board computer, as well as the radar system, appends the time stamp to the name. Now they treat the word obtained as the number x and compute $y = a^x \bmod p$, where a and p are non-secret. After that, the plane communicates the number y to the radar system. The latter compares its own y to the received value. If both values are equal the plane is admitted as legitimate.

The enemy cannot break this system. On the one hand, she does not know the secret name FALCON and cannot recover it from y, since finding

x given y requires, say, 10^{22} years. On the other hand, she cannot replay the same y in the future as the response to the radar system since the time of crossing the border will never be the same and the subsequent values of y will differ from the one stored by the enemy.

This way solving the "air defense" problem requires precise synchronization of the clocks on the plane and in the radar system. The issue can be easily settled. For instance, the navigation control service could periodically transmit time stamps and all radars and planes could use these to synchronize their clocks. But there are more delicate issues. A time stamp is appended to the word x in order to make all computed values of y different and to preclude replaying by the enemy. However, the enemy may try to replay y immediately within the current minute. How can we prevent this from happening? This is the first question. The other difficulty arises in a situation when the plane sends the number y at the end of the 45th minute, and the radar receives it at the beginning of the 46th. We give the reader an opportunity to independently offer a variant of the solution that takes into account these issues.

The other way of solving the "air defense" problem is possible if we use an extra communication channel to transmit data from the radar system to the plane. As before, each "legitimate" plane is assigned a secret name such as FALCON, which is also known to the radar. Having located a target, the radar sends a randomly generated number a (a "challenge"). The plane computes $y = a^x \bmod p$, where x is the secret word (FALCON) and communicates y (a "response") to the radar. The radar performs the same computations and compares the received and computed values of y. In this scheme, synchronizing clocks is not needed but, as in the earlier case, the enemy cannot replay y since the radar sends a different challenge (a) each time. It is interesting that this problem, apparently, was historically the first to be solved with the aid of one-way functions.

The third problem is solved quite similarly and both methods of transmitting passwords are applicable and used in practical network protocols.

2.2 The First Public-Key System — Diffie–Hellman Key Agreement

This cryptosystem was discovered in the mid-70-s by Whitfield Diffie and Martin Hellman [Diffie and Hellman (1976)] and caused a revolution in cryptography and its applications. It was the first system that allowed people to protect information without using secret keys transmitted over secure channels. As an example of one of the applications of such a system, consider a communication network with N users, where N is large. Suppose we are to organize secret communications for each pair of users. If we use an ordinary key distribution scheme, then each pair of users must be supplied with its dedicated secret key which results in the total number of keys being $\binom{N}{2} = N(N-1)/2 \approx N^2/2$.

So if we have 100 users then 5000 keys are required, and if we ever have 10^4 users then as many as 5×10^7 keys must be supplied. We can see that under the large number of users the system of supplying secret keys becomes very bulky and expensive.

Diffie and Hellman have solved this problem by means of the public distribution and computation of keys. The system suggested will be described in the following paragraphs.

Denote the users of a network by $A, B, C, \ldots$. For all the users the following common parameters are chosen: a large prime number p and an integer g, $1 < g < p-1$, such that all numbers from the set $\{1, 2, \ldots, p-1\}$ that might be represented as powers of g modulo p (i.e. $g^1, g^2, \ldots, g^{p-1} \pmod{p}$) are different numbers; such a g is called a *generator* and various approaches are known for finding generators, one of which will be presented below). The numbers p and g are assumed to be non-secret and known to all the users.

The users choose large numbers X_A, X_B, $X_C, \ldots$, which are kept in secret and called their *private keys* (it is usually recommended that the choice be made randomly with the aid of random number generators). Then every user computes a corresponding number Y and sends it to the other users in the clear,

$$Y_A = g^{X_A} \bmod p,$$
$$Y_B = g^{X_B} \bmod p, \qquad (2.9)$$
$$Y_C = g^{X_C} \bmod p.$$

The numbers $Y_A, Y_B, Y_C, \ldots$ are called the *public keys* of the users. All the information we know about the users is collected in Table 2.2.

Suppose user A wants to securely communicate with user B and they both have the public information from Table 2.2. User A asks B over an open channel to start a communication session. Then A computes

$$Z_{AB} = (Y_B)^{X_A} \bmod p \qquad (2.10)$$

Table 2.2   User keys in Diffie–Hellman system.

User	Private key	Public key
A	X_A	Y_A
B	X_B	Y_B
C	X_C	Y_C

(nobody else can do that since X_A is kept secret). Concurrently user B computes

$$Z_{BA} = (Y_A)^{X_B} \bmod p. \tag{2.11}$$

Proposition 2.2. $Z_{AB} = Z_{BA}$.

Proof. Indeed,

$$Z_{AB} = (Y_B)^{X_A} \bmod p = (g^{X_B})^{X_A} \bmod p$$
$$= g^{X_A X_B} \bmod p = (Y_A)^{X_B} \bmod p = Z_{BA}.$$

(Here the first equality follows from (2.10), the second and fourth from (2.9), and the last from (2.11).) $\square$

Review the main properties of the system:

(1) users A and B have obtained the same number $Z_{AB} = Z_{BA}$ that was not transmitted over the open channel;

(2) Eve cannot compute Z_{AB} since she does not know the secret numbers X_A and X_B (strictly speaking, she might try to find secret X_A from Y_A (see (2.9)), however under large p, this is practically impossible (or would require millions of years)).

Now users A and B can utilize Z_{AB} as a secret key for the encryption and decryption of their data. Similarly, each pair of users can compute a key which will be known only to that pair.

Let's now discuss briefly the abovementioned problem of selecting the generator g. The general method known so far relies on the factorization of $p - 1$. But, on the one hand, if p is randomly chosen, then there is a high probability that $p - 1$ will have a large prime divisor which is very difficult to determine. On the other hand, in the system considered, the number $p - 1$ has to have a large prime divisor since otherwise the Pohlig–Hellman algorithm ([Pohlig and Hellman (1978)]; see also [Menezes *et al.* (1996)]) would be able to quickly compute the discrete logarithm. So, under arbitrary chosen p, finding g is hard. Therefore it is often recommended that the following approach be used. The prime number p is chosen so that

$$p = 2q + 1$$

where q is also prime. Then g may be any number for which the following inequalities are satisfied:

$$1 < g < p - 1 \quad \text{and} \quad g^q \bmod p \neq 1.$$

Consider an example. Let $p = 23 = 2 \times 11 + 1 (q = 11)$. Now select g. Let's try $g = 3$. Check it: $3^{11} \bmod 23 = 1$, which means that this value is irrelevant. Take $g = 5$. Check it: $5^{11} \bmod 23 = 22 \neq 1$, that's OK. So we have chosen the parameters for the Diffie–Hellman system: $p = 23$, $g = 5$. Now each user chooses a secret number and computes a corresponding public number. Let $X_A = 7$, $X_B = 13$. Compute $Y_A = 5^7 \bmod 23 = 17$, $Y_B = 5^{13} \bmod 23 = 21$. Let A and B establish a common secret key. For that purpose A computes $Z_{AB} = 21^7 \bmod 23 = 10$ and B computes $Z_{BA} = 17^{13} \bmod 23 = 10$. They have now the common key, 10, which has never been transmitted over a communication channel.

2.3 The Elements of Number Theory

Many cryptographic algorithms are based on the results of the classical theory of numbers. We shall consider only the necessary elements of the whole theory. The classical theorems by Fermat and Euler, and a number of other number-theoretic results will be given without proofs since they may be found in almost any textbook on number theory, e.g. [Rosen (1992)]. The readers familiar with number theory may wish to proceed immediately to Sec. 2.4.

Definition 2.2. A positive integer p is *prime* if it has no divisors but 1 and itself.

For example, the numbers 11 and 23 are prime; the numbers 27 and 33 are composite (27 can be divided by 3 and by 9, 33 has divisors 3 and 11).

Theorem 2.1. (fundamental theorem of arithmetic) *Any positive integer can be represented as a product of prime numbers, this representation being unique.*

For example, $27 = 3 \times 3 \times 3$, $33 = 3 \times 11$.

Definition 2.3. Two numbers are said to be *coprime* (or *relatively prime*) if they have no common divisors but 1.

For example, the numbers 27 and 28 are coprime (the have no common divisors except 1), the numbers 27 and 33 are not (they have common divisor 3).

Definition 2.4. (Euler (totient) function) Let there be given an integer $N \geq 1$. The *Euler function* $\varphi(N)$ is the quantity of numbers among $1, 2, 3, \ldots, N-1$ that are coprime to N.

Consider an example.

$$\varphi(10) = ? \qquad\qquad \varphi(12) = ?$$
$$1, \not2, 3, \not4, \not5, \not6, 7, \not8, 9, \quad 1, \not2, \not3, \not4, 5, \not6, 7, \not8, \not9, \not{10}, 11$$
$$\varphi(10) = 4 \qquad\qquad \varphi(12) = 4$$

(the numbers which are not coprime to the argument have been struck out).

Proposition 2.3. *If p is prime then $\varphi(p) = p - 1$.*

Proof. In the series $1, 2, 3, \ldots, p-1$ all numbers are coprime to p since p is prime and, by definition, is not divisible by any other number. □

Proposition 2.4. *Let p and q be distinct primes ($p \neq q$). Then we have $\varphi(pq) = (p-1)(q-1)$.*

Proof. In the series $1, 2, \ldots, pq-1$ the numbers *not* relatively prime to pq are $p, 2p, 3p, \ldots, (q-1)p$ and $q, 2q, 3q, \ldots, (p-1)q$. The total of such numbers is $(q-1) + (p-1)$. Hence, the number of coprimes to pq is $pq - 1 - (p-1) - (q-1) = pq - q - p + 1 = (p-1)(q-1)$. □

Theorem 2.2. (Fermat) *Let p be prime and $0 < a < p$. Then*

$$a^{p-1} \bmod p = 1.$$

Consider an example. Let $p = 13$, $a = 2$;

$$2^{12} \bmod 13 = \left(2^2\right)^2 \times \left(\left(2^2\right)^2\right)^2 \bmod 13 = 3 \times 9 \bmod 13 = 1,$$
$$10^{10} \bmod 11 = 10^2 \times \left(\left(10^2\right)^2\right)^2 \bmod 11 = 1 \times 1 = 1.$$

Theorem 2.3. (Euler) *Let a and b be coprime. Then*

$$a^{\varphi(b)} \bmod b = 1.$$

The Fermat theorem is a special case of the Euler theorem when b is prime.

Consider an example.

$$\varphi(12) = 4,$$

$$5^4 \bmod 12 = \left(5^2\right)^2 \bmod 12 = \left(1^2\right)^2 \bmod 12 = 1.$$

$$\varphi(21) = 2 \times 6 = 12,$$

$$2^{12} \bmod 21 = 2^4 \times \left(2^4\right)^2 \bmod 21 = 16 \times 4 \bmod 21 = 1.$$

We shall need another theorem close to Euler's.

Theorem 2.4. *If p and q are distinct primes, $p \neq q$, and k is an arbitrary integer then*

$$a^{k\varphi(pq)+1} \bmod (pq) = a. \tag{2.12}$$

Consider an example. Let's take $p = 5$, $q = 7$. Then $pq = 35$ and the Euler function $\varphi(35) = 4 \times 6 = 24$. Consider the case of $k = 2$, i.e. we shall raise numbers to the power $2 \times 24 + 1 = 49$. We obtain $9^{49} \bmod 35 = 9$, $23^{49} \bmod 35 = 23$. This is not surprising because each of the numbers 9 and 23 is coprime to the modulus 35 and by the Euler theorem $9^{24} \bmod 35 = 1$, $23^{24} \bmod 35 = 1$. However, Theorem 2.4 remains right even for the following numbers: $10^{49} \bmod 35 = 10$, $28^{49} \bmod 35 = 28$, whereas the Euler theorem cannot be applied to these numbers (the numbers 10 and 28 are not coprime to the modulus 35 and $10^{24} \bmod 35 = 15$, $28^{24} \bmod 35 = 21$).

Definition 2.5. Let a and b be two positive integers. The *greatest common divisor* of a and b, denoted $\gcd(a, b)$, is the biggest number c which divides both a and b:

$$c = \gcd(a, b).$$

For example, $\gcd(10, 15) = 5$; $\gcd(8, 28) = 4$.

To find the greatest common divisor one may use the following algorithm which is known as the Euclidean algorithm.

Algorithm 2.1 EUCLIDEAN ALGORITHM

INPUT: Positive integers a, b, $a \geq b$.
OUTPUT: The greatest common divisor $\gcd(a, b)$.
1.   WHILE $b \neq 0$ DO
2. $r \leftarrow a \bmod b$, $a \leftarrow b$, $b \leftarrow r$.
3.   RETURN a.

For example, let us show how the Euclidean algorithm is used to compute $\gcd(28, 8)$:

$$a : 28\ 8\ 4$$
$$b : \ \ 8\ 4\ 0$$
$$r : \ \ 4\ 0$$

Here each column represents one iteration of the algorithm. The process continues until b turns to zero. Then the value of a holds the result (4).

For many of the cryptographic systems considered in this book the so-called *extended Euclidean algorithm* is important. The following theorem is associated with the extended Euclidean algorithm.

Theorem 2.5. *Let a and b be positive integers. Then the integer (not necessarily positive) numbers x and y exist such that*

$$ax + by = \gcd(a, b). \tag{2.13}$$

The extended Euclidean algorithm serves to find $\gcd(a, b)$ and x, y satisfying (2.13). Introduce three vectors $U = (u_1, u_2, u_3)$, $V = (v_1, v_2, v_3)$, and $T = (t_1, t_2, t_3)$. The algorithm is written as follows.

Algorithm 2.2 Extended Euclidean algorithm

INPUT:　　Positive integers a, b, $a \geq b$.
OUTPUT: $\gcd(a, b)$, x and y satisfying (2.13).
1.　　　　$U \leftarrow (a, 1, 0)$, $V \leftarrow (b, 0, 1)$.
2.　　　　WHILE $v_1 \neq 0$ DO
3.　　　　　　$q \leftarrow u_1$ div v_1;
4.　　　　　　$T \leftarrow (u_1 \bmod v_1, u_2 - qv_2, u_3 - qv_3)$;
5.　　　　　　$U \leftarrow V$, $V \leftarrow T$.
6.　　　　RETURN $U = (\gcd(a, b), x, y)$.

Vector U contains the result.

The operation, div, in the algorithm is integer division

$$a \text{ div } b = \lfloor a/b \rfloor.$$

The proof of correctness of Algorithm 2.2 may be found in [Aho *et al.* (1976); Knuth (1981)].

Consider an example. Let $a = 28$, $b = 19$. Find x and y satisfying (2.13).

$$
\begin{array}{lrrr}
U & 28 & 1 & 0 \\
V\,U & 19 & 0 & 1 \\
T\,V\,U & 9 & 1 & -1\ q=1 \\
T\,V\,U & 1 & -2 & 3\ q=2 \\
T\,V & 0 & 19 & -28\ q=9
\end{array}
$$

Let us comment on the presented schema. First, vector U is filled with numbers (28,1,0) and vector V with (19,0,1) (these are the first two rows in the schema). Vector T is computed (3rd row). After that the 2nd row becomes vector U, the 3rd row becomes vector V, and again vector T is computed (4th row). The process continues until the first element of V turns to 0. Then the next to last row holds the result. In our case, $\gcd(28,19) = 1$, $x = -2$, $y = 3$. Check the result: $28 \times (-2) + 19 \times 3 = 1$.

Consider one important application of the extended Euclidean algorithm. In many cryptographic schemes, it is required to find for the specified numbers c, m a number $d < m$ such that

$$cd \bmod m = 1. \tag{2.14}$$

Notice that such d exists if and only if c and m are coprime.

Definition 2.6. A number d satisfying (2.14) is called the *inverse* of c modulo m and often denoted $c^{-1} \bmod m$.

The above notation for the inverse is quite natural since we can now rewrite (2.14) as

$$cc^{-1} \bmod m = 1.$$

Multiplication by c^{-1} corresponds to division by c when operating modulo m. By analogy, arbitrary negative powers can be introduced:

$$c^{-e} = (c^e)^{-1} = (c^{-1})^e \pmod{m}.$$

Consider an example. We have $3 \times 4 \bmod 11 = 1$, therefore 4 is the inverse of 3 modulo 11. We can write $3^{-1} \bmod 11 = 4$. The number $5^{-2} \bmod 11$ can be found in two ways:

$$5^{-2} \bmod 11 = (5^2 \bmod 11)^{-1} \bmod 11 = 3^{-1} \bmod 11 = 4,$$

$$5^{-2} \bmod 11 = (5^{-1} \bmod 11)^2 \bmod 11 = 9^2 \bmod 11 = 4.$$

In the second variant, we used the equality $5^{-1} \bmod 11 = 9$. Indeed, $5 \times 9 \bmod 11 = 45 \bmod 11 = 1$.

Let us show how one computes the inverse by using the extended Euclidean algorithm. The equality (2.14) means that for some integer k

$$cd - km = 1. \qquad (2.15)$$

Taking into account that c and m are relatively prime, rewrite (2.15) as

$$m(-k) + cd = \gcd(m, c), \qquad (2.16)$$

which agrees with (2.13) up to the names of variables. Therefore to compute $c^{-1} \bmod m$, i.e. to find d, one can use the extended Euclidean algorithm for solving Eq. (2.16). Notice that the value of k is not interesting for us, so it makes sense not to compute the second element of vectors U, V, T. Besides, if the value of d is negative, we must add to it the modulus m because, by definition, $a \bmod m$ belongs to the set $\{0, 1, \ldots, m - 1\}$.

Consider an example. Compute $7^{-1} \bmod 11$. We use the same form of presentation as in the example on page 19.

$$
\begin{array}{ll}
11 & 0 \\
7 & 1 \\
4 & -1 \; q = 1 \\
3 & 2 \; q = 1 \\
1 & -3 \; q = 1 \\
0 & 11 \; q = 3.
\end{array}
$$

We obtain $d = -3$ and since it is negative we add the modulus: $-3 + 11 = 8$, i.e. $7^{-1} \bmod 11 = 8$. Check the result: $7 \times 8 \bmod 11 = 56 \bmod 11 = 1$.

One of the main operations in public-key cryptography is modular exponentiation. The idea of efficient algorithmic construction for exponentiation has already been shown in Eqs. (2.5) and (2.6). It is possible to implement this algorithm without storing in memory the series of numbers (2.5). Now we give the description of the algorithm in a form suitable for its immediate computer implementation. The name of the algorithm reflects the fact that the bits of exponent are examined from right to left, i.e. from the least-significant bit to the most-significant.

Algorithm 2.3 MODULAR EXPONENTIATION (FROM RIGHT TO LEFT)

INPUT: Integer numbers a, $x = (x_t x_{t-1} \ldots x_0)_2$, p.

OUTPUT: The number $y = a^x \bmod p$.

1. $y \leftarrow 1$, $s \leftarrow a$.

2.   FOR $i = 0, 1, \ldots, t$ DO

3.   IF $x_i = 1$ THEN $y \leftarrow y \times s \bmod p$;

4. $s \leftarrow s \times s \bmod p$.

5.   RETURN y.

To show how the algorithm works, trace the powers after each iteration. Let $x = 74 = (1001010)_2$ as in the example on page 9.

$i:$	0	1	2	3	4	5	6
$x_i:$	0	1	0	1	0	0	1
$y:$	1	a^2	a^2	a^{10}	a^{10}	a^{10}	a^{74}
$s:$	a^2	a^4	a^8	a^{16}	a^{32}	a^{64}	a^{128}.

There are situations where the following algorithm is more effective. It differs from the previous algorithm in that the bits of exponent are examined from left to right, i.e. from the most-significant bit to the least-significant.

Algorithm 2.4 MODULAR EXPONENTIATION (FROM LEFT TO RIGHT)

INPUT: Integer numbers a, $x = (x_t x_{t-1} \ldots x_0)_2$, p.

OUTPUT: The number $y = a^x \bmod p$.

1. $y \leftarrow 1$.

2.   FOR $i = t, t - 1, \ldots, 0$ DO

3. $y \leftarrow y \times y \bmod p$;

4.   IF $x_i = 1$ THEN $y \leftarrow y \times a \bmod p$.

5.   RETURN y.

To assure oneself that Algorithm 2.4 computes exactly the same value as Algorithm 2.3, trace again the powers after each iteration for $x = 73$.

$i:$	6	5	4	3	2	1	0
$x_i:$	1	0	0	1	0	1	0
$y:$	a	a^2	a^4	a^9	a^{18}	a^{37}	a^{74}

In fact, the number-theoretic results provided in this section will be enough to describe the basic cryptographic algorithms and methods in the rest of the book.

2.4   Shamir Cipher

This cipher attributed to Adi Shamir (see [Menezes *et al.* (1996)]) was one of the first public-key systems that allowed two parties to securely exchange messages over an open channel when these parties had neither secure channels nor secret keys and, perhaps, had never seen each other. (Recall that the Diffie-Hellman key-agreement scheme allows us to create a secret key but does not provide a cipher to be used with that key.)

The system will now be described. Let there be two users, A and B, connected by an open communication line. User A wants to send a message m to user B so that nobody but B will learn its contents. A randomly chooses a large prime number p and sends it to B. Then A selects two numbers c_A and d_A such that

$$c_A d_A \bmod (p-1) = 1. \tag{2.17}$$

A keeps these numbers secret, they will not be transmitted. B, similarly, selects two numbers c_B and d_B such that

$$c_B d_B \bmod (p-1) = 1, \tag{2.18}$$

and also keeps them secret.

After that, A transmits her message m using the three-step protocol described below. If $m < p$ (m is viewed as a number) then m is transmitted directly. If $m \geq p$ then the message is represented as a sequence of blocks $m_1, m_2, \ldots, m_t$, where all $m_i < p$, and these blocks are transmitted successively. For secure transmission of each m_i, it is better to randomly select new pairs (c_A, d_A) and (c_B, d_B), otherwise the security of the system decays. In present time, such a cipher is commonly used as a transport for secret keys whose values are less than p. So we shall focus on the case $m < p$. The protocol is as follows.

Step 1 A computes

$$x_1 = m^{c_A} \bmod p \qquad (2.19)$$

and sends x_1 to B.

Step 2 B, upon the receipt of x_1, computes

$$x_2 = x_1^{c_B} \bmod p \qquad (2.20)$$

and sends x_2 back to A.

Step 3 A computes

$$x_3 = x_2^{d_A} \bmod p \qquad (2.21)$$

and sends it to B.

Step 4 B, upon the receipt of x_3, computes

$$x_4 = x_3^{d_B} \bmod p. \qquad (2.22)$$

Proposition 2.5. (properties of the Shamir protocol)

(1) $x_4 = m$, *i.e. the realization of the protocol succeeds in transmitting the message m from A to B;*

(2) *the adversary cannot figure out what a message was transmitted (if p is large).*

Proof. Notice first that any integer $e \geq 0$ can be represented as $e = k(p-1) + r$ where $r = e \bmod (p-1)$. Therefore, by Fermat's theorem

$$x^e \bmod p = x^{k(p-1)+r} \bmod p = \left(x^{p-1}\right)^k \times x^r \bmod p$$

$$= (1^k \times x^r) \bmod p = x^{e \bmod (p-1)} \bmod p. \qquad (2.23)$$

By the protocol construction

$$x_4 = x_3^{d_B} \bmod p = (x_2^{d_A})^{d_B} \bmod p = (x_1^{c_B})^{d_A d_B} \bmod p$$

$$= (m^{c_A})^{c_B d_A d_B} \bmod p = m^{c_A d_A c_B d_B} \bmod p.$$

Taking into account Eq. (2.23) and then Eqs. (2.17) and (2.18)) we may continue

$$x_4 = m^{(c_A d_A c_B d_B) \bmod (p-1)} \bmod p$$

$$= m^{(c_A d_A \bmod (p-1))(c_B d_B \bmod (p-1))} \bmod p = m^{1 \times 1} \bmod p = m$$

which proves the first statement of the proposition.

The proof of the second statement is based on the assumption that for an adversary trying to recover m, there is no strategy more effective than the following. She computes c_B from (2.20), then finds d_B and computes $x_4 = m$ by (2.22). But to implement this strategy the adversary has to solve a discrete logarithm problem which is impossible if p is large. $\square$

Let us discuss a method of selecting pairs c_A, d_A and c_B, d_B satisfying (2.17) and (2.18). It suffices only to consider the actions of user A because user B acts the same way. The number c_A is chosen randomly but must be coprime to $p - 1$ (by searching through odd numbers since $p - 1$ is even). Then d_A may be computed by use of the extended Euclidean algorithm as was explained in Sec. 2.3.

Consider an example. If A wants to send B the message $m = 10$, A chooses $p = 23$ and sends it to B. Then A selects $c_A = 7$ ($\gcd(7, 22) = 1$) and computes $d_A = 19$. Similarly, B selects $c_B = 5$ (coprime to 22) and computes $d_B = 9$. The Shamir protocol begins.

Step 1 $A \longrightarrow B$: $x_1 = 10^7 \bmod 23 = 14$.
Step 2 $A \longleftarrow B$: $x_2 = 14^5 \bmod 23 = 15$.
Step 3 $A \longrightarrow B$: $x_3 = 15^{19} \bmod 23 = 19$.
Step 4 B computes $x_4 = 19^9 \bmod 23 = 10$.

We can see that B has received the message $m = 10$.

2.5   ElGamal Encryption

Let there be users A, B, $C, \ldots$, who wish to communicate secret messages to each other but have no secure communication channels. In this section, we consider a cipher suggested by Taher ElGamal [ElGamal (1985)] which solves the problem and uses only one message pass in contrast to the three-pass protocol by Shamir. In fact, the ElGamal scheme is based on the Diffie–Hellman key-agreement protocol which is used by pairs of users who wish to obtain a common secret key. The message is then encrypted by multiplication with that key. For any subsequent messages the secret key is computed anew. The details of the method are as follows.

For the whole group of users a large prime p and integer g are chosen so that distinct powers of g are distinct numbers modulo p (cf. Sec. 2.2). Numbers p and g are transmitted to users in the clear and may be used by all users of a network.

Then, every user selects his/her own secret number c_i (private key), $1 < c_i < p - 1$, and computes the corresponding public number d_i (public key),

$$d_i = g^{c_i} \bmod p. \tag{2.24}$$

This results in Table 2.3.

Table 2.3   User keys in the ElGamal system.

User	Private key	Public key
A	c_A	d_A
B	c_B	d_B
C	c_C	d_C

Let's show now how A transmits a message m to B. We shall assume, as in the case of the Shamir cipher, that the message is represented as a number $m < p$.

Step 1 A generates a random number k, $1 \leq k \leq p - 2$, computes

$$r = g^k \bmod p, \tag{2.25}$$

$$e = m \times d_B{}^k \bmod p \tag{2.26}$$

and transmits the pair of numbers (r, e) to user B.

Step 2 B, upon the receipt of (r, e), computes

$$m' = e \times r^{p-1-c_B} \bmod p. \tag{2.27}$$

Proposition 2.6. (properties of the ElGamal cipher)

(1) *User B has received the message, i.e. $m' = m$;*
(2) *An adversary who knows p, g, d_B, r, and e, cannot compute m.*

Proof. Substitute the value of e from (2.26) into (2.27):

$$m' = m \times d_B{}^k \times r^{p-1-c_B} \bmod p.$$

Now substitute (2.25) in place of r and (2.24) in place of d_B:

$$m' = m \times (g^{c_B})^k \times (g^k)^{p-1-c_B} \bmod p$$

$$= m \times g^{c_B k + k(p-1) - k c_B} \bmod p = m \times g^{k(p-1)} \bmod p. \tag{2.28}$$

By Fermat's theorem

$$g^{k(p-1)} \bmod p = 1^k \bmod p = 1$$

and thus we obtain the first statement of the proposition.

To prove the second statement, notice that the adversary cannot compute k in (2.25) since it is the discrete logarithm problem. Hence, she cannot compute m in (2.26) since m was multiplied by an unknown factor. The adversary also cannot reproduce the actions of the legitimate receiver (user B) because she does not know the secret number c_B (computation of c_B based on (2.24) is again the discrete logarithm problem). □

Consider an example. Transmit the message $m = 15$ from A to B. Choose the parameters in the same way as in the example on page 15. Let $p = 23$, $g = 5$. Let user B choose his secret number $c_B = 13$ and compute using (2.24)

$$d_B = 5^{13} \bmod 23 = 21.$$

User A generates a random number k, say $k = 7$, and computes using (2.25), (2.26):

$$r = 5^7 \bmod 23 = 17, \quad e = 15 \times 21^7 \bmod 23 = 15 \times 10 \bmod 23 = 12.$$

Then A sends B the encrypted message as a pair of numbers $(17, 12)$. B computes using (2.27)

$$m' = 12 \times 17^{23-1-13} \bmod 23 = 12 \times 17^9 \bmod 23 = 12 \times 7 \bmod 23 = 15.$$

We can see that B has been able to decrypt the message transmitted.

It is clear that the same scheme may be used by all the users in a network. Note that any user who knows the public key of user B (d_B) can send B messages encrypted using d_B. But it is only user B, and nobody else, who is able to decrypt those messages since decryption is done by utilizing the private key c_B which is known only to B. Note also that the length of the ciphertext is twice the length of the plaintext but only one pass is needed (provided the table with public keys was delivered to all users in advance).

2.6   RSA Encryption and Trapdoor Functions

Named after its developers Ron Rivest, Adi Shamir, and Leonard Adleman, this cipher proposed in [Rivest *et al.* (1978)] is so far one of the most widely used.

We have seen that Shamir's cipher completely solves the problem of secure message exchange in the case when only open channels are available. But it is a disadvantage that the message is passed three times from one user to another. The ElGamal cipher allows us to solve the same problem in only one pass, but also has the disadvantage of expanding the message: the ciphertext is twice as long as the plaintext. The RSA encryption is free of such disadvantages. It is interesting that this system is based on another one-way function, different from a discrete logarithm. Moreover, we meet here one more invention of contemporary cryptography — the *trapdoor function*.

The RSA system is based on the following two facts from number theory:

Fact 1 testing numbers for primality (and finding primes) is relatively easy (see, e.g. [Menezes *et al.* (1996)]);

Fact 2 the problem of factoring numbers of the form $n = pq$, where p and q are primes of roughly the same size, i.e. finding p and q given n, is very hard (or computationally infeasible) when p and q are sufficiently large (see also [Menezes *et al.* (1996)]).

Let there again be users A, B, C,.... Each user randomly chooses two large primes P and Q and computes

$$N = PQ. \tag{2.29}$$

Then the user computes the number $\phi = (P - 1)(Q - 1)$ and selects a number $d < \phi$ relatively prime to ϕ, after which he finds using the extended Euclidean algorithm a number c such that

$$cd \bmod \phi = 1. \tag{2.30}$$

The user keeps the number c (as well as P, Q, and ϕ, but these will not be needed any more) secret and publishes the numbers N and d. The number c is the private key of the user and the pair of numbers N, d is the corresponding public key. All information associated with the users is shown in Table 2.4.

Proceed to the description of RSA protocol. If Alice wants to send a message m to Bob, she will treat the message m as a number satisfying the inequality $m < N_B$ (further on subscript B indicates that the corresponding parameters belong to Bob).

Step 1 Alice encrypts the message as follows

$$e = m^{d_B} \bmod N_B \tag{2.31}$$

using Bob's public keys and transmits e over an open channel.

Table 2.4   User keys in the RSA system.

User	Private key	Public key
A	c_A	d_A, N_A
B	c_B	d_B, N_B
C	c_C	d_C, N_C

Step 2 Bob, having received the encrypted message, computes

$$m' = e^{c_B} \bmod N_B. \tag{2.32}$$

Proposition 2.7. *For the described protocol, $m' = m$, i.e. user B receives the message sent by A.*

Proof. By the protocol construction

$$m' = e^{c_B} \bmod N_B = m^{d_B c_B} \bmod N_B.$$

Equation (2.30) means that for some k

$$c_B d_B = k\phi_B + 1.$$

By Proposition 2.4

$$\phi_B = (P_B - 1)(Q_B - 1) = \varphi(N_B)$$

where $\varphi(\cdot)$ is the Euler function. Hence by Theorem 2.4

$$m' = m^{k\varphi(N_B)+1} \bmod N_B = m. \qquad \square$$

Proposition 2.8. (properties of RSA protocol)

(1) *The protocol encrypts and decrypts data correctly;*
(2) *An adversary who overhears all transmitted messages and knows all public information cannot recover the plaintext message if P and Q are large.*

Proof. The first property follows from Proposition 2.7. To prove the second property, notice that the adversary knows only public parameters N and d. In order to find c she must know the value $\phi = (P - 1)(Q - 1)$ for which, in turn, P and Q must be known. Generally speaking, P and Q can be found by factoring N but it is a hard problem (Fact 2). Note, however, that the selection of large random primes P and Q can be done in acceptable time (Fact 1). $\qquad \square$

The one-way function $y = x^d \bmod N$ employed in RSA has a so-called "trapdoor" which allows for easy computation of the inverse function $x = \sqrt[d]{y} \bmod N$ if the factorization of N is known. (Indeed, it is easy to compute $\phi = (P - 1)(Q - 1)$ and then $c = d^{-1} \bmod \phi$.) If P and Q are unknown then to compute the inverse function is practically impossible because to find P and Q given N is very hard (Fact 2), i.e. the knowledge of P and Q is a "trapdoor". The trapdoor functions are employed in other branches of cryptography, as well.

Notice that it is important for the RSA system that each user chooses his own pair of primes P and Q, i.e. that all moduli N_A, N_B, N_C,... be different (otherwise one user would be able to read encrypted messages destined for another user). But it is not required for the second public parameter d. The parameter d can be the same for all users. It is often recommended that $d = 3$ be chosen (for correspondingly chosen P and Q), see e.g. [Menezes *et al.* (1996)]. In this case encryption is maximally fast (it requires only 2 modular multiplications).

Consider an example. Suppose Alice wants to send Bob the message $m = 15$. Let Bob's parameters be

$$P_B = 3, \quad Q_B = 11, \quad N_B = 33, \quad d_B = 3$$

(3 is coprime to $\varphi(33) = 20$). Find c_B using the extended Euclidean algorithm: $c_B = 7$ (check it: $3 \times 7 \bmod 20 = 1$). Encrypt m using Eq. (2.31):

$$e = 15^3 \bmod 33 = 15^2 \times 15 \bmod 33 = 27 \times 15 \bmod 33 = 9.$$

Alice sends the number 9 to Bob over an open channel. Only Bob knows $c_B = 7$ so he decrypts by (2.32):

$$m' = 9^7 \bmod 33 = \left(9^2\right)^2 \times 9^2 \times 9 \bmod 33 = 15^2 \times 15 \times 9 \bmod 33 = 15.$$

We can see that Bob has deciphered the message.

The system is considered unbreakable if P and Q are large, but has the following imperfection: A sends a message to B by utilizing B's public information (the numbers N_B and d_B). Adversary E cannot read the messages destined for B but she is able to send a message to B on behalf of A, i.e. E can impersonate A. Surely, we need more complex protocols to avoid this. It is interesting that one of the possible solutions may be based entirely on the RSA scheme, as the following.

A wants to send B a message m. First A computes the number $e = m^{c_A} \bmod N_A$. E cannot do that since c_A is secret. Then A computes the number $f = e^{d_B} \bmod N_B$ and sends f to B. B receives f and computes sequentially $u = f^{c_B} \bmod N_B$ and $w = u^{d_A} \bmod N_A$.

As a result, B obtains the message $w = m$. As in the conventional RSA system, E cannot recover the message but, in contrast to RSA, she also cannot send a message on behalf of A (because she does not know the secret c_A).

Here we meet a new situation. B knows that the message originated from A as it was signed by A. A virtually signs the message by encrypting it with the use of her secret parameter c_A. This is an example of the so-called *digital signature.* The digital signature is one of the widely used inventions of modern cryptography. It will be systematically studied in Chapter 4.

Problems and Exercises

2.1 Reduce the results of expressions 5, 16, 27, -4, -13, $3 + 8$, $3 - 8$, $3 \cdot 8$, $3 \cdot 8 \cdot 5$

    (a) modulo 10,

    (b) modulo 11.

2.2 Compute using fast modular exponentiation algorithms 2^8 mod 10, 3^7 mod 10, 7^{19} mod 100, 7^{57} mod 100.

2.3 Factor numbers 108, 77, 65, 30, 159.

2.4 Determine which pairs of numbers $(25, 12)$, $(25, 15)$, $(13, 39)$, $(40, 27)$ are relatively prime.

2.5 Find the values of the Euler functions $\varphi(14)$, $\varphi(20)$.

2.6 Compute using the properties of Euler functions $\varphi(53)$, $\varphi(21)$, $\varphi(159)$.

2.7 Compute the quantities 3^{13} mod 13, 5^{22} mod 11, 3^{17} mod 5 using the Fermat theorem.

2.8 Compute the quantities 3^9 mod 20, 2^{14} mod 21, 2^{107} mod 159 using the Euler theorem.

2.9 Find using the Euclidean algorithm $\gcd(21, 12)$, $\gcd(30, 12)$, $\gcd(24, 40)$, $\gcd(33, 16)$.

2.10 Using the extended Euclidean algorithm, find x and y in equations

    (a) $21x + 12y = \gcd(21, 12)$,

    (b) $30x + 12y = \gcd(30, 12)$,

    (c) $24x + 40y = \gcd(24, 40)$,

    (d) $33x + 16y = \gcd(33, 16)$.

2.11 Compute 3^{-1} mod 7, 5^{-1} mod 8, 3^{-1} mod 53, 10^{-1} mod 53.

2.12 Write out all primes less than 100. Which of them are of the form $p = 2q + 1$, where q is also prime?

2.13 Find all relevant values for the parameter g in the Diffie–Hellman system with $p = 11$.

2.14 Compute public keys Y_A, Y_B and a corresponding common key Z_{AB} in the Diffie–Hellman system with parameters

    (a) $p = 23$, $g = 5$, $X_A = 5$, $X_B = 7$;

    (b) $p = 19$, $g = 2$, $X_A = 5$, $X_B = 7$;

    (c) $p = 23$, $g = 7$, $X_A = 3$, $X_B = 4$;

(d) $p = 17$, $g = 3$, $X_A = 10$, $X_B = 5$;

(e) $p = 19$, $g = 10$, $X_A = 4$, $X_B = 8$.

2.15 For Shamir's cipher with specified parameters p, c_A, c_B find the missing parameters and describe the process of transmitting message m from A to B.

(a) $p = 19$, $c_A = 5$, $c_B = 7$, $m = 4$;

(b) $p = 23$, $c_A = 15$, $c_B = 7$, $m = 6$;

(c) $p = 19$, $c_A = 11$, $c_B = 5$, $m = 10$;

(d) $p = 23$, $c_A = 9$, $c_B = 3$, $m = 17$;

(e) $p = 17$, $c_A = 3$, $c_B = 13$, $m = 9$.

2.16 For ElGamal's cipher with specified parameters p, g, c_B, k find the missing parameters and describe the process of transmitting message m to user B.

(a) $p = 19$, $g = 2$, $c_B = 5$, $k = 7$, $m = 5$;

(b) $p = 23$, $g = 5$, $c_B = 8$, $k = 10$, $m = 10$;

(c) $p = 19$, $g = 2$, $c_B = 11$, $k = 4$, $m = 10$;

(d) $p = 23$, $g = 7$, $c_B = 3$, $k = 15$, $m = 5$;

(e) $p = 17$, $g = 3$, $c_B = 10$, $k = 5$, $m = 10$.

2.17 For the RSA system with specified parameters P_A, Q_A, d_A find the missing parameters and describe the process of transmitting message m to user A.

(a) $P_A = 5$, $Q_A = 11$, $d_A = 3$, $m = 12$;

(b) $P_A = 5$, $Q_A = 13$, $d_A = 5$, $m = 20$;

(c) $P_A = 7$, $Q_A = 11$, $d_A = 7$, $m = 17$;

(d) $P_A = 7$, $Q_A = 13$, $d_A = 5$, $m = 30$;

(e) $P_A = 3$, $Q_A = 11$, $d_A = 3$, $m = 15$.

2.18 The encrypted message $e = 100$ is sent to the RSA user with parameters $N = 187$, $d = 3$. Decrypt the message by breaking the RSA system of the user.

Themes for Labs

2.19 Write and debug the set of program functions implementing the basic algorithms used in the cryptosystems studied: modular exponentiation ($a^x \bmod m$), greatest common divisor ($\gcd(a, b)$), inversion ($x^{-1} \bmod m$).

2.20 Write a program implementing the Diffie–Hellman key agreement. The following parameter values are recommended: $p = 30803, g = 2$. Secret keys are to be randomly generated.

2.21 Write a program implementing the Shamir cipher. The number $p = 30803$ may be taken as a prime modulus. The other parameters are to be randomly generated.

2.22 Write a program implementing the ElGamal cipher. The following parameter values are recommended: $p = 30803, g = 2$. Private keys and the other parameters are to be randomly generated.

2.23 Write a program implementing the RSA cipher for transmitting messages to users A or B. The following parameter values are recommended: $P_A = 131, Q_A = 227, P_B = 113, Q_B = 281, d_A = d_B = 3$.

Chapter 3

Solving Discrete Logarithm Problem

3.1 Problem Setting

In order to construct a reliable cryptosystem one should take into account the methods of disclosure the adversary can employ. This allows one to choose cryptosystem parameters (e.g. the length of numbers) so that the adversary's methods become infeasible. In the present section, we shall consider two such methods to give the reader some insight into this "mysterious" field.

We have seen that many public-key ciphers are based on the one-way function

$$y = a^x \bmod p \qquad (3.1)$$

and we know that given a and x the value of y can be computed with not more than $2 \log x$ operations (Proposition 2.1). But finding x given a and y, i.e. computing the discrete logarithm, is assumed to be a much more complex problem.

As it was shown in the justification of the Shamir cipher (see (2.23)), by Fermat's theorem, when exponentiating modulo a prime p exponents are reduced modulo $p-1$. Therefore it suffices to deal with only the exponents x satisfying the inequality $0 \le x \le p-1$.

Denote by t_y the number of multiplications needed for computation of y in (3.1) given a and x and, for brevity, we shall call t_y time of computation. Time of exponentiation with the algorithms of Sec. 2.1 is not more than $2 \log x$ and $x < p$. Hence

$$t_y \le 2 \log p \qquad (3.2)$$

for any exponent x.

33

Now proceed to the problem of finding x in (3.1) given a and y. First estimate the complexity of the exhaustive search. In the exhaustive search, we begin with a^1 and check whether $a^1 = y$. If it is not the case, check whether $a^2 = y$, $a^3 = y$, and so on until $a^i = y$ is found (then $x = i$). On average, it will require us to multiply by a and check for equality $(p-1)/2$ times. So the time of exhaustive search

$$t_{\text{e.s.}} \approx p/2.$$

With the "baby-step giant-step" algorithm described below the time of finding x is noticeably smaller:

$$t_{\text{b.s.g.s.}} \approx 2 \times \sqrt{p},$$

and with the index calculus algorithm also described below this time is even substantially smaller:

$$t_{\text{i.c.}} \approx c_1 \times 2^{c_2 \sqrt{\log p \log \log p}}$$

where c_1, c_2 are some positive constants.

To make the comparison more illustrative, express the time of computation through the bitlength of the numbers in (3.1). Denote the bitlength of p by n. When making computations modulo p we have $n \approx \log p$. Therefore the order of complexity (time of computation) for the above mentioned algorithms will be the following:

$$t_y \approx n,$$

$$t_{\text{e.s.}} \approx 2^{n-1},$$

$$t_{\text{b.s.g.s.}} \approx 2^{n/2},$$

$$t_{\text{i.c.}} \approx 2^{c_2 \sqrt{n \log n}},$$

where $\approx$ loosely denotes "proportional".

We can see that the time of exponentiation grows linearly as the length of numbers (n) increases but the time of solving the inverse problem grows exponentially or (for the index calculus algorithm) subexponentially. The issue of the existence of faster algorithms for computing discrete logarithms, as well as for solving other inverse problems in cryptography, remains an open question.

3.2   The Baby-step Giant-step Algorithm

This method was described by Daniel Shanks (see [Knuth (1973)]) in 1971. However in [Nechaev (1994)] it is stated that the method had been invented in 1962 by Soviet mathematician Alexander Gelfond. It was one of the first methods to show that the discrete logarithm problem can be solved much faster than by the exhaustive search. The algorithm is as follows.

Step 1 Take two integers m and k such that

$$mk > p. \tag{3.3}$$

Step 2 Compute two number series

$$y, \quad ay, \quad a^2y, \quad \ldots, \quad a^{m-1}y \quad (\text{mod } p); \tag{3.4}$$

$$a^m, \quad a^{2m}, \quad \ldots, \quad a^{km} \quad (\text{mod } p) \tag{3.5}$$

(all computations are carried out modulo p).

Step 3 Find such i and j that

$$a^{im} = a^j y. \tag{3.6}$$

Proposition 3.1. *A number*

$$x = im - j \tag{3.7}$$

is the solution of Eq. (3.1). Besides, the integers i, j satisfying (3.6) exist.

Proof. The correctness of (3.7) follows from the chain of equalities below, where all computations are modulo p and division corresponds to multiplication by an inverse number:

$$a^x = a^{im-j} = \frac{a^{im}}{a^j} = \frac{a^{im}y}{a^j y} = \frac{a^{im}y}{a^{im}} = y$$

(here the next to last equality follows from (3.6)). Next, show that the numbers i and j satisfying (3.6) exist. For that purpose place all numbers of the form (3.7) into the table (Table 3.1).

We can see that all numbers from 1 to km are contained in the table. It means by (3.3) that the table contains all numbers from 1 to p. So any exponent $x < p$ is present in the table, i.e. the number x satisfying (3.1) can be represented in the form (3.7), and (3.6) always has a solution.   □

Table 3.1   Numbers of the form $im - j$.

$i \downarrow \quad j \rightarrow$	0	1	2	...	$m-1$
1	m	$m-1$	$m-2$	...	1
2	$2m$	$2m-1$	$2m-2$	...	$m+1$
...	...	...	...	...	...
k	km	$km-1$	$km-2$	...	$(k-1)m+1$

Consider an example. Find the solution of the equation $2^x \bmod 23 = 9$ with the aid of the baby-step giant-step algorithm.

Choose m and k. Let $m = 6$, $k = 4$. We can see that (3.3) is fulfilled. Compute the series (3.4), (3.5):

$$(3.4): \ 9, 18, 13, 3, 6, 12;$$

$$(3.5): \ 18.$$

Here we stop computations since there are equal numbers in (3.4) and (3.5) under $i = 1$, $j = 1$. By (3.7) we obtain

$$x = 1 \times 6 - 1 = 5.$$

Check it: $2^5 \bmod 23 = 9$. Indeed, $x = 5$ is the solution.

Let us explain the name of the algorithm considered. We know that in cryptography, p is a large number, hence m and k are also large. In the series (3.4), the exponent is increased by 1 (baby step), and in the series (3.5), the exponent is increased by m (giant step).

Let's now estimate the complexity of the method.

Proposition 3.2. *With the given method and for large p, computation time satisfies the inequality*

$$t_{\text{b.s.g.s.}} \leq \text{const} \times \sqrt{p} \log^2 p. \tag{3.8}$$

(Here we speak of the total time rather than of the number of multiplications.)

Proof. We can take

$$k = m = \lfloor \sqrt{p} \rfloor + 1 \tag{3.9}$$

which, obviously, satisfies (3.3). Then no more than $2\sqrt{p}$ multiplications are required for computation of (3.4) and (3.5). We know that for "usual" ("secondary school") methods of multiplication and division, the time of computation with r-digit operands is proportional to r^2. We have all the numbers taken from the set $\{1, \ldots, p\}$, so $r \leq \log p$ and computation time is proportional to $\log^2 p$. Hence we immediately obtain the time needed for computation of the series (3.4) and (3.5). Now we have to consider the time required for the search of equal numbers between the two series. Under large k and m this is far from being simple. The problem can be solved in the following way: first ascribe to each number in a series the corresponding value of i or j and one extra bit indicating the series (3.4) or (3.5). Then join both series in one and sort with respect to the values of numbers. The length of the joint series is $k + m \approx 2\sqrt{p}$. For the best sorting methods, $S \log S$ comparisons are required, where S is the number of elements to sort (see e.g. [Aho *et al.* (1976)]). In our case $S = 2\sqrt{p}$ and consequently $2\sqrt{p} \log \left(2\sqrt{p}\right) \approx \sqrt{p} \log p$ comparisons with words of length $\log p$ bits are required, which totals to about $\sqrt{p} \log^2 p$ bit operations. After having sorted the joint series we look it through and find two equal numbers from different initial series (using the bit flag). Finally, summing up the times on all stages of the algorithm we obtain the estimate (3.8). □

3.3 Index Calculus Algorithm

The main ideas behind the *index calculus algorithm* had been known in number theory since the 1920s. But it was only in 1979 that Adleman, one of the inventors of RSA, pointed out this algorithm as a means for solving Eq. (3.1) and investigated its complexity [Adleman (1979)]. At the present time, the index calculus algorithm and its enhanced variants offer the fastest methods for the computation of discrete logarithms in equations like (3.1).

Before describing the algorithm we introduce the following notion.

Definition 3.1. A number n is said to be *p-smooth* if all its prime factors are less than or equal to p.

For instance, the numbers 15, 36, 45, 270, 2025 are 5-smooth (their factorization includes only the prime factors 2, 3, and 5).

Proceed to the description of the algorithm.

Step 1 Select a factor base

$$S = \{p_1, p_2, \ldots, p_t\}$$

which consists of the first t primes $(2, 3, 5, \ldots,$ a remark concerning the choice of t will be given below).

Step 2 By randomly selecting k find $t + \epsilon$ (ϵ is a small integer, see below) p_t-smooth numbers of the form $a^k \bmod p$. That is, for each k, we compute the number $a^k \bmod p$ and check its smoothness by trial division over the elements of S. If the number is p_t-smooth then we pick it for further use, else we discard it and proceed with the next k. Write each p_t-smooth number found as a product of elements in S:

$$a^k \bmod p = \prod_{i=1}^{t} p_i^{c_i}, \quad c_i \geq 0 \qquad (3.10)$$

(for each value of k we obtain the corresponding set of numbers c_i).

Step 3 Take logarithms on both sides of (3.10):

$$k = \sum_{i=1}^{t} c_i \log_a p_i \qquad (3.11)$$

for each p_t-smooth number found at Step 2. We obtain a system of $t + \epsilon$ linear equations of the form (3.11) with t unknowns ($\log_a p_i$). We know that, in principle, t equations are enough for finding t unknowns. However, it may happen that some of the equations will be linearly dependent. That is why the number of equations is greater by ϵ than the number of unknowns. This increases the probability of obtaining a unique solution should some relations be linearly dependent. Now we solve the system using linear algebra methods with all calculations carried out modulo $p - 1$ (recall that exponents and hence logarithms are reduced modulo $p - 1$). As a result, we obtain the values of logarithms of elements from S : $\log_a p_1, \log_a p_2, \ldots, \log_a p_t$.

Step 4 By randomly selecting r find a p_t-smooth number of the form $y \times a^r \bmod p$:

$$y \times a^r \bmod p = \prod_{i=1}^{t} p_i^{e_i}, \quad e_i \geq 0. \qquad (3.12)$$

Similarly to Step 2, compute the number $y \times a^r \bmod p$ and check whether it is p_t-smooth. If not, try the next r.

Step 5 Taking logarithms on both sides of (3.12), obtain the final result

$$x = \log_a y = \left(\sum_{i=1}^{t} e_i \log_a p_i - r \right) \bmod (p-1). \qquad (3.13)$$

The correctness of the described algorithm is quite obvious and its effectiveness is connected with the following observation. If we randomly select a number from the infinite set of integers then with probability $1/2$ it is divisible by 2, with probability $1/3$ it is divisible by 3, with probability $1/5$ it is divisible by 5, and so on. So we may expect that in the interval from 1 to $p-1$ there are sufficiently many numbers whose prime factors are only the elements of our factor base S. It is exactly these numbers which are being sought at steps 2 and 4 of the algorithm.

As we have mentioned above, the parameter ϵ must ensure a unique solution at Step 3. It is believed that given a large p the value of ϵ of about 10 guarantees the uniqueness of a solution with high probability (see [Menezes *et al.* (1996)]). If it is not the case then it is necessary to revert to Step 2 and use other values of k.

Now let's discuss the complexity issues. The running time of the algorithm depends on the choice of t. The greater t, or the number of prime factors in S, is the fewer failures we meet when searching for smooth numbers at steps 2 and 4 (it is easy to see that the complexity of Step 2 is $t + \epsilon$ times greater than that of Step 4). But with large t the complexity of Step 3 drastically increases since we have to solve the system with $t + \epsilon$ equations. Finding an optimum t which minimizes the overall time can usually be done with numerical methods. Adleman [Adleman (1979)] showed that when an optimal choice of t is made, the complexity of the algorithm is estimated as

$$t_{\text{i.c.}} < c_1 \times 2^{(c_2 + o(1))\sqrt{\log p \log \log p}}$$

where c_1, c_2 are some positive constants.

Consider an example. Apply the index calculus algorithm to solve the equation

$$37 = 10^x \bmod 47. \qquad (3.14)$$

We have $y = 37$, $a = 10$, $p = 47$. Take as a factor base $S = \{2, 3, 5\}$, $t = 3$, and assume $\epsilon = 1$, i.e. we shall construct a system of 4 equations. We completed the first step of the algorithm and will proceed to the second.

Let's find four 5-smooth numbers (taking $k = 1, 2, 3, \ldots$):

$$10^1 \bmod 47 = 10 = 2 \times 5 \qquad \checkmark$$
$$10^2 \bmod 47 = 6 = 2 \times 3 \qquad \checkmark$$
$$10^3 \bmod 47 = 13 = 13$$
$$10^4 \bmod 47 = 36 = 2 \times 2 \times 3 \times 3 \quad \checkmark$$
$$10^5 \bmod 47 = 31 = 31$$
$$10^6 \bmod 47 = 28 = 2 \times 2 \times 7$$
$$10^7 \bmod 47 = 45 = 3 \times 3 \times 5 \qquad \checkmark$$

We have found four 5-smooth numbers (marked with a $\checkmark$) corresponding to the exponents 1, 2, 4, and 7.

Begin with the third step of the algorithm. For ease of exposition, denote the logarithms of the numbers p_1, p_2, p_3 from S by u_1, u_2, u_3, respectively, e.g. $u_3 = \log_{10} 5 \bmod 47$. For the equations checked with a $\checkmark$ at the previous step, turn to the logarithms and construct a system

$$1 = u_1 + u_3, \tag{3.15}$$

$$2 = u_1 + u_2, \tag{3.16}$$

$$4 = 2u_1 + 2u_2, \tag{3.17}$$

$$7 = 2u_2 + u_3. \tag{3.18}$$

We can see that in the system obtained, Eqs. (3.16) and (3.17) are linearly dependent, so it was not in vain that we have found the 4th smooth number. To solve the system, subtract (3.15) from (3.16). We obtain

$$1 = u_2 - u_3. \tag{3.19}$$

Add (3.19) to (3.18). We obtain

$$8 = 3u_2. \tag{3.20}$$

From (3.20) we immediately find u_2 (recall that the logarithms are reduced modulo $47 - 1 = 46$):

$$u_2 = (8/3) \bmod 46 = 8 \times 3^{-1} \bmod 46 = 8 \times 31 \bmod 46 = 18.$$

We can make a check by computing $10^{18} \bmod 47 = 3$, so u_2 is actually the logarithm of 3. Now from (3.19) find u_3:

$$u_3 = u_2 - 1 = 18 - 1 = 17$$

(actually, 10^{17} mod $47 = 5$). Finally, from (3.16) find u_1:

$$u_1 = 2 - u_2 = (2 - 18) \bmod 46 = -16 \bmod 46 = 30$$

(10^{30} mod $47 = 2$).

Thus we know the logarithms of the elements of S. The most complex part of the algorithm is left behind. Proceed to the fourth step. Select (randomly) $r = 3$ and compute

$$37 \times 10^3 \bmod 47 = 37 \times 13 \bmod 47 = 11.$$

The number 11 is not 5-smooth, so try the next r:

$$37 \times 10^4 \bmod 47 = 37 \times 36 \bmod 47 = 16 = 2 \times 2 \times 2 \times 2.$$

The number 16 is 5-smooth and the fourth step is completed.

Turn to logarithms in the last equality (this is the fifth step) and obtain the final result:

$$\log_{10} 37 = 4 \log_{10} 2 - 4 = (4 \times 30 - 4) \bmod 46 = 24.$$

We have found the solution of Eq. (3.14) $x = 24$. We may check it: 10^{24} mod $47 = 37$.

The fastest to the date is the variant of the described index calculus algorithm called Number Field Sieve, see [Lenstra and Lenstra (1993)]. This method is based upon subtle algebraic constructions so we do not describe it in this book. Its time complexity is estimated as

$$t_{\text{n.f.s.}} < c_1 \times 2^{(c_2 + o(1)) \sqrt[3]{\log p (\log \log p)^2}} \tag{3.21}$$

where c_1, c_2 are some positive constants. It is this method which dictates the conditions for choosing the length of modules in the cryptosystem that rely on the intractability of the discrete logarithm problem (among the systems considered in Chapter 2 are the Diffie–Hellman, Shamir, and ElGamal schemes). To achieve long-term security it is recommended that the length of modulus be at least 1024 bits.

The remark at the conclusion of this chapter is that in our book, we do not consider the methods of breaking the cryptosystems whose security is based on integer factorization problem (such as RSA). The fact is that this discussion would require us to introduce some extra notions and algorithms from number theory that are of no use elsewhere in this book. However we may say that to date the fastest methods of factorization are characterized by the same estimate of complexity as given by Eq. (3.21). As a consequence, to ensure long-term security of the RSA system, the modulus length must also be at least 1024 bits (i.e. prime numbers producing a modulus must be at least 512 bits each).

Problems and Exercises

3.1 Using the baby-step giant-step algorithm, solve the following equations:

(a) $2^x \bmod 29 = 21$,
(b) $3^x \bmod 31 = 25$,
(c) $2^x \bmod 37 = 12$,
(d) $6^x \bmod 41 = 21$,
(e) $3^x \bmod 43 = 11$.

3.2 Using the index calculus algorithm, solve the following equations:

(a) $2^x \bmod 53 = 24$,
(b) $2^x \bmod 59 = 13$,
(c) $2^x \bmod 61 = 45$,
(d) $2^x \bmod 67 = 41$,
(e) $7^x \bmod 71 = 41$.

Themes for Labs

3.3 Create programs implementing the baby-step giant-step and index calculus algorithms and solve on a computer the following equations:

(a) $2^x \bmod 30203 = 24322$,
(b) $2^x \bmod 30323 = 21740$,
(c) $2^x \bmod 30539 = 28620$,
(d) $2^x \bmod 30803 = 16190$,
(e) $5^x \bmod 31607 = 30994$

(due to lack of time, the program implementation of only some steps of the algorithms would be enough).

Chapter 4

Digital Signatures

4.1   RSA Digital Signature

Public-key cryptography has made a real revolution in contemporary computer and network technologies. There emerged a possibility to solve problems that earlier had seemed insoluble but now are widely called for in practice. One of the important elements of these new technologies is the digital signature. In many countries, including the USA and Russia, digital signature standards have been adopted and the notion of the digital signature is made part of civil legislation.

Before studying cryptographic digital signatures, let us formulate the main requirements which, ideally, should be met by any signature (including handwritten).

(1) It must be only the entity A that can sign documents on behalf of A, i.e. no one should be able to forge signatures.
(2) If the signed document is somehow altered or damaged, the signature must become invalid.
(3) The author of the signature should not be able to repudiate it.
(4) The signature must be verifiable by all interested parties, and moreover, a third party (e.g. the court) should be able to decide on the authenticity of the signature in cases of contention.

Of course, digital signatures should meet all these requirements but the signer and verifier may be thousands of kilometers from each other and communicate via an open computer network (e.g. the Internet).

In this section, we consider a digital signature scheme based on the RSA algorithm [Rivest *et al.* (1978)]. Historically, it was the first method discovered for creating digital signatures. Let's proceed to its description.

Suppose Alice intends to sign documents. Then she has to choose the RSA parameters in the same way as was described in Sec. 2.6. To do that, Alice selects two large primes P and Q, computes $N = PQ$ and $\phi = (P-1)(Q-1)$. Then she selects a number d relatively prime to ϕ and finds

$$c = d^{-1} \bmod \phi. \tag{4.1}$$

At last, she publishes the numbers N and d (her public key), e.g. exposes them at her Internet site in association with her name, and keeps secret the number c (her private key, the other numbers P, Q, and ϕ are no longer required). Now Alice is ready to sign documents and messages.

Assume that Alice wishes to sign a message $\bar{m} = m_1, \ldots, m_n$. First, she computes a so-called *hash function*

$$h = h(m_1, \ldots, m_n)$$

which maps the message $\bar{m}$ into a number h. It is assumed that the hash function algorithm is publicly known. For the time being, we shall not speak of the properties and ways of computation of hash functions, as this question will be considered in detail in Sec. 8.5. Point out only the property most important for us here: it is practically impossible to alter the main text $m_1, \ldots, m_n$ without altering $h(\bar{m})$. So, it is enough for Alice to sign only the number h, and this will act as a signature to the whole message $\bar{m}$.

Alice computes the number

$$s = h^c \bmod N, \tag{4.2}$$

i.e. she raises h to her secret power. The number s is nothing else but the digital signature. Alice simply appends s to the message $\bar{m}$ and obtains the signed message

$$\langle \bar{m}, \ s \rangle . \tag{4.3}$$

Now everybody who knows Alice's public key, i.e. the numbers N and d associated with her name, can verify the authenticity of her signature. To do that, given the signed message (4.3), one needs to compute hash function $h(\bar{m})$ and the number

$$w = s^d \bmod N, \tag{4.4}$$

after which one needs to check the equality $w = h(\bar{m})$.

Proposition 4.1. *If the signature is authentic, $w = h(\bar{m})$.*

Proof. It follows from (4.4), (4.2) and (4.1) that

$$w = s^d \bmod N = h^{cd} \bmod N = h = h(\bar{m}).$$ □

Proposition 4.2. *The described digital signature satisfies all the requirements the signature must meet.*

Proof. The first requirement is met since nobody who knows only the public parameters N and d can derive secret c which is needed to produce a signature (we have already discussed this problem in Sec. 2.6). The second requirement is fulfilled due to hash function: any change in the message contents will (with overwhelming probability) also change the value of h, which makes the previously computed signature invalid. The third requirement is met as a consequence of the former two (the author cannot repudiate the signature since nobody is able to alter the document and forge the signature). Finally, everybody who knows the public parameters N and d can verify the signature. In case of contention, the court can reproduce all computations. □

Consider an example. Let $P = 5$, $Q = 11$. Then $N = 5 \times 11 = 55$, $\phi = 4 \times 10 = 40$. Let $d = 3$. Such a choice of d is valid since $\gcd(40,3) = 1$. Compute the private key $c = 3^{-1} \bmod 40$ with the extended Euclidean algorithm (see Sec. 2.3), $c = 27$.

Assume that Alice wishes to sign the message $\bar{m} = abbbaa$, the value of hash function being, say, 13:

$$h = h(abbbaa) = 13.$$

Alice computes by (4.2)

$$s = 13^{27} \bmod 55 = 7$$

and obtains the signed message

$$\langle abbbaa,\ 7 \rangle.$$

Now the one who knows Alice's public key $N = 55$, $d = 3$ can verify the signature. Having received the signed message, one computes hash function

$$h(abbbaa) = 13$$

(if the contents of the message are not changed, the value of hash function equals that computed by Alice) and computes using (4.4)

$$w = 7^3 \bmod 55 = 13.$$

The values of w and the hash function are equal, hence, the signature is valid.

Remark 4.1. Notice that the same RSA scheme generated by Alice can be used for solving two problems. First, Alice can sign messages as was shown in the present section, by utilizing her *secret key c*. Second, anybody can encrypt messages to be read by Alice as was shown in Sec. 2.6, by utilizing her *public key d*.

4.2 ElGamal Digital Signature

In the previous section, a digital signature scheme was described whose security is based on the intractability of the integer factorization problem. In this section, we present a scheme that relies upon another hard problem, namely, computing discrete logarithms. This scheme was suggested in [ElGamal (1985)] and utilizes the ElGamal encryption (see Sec. 2.5).

Assume as before that Alice is going to sign documents. Alice chooses a large prime p and a number g such that different powers of g are different numbers modulo p (see Sec. 2.2). These numbers are transmitted or stored in the clear and may be used by the whole community of users. Alice then selects a random number x, $1 < x < p - 1$, which she keeps secret. This is her private key unknown to anybody. Alice computes the number

$$y = g^x \bmod p \tag{4.5}$$

and publishes it as her public key. Due to the hardness of the discrete logarithm problem, it is assumed impossible to find x given p and y.

Now Alice is ready to sign messages. Suppose she wants to sign a message $\bar{m} = m_1, \ldots, m_n$. Describe the steps needed to create a signature.

Alice begins with computing a hash function of the message $h = h(\bar{m})$, $1 < h < p$. Then Alice selects a random number k ($1 < k < p-1$) relatively prime to $p - 1$, and computes

$$r = g^k \bmod p. \tag{4.6}$$

Then Alice computes

$$u = (h - xr) \bmod (p - 1), \tag{4.7}$$

$$s = k^{-1} u \bmod (p - 1). \tag{4.8}$$

(Remark that k^{-1} in (4.8) denotes a number satisfying the equality

$$k^{-1} k \bmod (p - 1) = 1. \tag{4.9}$$

Such a k^{-1} exists since k and $p - 1$ are coprime, and can be found with the extended Euclidean algorithm.) Eventually, Alice forms the signed message

$$\langle \bar{m}; \quad r, \ s \rangle. \tag{4.10}$$

The receiver of the signed message (4.10), first of all, computes again the hash function $h = h(\bar{m})$. Then he verifies the signature using the equality

$$y^r r^s = g^h \bmod p. \tag{4.11}$$

Proposition 4.3. *If the signature is authentic then* (4.11) *holds.*

Proof. Recall that in all computations the exponents are reduced modulo $p - 1$. Substitute y and r into Eq. (4.11) using their defining equations (4.5) and (4.6), and then replace s with (4.8), (4.7):

$$y^r r^s = (g^x)^r \left(g^k \right)^s = g^{xr} g^{k\left(k^{-1}(h - xr) \right)}$$

$$= g^{xr} g^h g^{-xr} = g^h \bmod p. \qquad \square$$

Proposition 4.4. *The described digital signature satisfies all the requirements the signature must meet.*

Proof. The proof is virtually the same as for an RSA signature. First, a secret number x is used in the process of signature generation, moreover, the factor xr in (4.7) changes from message to message since k is selected at random. Therefore nobody can forge the signature. Second, the hash function prevents from altering signed messages. Third, the author cannot repudiate the signature as a consequence of the former items. Finally, everybody who knows the public key y and common parameters p and g can verify the signature. In case of contention, the court can reproduce all computations. $\square$

Consider an example. Let common parameters for a community of users be $p = 23$, $g = 5$. Alice chooses her private key $x = 7$ and computes her public key y by (4.5):

$$y = 5^7 \bmod 23 = 17.$$

Let Alice create the document $\bar{m} = baaaab$ and wish to sign it.

Proceed to signature generation. First of all, Alice computes the hash function of the message. Let $h(\bar{m}) = 3$. Then Alice selects a random number k, e.g. $k = 5$. Computations by (4.6), (4.7) give

$$r = 5^5 \bmod 23 = 20,$$

$$u = (3 - 7 \times 20) \bmod 22 = 17.$$

Then Alice finds $k^{-1} \bmod 22$:

$$k^{-1} \bmod 22 = 5^{-1} \bmod 22 = 9.$$

Computations by (4.8) give

$$s = 9 \times 17 \bmod 22 = 21.$$

At last, Alice forms the signed message (4.10) that looks like

$$\langle baaaab, \ 20, \ 21 \rangle.$$

The signed message is transmitted. Bob (or someone else) receives it and verifies the signature. First, he computes the hash function

$$h(baaaab) = 3,$$

then he computes the left of (4.11)

$$17^{20} \times 20^{21} \bmod 23 = 16 \times 15 \bmod 23 = 10,$$

and the right of (4.11)

$$5^3 \bmod 23 = 10.$$

Since the results of both computations are the same, Bob concludes that the signature is valid, i.e. the message is authentic.

The considered digital signature scheme is somewhat more complex than RSA but its security is based on a different one-way function. It is important for cryptography because should one system be broken or compromised, the other may be used instead. Besides, the ElGamal signature is a basis for a more efficient algorithm in which computation time is substantially reduced due to the use of "short" exponents. Such an algorithm is presented in the following section.

4.3   Digital Signature Standards

Today, digital signature standards exist in many countries. In this section, we describe the US standard FIPS-186 [FIPS 186-1 (1998)] and the Russian standard GOST R34.10-94 [RFC 4491 (2006)]. Both standards are based on essentially the same algorithm, called DSA (Digital Signature Algorithm), which, in turn, is a variant of ElGamal signature. We consider in detail an American version of the algorithm and then show the distinctive features of the Russian variant. Note that today there are newer digital signature standards based on elliptic curves (Chapter 6). However, as we shall see, the algorithms described in this section form the basis for elliptic curve methods.

As a preliminary setup, for a community of users, common open parameters are to be chosen. First, two prime numbers, q (of length 160 bits) and p (of length up to 1024 bits) are chosen related by the equation

$$p = bq + 1 \qquad (4.12)$$

for some integer b. The most significant bits in p and q must be 1. (FIPS-186 also suggests more secure pairs (q, p) of lengths (224, 2048), (256, 2048) and (256, 3072)).

Second, a number $a > 1$ is chosen such that

$$a^q \bmod p = 1. \qquad (4.13)$$

As a result, we have three common parameters p, q, and a.

Note that Eq. (4.13) means that, operating modulo p, the exponents of a are reduced modulo q, i.e.

$$a^c \bmod p = a^{c \bmod q} \bmod p \quad \text{for all } c. \qquad (4.14)$$

Indeed, if $c = mq + r$, where $0 \le r < q$, then $a^c \bmod p = (a^q)^m \times a^r \bmod p = 1 \times a^r \bmod p$, see (4.13). This reduction will always be made during signature generation and verification to ensure that the length of exponents will never exceed 160 bits, which simplifies computations.

Every user then chooses a random number x satisfying the condition $0 < x < q$ and computes

$$y = a^x \bmod p. \qquad (4.15)$$

The number x will be the private key of the user and the number y the public key. It is assumed that the public keys for all users are collected in a non-secret but "certified" directory which is made available to the whole community. Note that nowadays it is impossible to find x given y under the length of p indicated above. This completes the setup stage of the scheme and now all users are ready to generate and verify signatures.

Let there be given a message $\bar{m}$ to be signed. Signature generation is done as follows.

1 Compute hash function $h = h(\bar{m})$ for message m, the hash function value should lie within the limits $0 < h < q$ (in the American standard, SHA-1 or SHA-2 hash function [FIPS 180-4 (2015)] must be used).
2 Select a random integer k, $0 < k < q$.
3 Compute $r = (a^k \bmod p) \bmod q$. If $r = 0$, revert to Step 2.
4 Compute $s = k^{-1}(h + xr) \bmod q$. If $s = 0$, revert to Step 2.
5 Obtain the signed message $\langle \bar{m}; \ r, \ s \rangle$.

To verify the signature do the following.

6 Compute hash function of the message $h = h(\bar{m})$.
7 Verify that $0 < r < q$ and $0 < s < q$.
8 Compute $u_1 = h \times s^{-1} \bmod q$, $u_2 = r \times s^{-1} \bmod q$.
9 Compute $v = (a^{u_1} y^{u_2} \bmod p) \bmod q$.
10 Verify that $v = r$.

If at least one test at Step 7 or 10 fails one should reject the signature. And vice versa, if all the tests pass, the signature is declared valid.

Proposition 4.5. *If the signature on the message was created by a legitimate user, i.e. by the owner of private key x, then $v = r$.*

Proof. Recall that Eq. (4.14) holds for all exponentials with base a. Since y defined by Eq. (4.15) is a power of a, Eq. (4.14) also holds for all exponentials with y as a base. Now, using the definition of v (Step 9) and substituting the defining equations for u_1, u_2 (Step 8) we obtain

$$v = \left(a^{hs^{-1}} y^{rs^{-1}} \bmod p\right) \bmod q. \tag{4.16}$$

Using the definition of s (Step 4) we can write

$$s^{-1} \bmod q = k(h + xr)^{-1} \bmod q. \tag{4.17}$$

Substituting the right of Eq. (4.17) for s^{-1} in Eq. (4.16) we obtain

$$v = \left(a^{hk(h+xr)^{-1}} a^{xrk(h+xr)^{-1}} \bmod p\right) \bmod q$$

$$= \left(a^{(h+xr)^{-1}(h+xr)k} \bmod p\right) \bmod q$$

$$= (a^k \bmod p) \bmod q.$$

Taking into account the definition of r (Step 3) we conclude that $v = r$, which completes the proof. ☐

Remark 4.2. To find an integer a satisfying (4.13) the following method is recommended. Select a random integer $g > 1$ and compute

$$a = g^{(p-1)/q} \bmod p. \tag{4.18}$$

If $a > 1$ then it is what we need. Indeed, by (4.18) and Fermat's theorem

$$a^q \bmod p = g^{((p-1)/q)q} \bmod p = g^{p-1} \bmod p = 1,$$

i.e. (4.13) holds. If after computation by (4.18) we obtain $a = 1$ (extremely improbable case) then we should try another value of g.

Consider an example. Choose the common parameters

$$q = 11, \quad p = 6q + 1 = 67,$$

select $g = 10$ and compute

$$a = 10^6 \bmod 67 = 25.$$

Choose a private key $x = 6$ and compute the corresponding public key

$$y = 25^6 \bmod 67 = 62.$$

Generate a signature for the message $\bar{m} = baaaab$. Let hash function $h(\bar{m}) = 3$. Randomly select an integer $k = 8$. Compute

$$r = \left(25^8 \bmod 67\right) \bmod 11 = 24 \bmod 11 = 2,$$

$$k^{-1} \bmod q = 8^{-1} \bmod 11 = 7,$$

$$s = (7(3 + 6 \times 2) \bmod 11 = 105 \bmod 11 = 6.$$

We obtain the signed message

$$\langle baaaab;\ 2,\ 6 \rangle.$$

Now verify the signature. If the message is intact then $h = 3$. Compute

$$s^{-1} \bmod q = 6^{-1} \bmod 11 = 2,$$

$$u_1 = 3 \times 2 \bmod 11 = 6,$$

$$u_2 = 2 \times 2 \bmod 11 = 4,$$

$$v = \left(25^6 \times 62^4 \bmod 67\right) \bmod 11$$

$$= (62 \times 22 \bmod 67) \bmod 11 = 24 \bmod 11 = 2.$$

We see that $v = r$, hence, the signature is valid.

Let us now discuss the differences between the Russian standard and the American. They are as follows.

(1) The length of q is 256 bits.
(2) As a hash function, the Russian GOST R34.11-94 [RFC 4491 (2006)] is used.
(3) In the signature generation process, at Step 4, the parameter s is computed by the formula $s = (kh + xr) \bmod q$.
(4) In the signature verification process, at Step 8, u_1 and u_2 are computed by the formulas $u_1 = s \times h^{-1} \bmod q$, $u_2 = -r \times h^{-1} \bmod q$.

Taking into account these differences one can easily rewrite the whole scheme in the "Russian" style. The proof of correctness is quite similar.

Problems and Exercises

Assume in all tasks that $h(m) = m$ for all m.

4.1 Generate the RSA signature for m given the following parameters:

(a) $P = 5$, $Q = 11$, $c = 27$, $m = 7$;
(b) $P = 5$, $Q = 13$, $c = 29$, $m = 10$;
(c) $P = 7$, $Q = 11$, $c = 43$, $m = 5$;
(d) $P = 7$, $Q = 13$, $c = 29$, $m = 15$;
(e) $P = 3$, $Q = 11$, $c = 7$, $m = 24$.

4.2 For the specified public keys of each RSA user, verify the authenticity of the signed messages

(a) $N = 55$, $d = 3$: $\langle 7, 28 \rangle$, $\langle 22, 15 \rangle$, $\langle 16, 36 \rangle$;
(b) $N = 65$, $d = 5$: $\langle 6, 42 \rangle$, $\langle 10, 30 \rangle$, $\langle 6, 41 \rangle$;
(c) $N = 77$, $d = 7$: $\langle 13, 41 \rangle$, $\langle 11, 28 \rangle$, $\langle 5, 26 \rangle$;
(d) $N = 91$, $d = 5$: $\langle 15, 71 \rangle$, $\langle 11, 46 \rangle$, $\langle 16, 74 \rangle$;
(e) $N = 33$, $d = 3$: $\langle 10, 14 \rangle$, $\langle 24, 18 \rangle$, $\langle 17, 8 \rangle$.

4.3 The users of some network apply the ElGamal signature with common parameters $p = 23$, $g = 5$. For the specified private key, find the corresponding public key and generate a signature for message m.

(a) $x = 11$, $k = 3$, $m = h = 15$;
(b) $x = 10$, $k = 15$, $m = h = 5$;
(c) $x = 3$, $k = 13$, $m = h = 8$;
(d) $x = 18$, $k = 7$, $m = h = 5$;
(e) $x = 9$, $k = 19$, $m = h = 15$.

4.4 For the specified public key (y) of the ElGamal system with the common parameters $p = 23$, $g = 5$, verify the authenticity of the signed messages

(a) $y = 22$: $\langle 15; 20, 3 \rangle$, $\langle 15; 10, 5 \rangle$, $\langle 15; 19, 3 \rangle$;
(b) $y = 9$: $\langle 5; 19, 17 \rangle$, $\langle 7; 17, 8 \rangle$, $\langle 6; 17, 8 \rangle$;
(c) $y = 10$: $\langle 3; 17, 12 \rangle$, $\langle 2; 17, 12 \rangle$, $\langle 8; 21, 11 \rangle$;
(d) $y = 6$: $\langle 5; 17, 1 \rangle$, $\langle 5; 11, 3 \rangle$, $\langle 5; 17, 10 \rangle$;
(e) $y = 11$: $\langle 15; 7, 1 \rangle$, $\langle 10; 15, 3 \rangle$, $\langle 15; 7, 16 \rangle$.

4.5 A community of DSA users have the common parameters $q = 11$, $p = 67$, $a = 25$. Compute the public key (y) and generate a signature for message m given the following secret parameters:

(a) $x = 3$, $h = m = 10$, $k = 1$;
(b) $x = 8$, $h = m = 1$, $k = 3$;
(c) $x = 5$, $h = m = 5$, $k = 9$;
(d) $x = 2$, $h = m = 6$, $k = 7$;
(e) $x = 9$, $h = m = 7$, $k = 5$.

4.6 For the specified public keys of DSA users with the common parameters $q = 11$, $p = 67$, $a = 25$, verify the authenticity of the signed messages

(a) $y = 14$: $\langle 10; 4, 5 \rangle$, $\langle 10; 7, 4 \rangle$, $\langle 10; 3, 8 \rangle$;
(b) $y = 24$: $\langle 1; 3, 1 \rangle$, $\langle 1; 9, 1 \rangle$, $\langle 1; 4, 5 \rangle$;
(c) $y = 40$: $\langle 7; 7, 4 \rangle$, $\langle 7; 9, 2 \rangle$, $\langle 5; 9, 8 \rangle$;
(d) $y = 22$: $\langle 6; 9, 5 \rangle$, $\langle 8; 8, 3 \rangle$, $\langle 7; 4, 7 \rangle$;
(e) $y = 64$: $\langle 10; 7, 8 \rangle$, $\langle 7; 7, 3 \rangle$, $\langle 8; 7, 5 \rangle$.

Themes for Labs

4.7 Work out programs for the generation and verification of RSA signatures. The user parameters should be chosen on one's own. To test the signature verification program, the signed message $\langle 500, 46514 \rangle$ constructed under the public parameters $N = 52891$, $d = 3$ may be used (assume that $h(m) = m$). This message should be declared authentic. Any change in the components of the signed message, with high probability, should make the signature invalid.

4.8   Work out programs for the generation and verification of ElGamal signatures. The recommended values of common parameters are $p = 31259$, $g = 2$. The other parameters should be chosen on one's own. To test the signature verification program, the signed message $\langle 500; 27665, 26022 \rangle$ constructed under the public key $y = 16196$ may be used (assume that $h(m) = m$). This message should be declared authentic. Any change in the components of the signed message, with high probability, should make the signature invalid.

4.9   Work out programs for the generation and verification of DSA signatures. The recommended values of common parameters are $q = 787$, $p = 31481$, $a = 1928$. The other parameters should be chosen on one's own. To test the signature verification program, the signed message $\langle 500; 655, 441 \rangle$ constructed under the public key $y = 12785$ may be used (assume that $h(m) = m$). This message should be declared authentic. Any change in the components of the signed message, with high probability, should make the signature invalid.

Chapter 5

Cryptographic Protocols

5.1 Introduction

The cryptographic methods considered in the previous chapters are often used as tools for solving many other important problems. Not long ago some of those problems seemed completely insoluble. For example, it seemed impossible to securely commit commercial transactions between remote participants connected through open communications media, to make secure money transfers over public channels, to conduct elections without personal attendance and so on. Now all these problems can be solved by applying cryptographic techniques. The methods involved are usually described in the form of so-called *cryptographic protocols*. Several such protocols will be presented in this chapter.

Notice that cryptographic algorithms not only offer new facilities to the user (e.g. she can use a home computer and does not need to go to the bank to make payments) but are able to provide a considerably higher level of security compared to traditional mechanisms. For example, a traditional paper bank note can be fabricated, and the acts of fabricating money occur quite frequently, but by contrast, a digital bank note created with the use of cryptographic methods is practically impossible to fabricate.

Quite often important problems are formulated in the form of amusing games in order to make a solution "pure", not overladen with technical details. One of such problems, "mental poker", is considered in the next section.

5.2   Mental Poker

Consider the problem of playing a fair card game when the players are far from each other and can communicate only via some public channel, e.g. exchange messages via electronic mail. We consider an extremely simplified version of the problem where there are only two players and three cards. Nevertheless, all basic ideas will be demonstrated with obvious generalizations to other cases.

The problem is stated as follows. There are two players, Alice and Bob, and three cards, α, β, γ. It is required that cards be dealt so that each player gets one card and one card remains in the deck. Moreover, at the end of the game the following conditions must be fulfilled:

(1) each player gets any of three cards with equal probabilities;
(2) each player knows only his/her card but not the card of the opponent and/or the deck;
(3) in cases of contention, a third party is able to judge who has cheated;
(4) anyone who overhears the transmitted messages is unable to determine which cards are dealt to whom.

Let's describe the protocol that allows us to arrange such distributions of cards. A preliminary stage is needed for selecting the parameters of protocol. The participants publicly choose a large prime p. Then Alice randomly selects a number c_A coprime to $p-1$ and finds with the extended Euclidean algorithm the number d_A such that

$$c_A d_A \bmod (p-1) = 1. \tag{5.1}$$

Independently and similarly, Bob finds a pair c_B, d_B such that

$$c_B d_B \bmod (p-1) = 1. \tag{5.2}$$

These numbers are kept secret by each player. Then Alice randomly selects three different numbers $\hat{\alpha}$, $\hat{\beta}$, $\hat{\gamma}$ in the interval from 1 to $p-1$, sends them to Bob in clear and tells him that $\hat{\alpha}$ corresponds to α, $\hat{\beta}$ to β, $\hat{\gamma}$ to γ (e.g. 3756 denotes the ace).

After that we go to the second stage — the distribution of cards which is described by the following steps.

Step 1 Alice computes the numbers

$$u_1 = \hat{\alpha}^{c_A} \bmod p,$$

$$u_2 = \hat{\beta}^{c_A} \bmod p,$$

$$u_3 = \hat{\gamma}^{c_A} \bmod p,$$

and sends u_1, u_2, u_3 to Bob having shuffled them beforehand.

Step 2 Bob receives the three numbers, selects randomly one of them, say, u_2, and sends it back to Alice. It will be the card dealt to her in the game. Upon the receipt of u_2, Alice can compute

$$\hat{u} = u_2^{d_A} \bmod p = \hat{\beta}^{c_A d_A} \bmod p = \hat{\beta}, \tag{5.3}$$

i.e. she learns that her hand is β (she could learn this without computation since she knows the correspondence between all u_i and the cards).

Step 3 Bob continues. He computes for the two numbers left

$$v_1 = u_1^{c_B} \bmod p, \tag{5.4}$$

$$v_3 = u_3^{c_B} \bmod p. \tag{5.5}$$

With probability $1/2$ he rearranges v_1 and v_3 and sends them to Alice.

Step 4 Alice selects randomly one of the numbers received, say, v_1, computes the number

$$w_1 = v_1^{d_A} \bmod p \tag{5.6}$$

and sends w_1 to Bob. Bob computes

$$z = w_1^{d_B} \bmod p \tag{5.7}$$

and learns his card (his hand is $\hat{\alpha}$). Indeed,

$$z = w_1^{d_B} = v_1^{d_A d_B} = u_1^{c_B d_B d_A} = \hat{\alpha}^{c_A c_B d_A d_B} = \hat{\alpha} \bmod p.$$

The card corresponding to v_2 remains in the deck.

Proposition 5.1. *The described protocol satisfies all requirements for the fair distribution of cards.*

Proof. We give only the idea of proof. Alice shuffles the numbers u_1, u_2, u_3 prior to sending them to Bob. Then Bob selects one of these numbers without any knowledge of what corresponds to what. If he selects a number randomly, Alice gets any card with probability $1/3$. Similarly, if Alice selects one of the two remaining cards randomly (with equal probabilities) then Bob gets the card which can be any card with probability $1/3$. It is plain that under these conditions, the card in the deck can also be any card with probability $1/3$.

It is interesting to note that if any of the players violate the protocol specifications, it may be used against that player. Therefore each player is concerned with the exact observance of the rules. Let's check it assuming that the game repeats many times.

Suppose that Alice does not shuffle the numbers u_1, u_2, u_3, but always sends them in one order or follows some other simple rule. If the distribution of cards is carried out several times, Bob can benefit from Alice's behavior (e.g. he will always send back to Alice the first number and will know what card she is dealt). So it is advantageous to Alice to shuffle the cards. Similarly, it can be easily confirmed that it is better for Bob to shuffle and select cards randomly (with equal probabilities).

Check the second requirement of a fair card game. When Bob selects u_i to be Alice's card (Step 2) he does not know the secret c_A, so he cannot determine to which card u_i corresponds and the computation of c_A given u_i is equivalent to solving the discrete logarithm problem which is impossible when p is large. As a matter of fact, when Alice selects a card for Bob, and Bob for Alice, neither of them can determine the value of the card because it is encrypted with either c_A or c_B.

Notice also that neither Alice nor Bob can determine the card remaining in the deck because the corresponding number has the form $a^{c_A c_B}$ (see (5.4) and (5.5)). Alice does not know d_B and Bob does not know d_A to decrypt this.

Check the third requirement. In case of contention between Alice and Bob, they reveal their cards together with the record of all computations to the judge who is able to repeat all computations and bring in a verdict.

Finally, check the fourth requirement. Eve, who overhears all communication between Alice and Bob, has the numbers u_1, u_2, u_3, v_1, v_2, v_3, and w_1. Each of these numbers can be represented as $a^x \bmod p$ where x is unknown to Eve. But to find x one has to solve the discrete logarithm problem which is practically impossible. So Eve cannot learn anything. $\square$

Consider an example. Assume that Alice and Bob wish to honestly deal the three cards: the three (α), the seven (β), and the ace (γ). (More exactly, it is usually assumed in cryptography that neither of them wants to be cheated and "greater" honesty is not required.) Let the following parameters be chosen at the preliminary stage:

$$p = 23, \quad \hat{\alpha} = 2, \quad \hat{\beta} = 3, \quad \hat{\gamma} = 5.$$

Let Alice choose $c_A = 7$ and Bob $c_B = 9$. Then they find using the extended Euclidean algorithm that $d_A = 19$ and $d_B = 5$.

(Step 1) Alice computes

$$u_1 = 2^7 \bmod 23 = 13,$$
$$u_2 = 3^7 \bmod 23 = 2,$$
$$u_3 = 5^7 \bmod 23 = 17.$$

Then she shuffles u_1, u_2, u_3 and sends them to Bob.

(Step 2) Bob selects one of the numbers received. Let it be 17. He sends the number 17 to Alice. She knows that 17 corresponds to γ and so her hand is the ace.

(Step 3) Bob computes

$$v_1 = 13^9 \bmod 23 = 3,$$
$$v_2 = 2^9 \bmod 23 = 6$$

and sends these numbers to Alice, perhaps, having swapped them.

(Step 4) Alice receives the numbers 3 and 6, selects one of them, let it be 3, and computes the number

$$w_1 = 3^{19} \bmod 23 = 6.$$

She sends this number to Bob, who computes

$$z = 6^5 \bmod 23 = 2$$

and learns his card α, i.e. his hand is the three. The seven remains in the deck but neither Alice nor Bob know that. As for Eve who has intercepted all messages, she cannot learn the cards without having computed the inverse functions of the messages which is impossible when p is large.

5.3 Zero Knowledge Proofs

Consider the following problem which arises in some cryptographic applications. The participants are again Alice and Bob. Alice knows the solution of some complex problem and wishes to convince Bob thereof but in such a way that he would not learn the solution. In other words, Bob must become sure that Alice knows the solution but must know nothing about that solution. At first glance the very problem statement seems absurd and the possibility of its being settled fantastic! In order to realize the situation better, consider a scenario from the lives of pirates. Let Alice know of the map of an island where there is buried treasure. And let Bob be the captain of the ship which can get her to the island. Alice wishes to prove to Bob that she really possesses the map without showing it to him (or else Bob could manage without her and obtain all the treasure himself).

A similar problem occurs in computer networks in the cases when Bob (server or domain controller) has to decide whether Alice should be able to access the information stored in the network but Alice does not wish anybody who overhears the communications channels, including Bob himself, to learn anything about her password. That is, Bob gets zero knowledge about her password (or map) but is sure that Alice possesses that password (or map).

So our goal is to construct a "zero-knowledge proof" protocol. To that end we assume that the participants can play an unfair game and try to cheat one another.

As an example of a complex problem whose solution is known to Alice, we first consider the graph coloring problem with three colors. We describe a quite simple (in the sense of ideas) protocol for that problem. Then we consider the problem of finding the Hamiltonian cycle in a graph with a more complicated (in the sense of ideas) but more computationally efficient proof protocol. Note that both problems, the graph coloring and the finding of the Hamiltonian cycle, are NP-complete. We do not give a formal definition of NP-completeness, which can be found, e.g. in [Aho *et al.* (1976); Papadimitriou (1994)]. For the reader who is not familiar with this definition, note only that, informally, NP-completeness means the exponential growth of problem solving time as the problem size (the amount of initial data) increases.

5.3.1 *Graph Coloring Problem*

In the problem of graph coloring, a graph is considered with the set of vertices V and the set of edges E (denote the number of elements in these

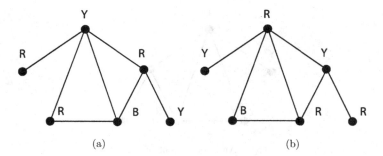

Fig. 5.1   Coloring: (a) — right coloring, (b) — wrong coloring.

sets by $|V|$ and $|E|$). Alice knows the right coloring of the graph with three colors, red (R), blue (B), and yellow (Y). The right coloring is the one where any two adjacent vertices, i.e. connected by an edge, are colored with different colors. Consider an example (Fig. 5.1).

In order to find a correct coloring with three colors, only exponential algorithms can be used, i.e. those whose computation time grows exponentially as the number of vertices and edges in a graph increases. Therefore, in the case of large $|V|$ and $|E|$ this problem is intractable.

So, Alice knows a right coloring in a graph with large $|V|$ and $|E|$. She wishes to prove that to Bob in such a way that he would not learn the coloring.

The protocol of proof consists of a number of realizations of the following procedure.

Step 1 Alice chooses a random permutation Π of three letters R, B, Y and changes the coloring of the graph according to that permutation. Obviously, the coloring remains correct. For example, if $\Pi = (Y, R, B)$ then the coloring on the left (Fig. 5.1) turns into the coloring shown in Fig. 5.2.

Step 2 For every vertex v from set V, Alice generates a large random integer r and replaces its two least significant bits by the color code: 00 for red, 01 for blue, 10 for yellow.

Step 3 For every vertex v, Alice generates the data used in RSA, namely, P_v, Q_v, $N_v = P_v Q_v$, c_v, and d_v.

Step 4 Alice computes

$$Z_v = r_v^{d_v} \bmod N_v$$

and sends Bob the values N_v, d_v, and Z_v, for each vertex.

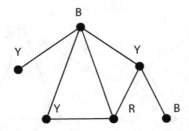

Fig. 5.2 Another variant of coloring.

Step 5 Bob selects randomly one edge from set E and tells Alice what edge he has selected. Alice responds with the numbers c_{v_1} and c_{v_2} corresponding to the vertices of this edge. After that Bob computes

$$\hat{Z}_{v_1} = Z_{v_1}^{c_{v_1}} \bmod N_{v_1} = r_{v_1}, \quad \hat{Z}_{v_2} = Z_{v_2}^{c_{v_2}} \bmod N_{v_2} = r_{v_2}$$

and checks the two least significant bits in these numbers. Under the right coloring, the least significant bits in $\hat{Z}_{v_1}$ and $\hat{Z}_{v_2}$ must be different. If it is not the case, Alice is declared to be cheating and the protocol stops. Otherwise, the described procedure repeats once again. The total number of repetitions is $a|E|$ where $a > 0$ is a protocol parameter.

Proposition 5.2. *If Alice does not know the right coloring of the graph then the probability of deceiving Bob does not exceed* e^{-a} *where* e ≈ 2.718 *is the Euler number (the base of a natural logarithm).*

Remark 5.1. If one takes a large a then the probability of deception can be made as small as desired. For instance, with $a = 5$ this probability is less than 0.01.

Proof. Assume that Alice does not know the right coloring, i.e. her coloring is not correct. In this case, at least for one edge the vertices are equally colored. If Alice obeys the protocol then the probability of Bob selecting that edge is not less than $1/|E|$ (in this case Alice is denounced). Hence, the probability that Alice can deceive at one realization of the protocol procedure does not exceed $1 - 1/|E|$ and, consequently, the probability that Alice can deceive at $a|E|$ realizations does not exceed $(1 - 1/|E|)^{a|E|}$. Using a well-known inequality $1 - x \le e^{-x}$ we obtain

$$(1 - 1/|E|)^{a|E|} \le \left(e^{-1/|E|}\right)^{a|E|} = e^{-a}.$$

$\square$

Check the properties zero-knowledge proof must have.

(1) We see that the probability of Alice's deception can be made as small as desired by selecting large a.

(2) Let us explain why Bob does not receive any information about coloring. Because the colors are permuted randomly in each realization (see Step 1), he cannot learn the right coloring by examining all the edges one after another. All he learns is that two adjacent vertices are differently colored but it gives him no information about the coloring. Besides, he cannot find the codes of the colors given the set of N_v and d_v since r_v is random (Step 2). He also cannot decrypt Z_v since he does not know c_v (these are not sent for all vertices) and cannot compute c_v without P_v and Q_v.

(3) Consider one more chance to deceive that Alice seems to have. It seems that Alice can substitute c_{v_1} and c_{v_2} with other values at Step 5. But it is impossible since the value c_v satisfying the equation

$$c_v d_v \bmod ((P_v - 1)(Q_v - 1)) = 1$$

is unique and Bob knows d_v.

So, all requirements are fulfilled:

(1) Alice proves to Bob that she knows the problem's solution and the probability of deception does not exceed e^{-a};
(2) Bob obtains no information about the coloring.

Consider the last chance for deception for all participants. What will ensue should they disobey the described protocol by not making their choices randomly?

Let it be, for instance, that Bob does not ask for edges randomly but by some simple rule (e.g. in their order). In this case Alice, not actually knowing the coloring, can deceive him by preparing "right" colors only for the edges he will ask for. Therefore Bob is interested in making random selections without any regularity.

The security of other protocol actions is determined by security of RSA and under large P_v and Q_v the system is quite reliable.

5.3.2 *Hamiltonian Cycle Problem*

The problem considered in this subsection not only gives us an opportunity to describe one more scheme of constructing zero-knowledge proofs but also plays an important theoretical role. Manuel Blum showed that, speaking

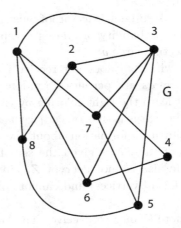

Fig. 5.3   Graph with Hamiltonian cycle (8, 2, 4, 6, 3, 5, 7, 1).

informally, any mathematical statement can be represented as a graph, the proof of the statement being in correspondence with the Hamiltonian cycle of the graph (see [Goldreich *et al.* (1987); Schneier (1996)]). Therefore the existence of zero-knowledge proof for a Hamiltonian cycle implies that the proof of any mathematical statement can be presented in the form of zero-knowledge proof.

Definition 5.1. *The Hamiltonian cycle in a graph is a continuous circular path that passes through all vertices. Each vertex is visited exactly once.*

Consider for example the graph shown in Fig. 5.3. The path that sequentially passes through vertices 8, 2, 4, 6, 3, 5, 7, 1, is a Hamiltonian cycle. Actually, this path contains all vertices of the graph and each vertex is visited only once.

It is plain that if a Hamiltonian cycle exists in a graph G with n vertices, then, under a certain numbering of vertices, it will pass exactly through vertices with sequential numbers $1, 2, 3, \ldots, n$. So by examining all possible enumerations of vertices we shall necessarily find a Hamiltonian cycle. But the number of enumerations equals $n!$ and therefore, already under moderately large n, say, $n = 100$, this approach becomes infeasible in practice. It is proved that the problem of finding a Hamiltonian cycle in a graph is NP-complete (we have already mentioned this). Informally, NP-completeness of the considered problem means that, for solving it, no algorithms exist (more exactly, no algorithms are known) which are essentially faster than the exhaustive search method mentioned above.

Our task is to construct a protocol that shall be used by Alice to prove to Bob that she knows a Hamiltonian cycle in a certain graph G in such a way that Bob will not get any knowledge of this cycle. The first construction of the protocol was suggested in [Blum (1986)]. Recall once more that "zero knowledge" means that, independently of the number of realizations of the protocol, Bob will have the same knowledge about the Hamiltonian cycle as he might have if he had just studied the graph G.

So, assume that Alice knows a Hamiltonian cycle in graph G. She can prove this to Bob (and anybody else who has the graph) with the help of a protocol described below. She may use this proof, e.g. for her personal identification. But before giving the protocol description, let us agree on some notation.

We shall denote graphs by letters G, H, F, implying simultaneously corresponding adjacency matrices. The matrix element $H_{i,j} = 1$ if there is an edge in graph H which connects the vertices i and j; $H_{i,j} = 0$ otherwise. The symbol $\|$ will denote the concatenation of two numbers, more exactly, of two corresponding binary words. For example, $10010\|1 = 100101$. We need a public-key cipher. Generally speaking, it may be any cipher, but for concreteness we shall use RSA (Sec. 2.6). Assume that Alice has generated the RSA system with public parameters N and d. It is essential that the messages encrypted with that system can only be decrypted by Alice and no one else (since only Alice knows the corresponding private key).

Proceed now to the description of the protocol. Each protocol realization comprises the following four steps (explanations will be given below).

Step 1 Alice constructs a graph H which is the copy of G with a new (random) numbering of vertices. In terms of graph theory, H is said to be isomorphic to G. Alternatively, H is obtained by some permutation of vertices in G (preserving connections between vertices). Alice encodes matrix H by ascribing to initial zeros and ones random numbers $r_{i,j}$ according to the scheme $\tilde{H}_{i,j} = r_{i,j}\|H_{i,j}$. Then she encrypts the elements of matrix $\tilde{H}$ and obtains the encrypted matrix F, $F_{i,j} = \tilde{H}_{i,j}^d \bmod N$. Alice sends matrix F to Bob.

Step 2 Upon the receipt of encrypted matrix F, Bob asks Alice one of two questions:

(1) What is the Hamiltonian cycle in graph H?
(2) Is graph H isomorphic to G?

Step 3 Alice answers the question Bob asked:

(1) In response to the first question, she decrypts in F the edges that constitute the Hamiltonian cycle.

(2) In response to the second question, she decrypts F completely (in fact, she sends Bob the graph $\tilde{H}$) and reveals the permutations used to produce graph H from G.

Step 4 Having received the reply, Bob checks the correctness of decrypting by repeated encrypting and comparing to F and makes certain that either the edges decrypted constitute a Hamiltonian cycle, or the permutations revealed convert graph G to graph H.

The described process repeats t times.

We briefly discuss several issues on the protocol construction in the form of questions and answers.

(1) Why does Alice construct an isomorphic graph? If she had not done that, Bob, upon receiving the reply to his Question 1, would have learned the Hamiltonian cycle in graph G.

(2) Why does Alice encode the matrix H? We have already met with this trick when encrypting the colors of vertices. The issue is that it is impossible to encrypt individual zeros and ones (with RSA cipher they are not changed at all). Even if we replace 0 and 1 by some numbers a and b then we will obtain as few as two different ciphertexts and it will be straightforward to determine their correspondence to a and b, i.e. the graph's structure will not be concealed. Here we face a typical situation where a so-called *randomized cipher* is necessary. And this cipher is constructed by introducing random numbers into the matrix H prior to encrypting. The encoded matrix $\tilde{H}$ completely describes the graph (odd numbers denote the presence of edge, even numbers the absence of it) but after encryption the graph's structure becomes completely concealed.

(3) Why does Bob ask two questions? If he had asked only Question 1 which is, in a sense, the main question, then Alice, not actually knowing a Hamiltonian cycle in graph G, would have been able to present another graph with the same number of vertices and an artificially enclosed Hamiltonian cycle. Therefore Bob sometimes asks Alice to prove the isomorphism of H and G. The point is that Alice does not know in advance what question she will be asked.

(4) Why can Bob not ask the two questions at once? In this case he would have learned the Hamiltonian cycle in G, since he had obtained a Hamiltonian cycle in H and the way of converting H into G.

(5) Why does Bob check the correctness of decrypting? If he had not done that then Alice at Step 4 would have sent some "favorable" information not connected with that sent at Step 2.

The main details of the protocol are more strictly justified in the proofs of the following two propositions.

Proposition 5.3. *The probability of deception under t protocol realizations does not exceed 2^{-t}.*

Proof. First we show that the probability of deception in one realization of the protocol equals $1/2$. Notice that if Alice knows the Hamiltonian cycle in graph G, she can answer right to any of Bob's questions. On the contrary, if she does not know the Hamiltonian cycle then the most she can do is to prepare an answer to either the first or the second question. In expectation of Question 1 she creates a new graph with artificially enclosed Hamiltonian cycle. But in this case she will not be able to prove its isomorphism to graph G. In expectation of Question 2 she creates a graph isomorphic to G. But in this case she will not be able to show a Hamiltonian cycle therein. So the probability of deception equals the probability of guessing the question number. Assuming that Bob asks both questions with equal probabilities we obtain that the probability of deception equals $1/2$.

Since Bob stops the game upon a first incorrect answer, the probability of deception under t realizations of the protocol does not exceed $(1/2)^t$. $\square$

Proposition 5.4. *The described protocol implements a zero-knowledge proof.*

Proof. In order to prove that Bob does not get any knowledge in realization of the protocol it suffices to show that all he receives from Alice he would obtain himself without entering into any communication with Alice.

Let's begin with Bob's second question. As a reply to this question he receives a graph isomorphic to G. But he could himself construct as many isomorphic graphs as he wished and what he obtains from Alice is one of such graphs.

The case of Bob's first question is not that simple. As a reply to his first question he obtains a Hamiltonian cycle in a graph isomorphic to graph G. At first glance it may seem that this provides Bob with some information. But it is not so. Notice that if G possesses a Hamiltonian cycle then under some numbering of vertices, there exists an isomorphic graph defined by the adjacency matrix of the form

$$
\begin{pmatrix}
* & 1 & * & \cdots & * & * & * \\
* & * & 1 & \cdots & * & * & * \\
 & & & \cdots & & & \\
* & * & * & \cdots & * & 1 & * \\
* & * & * & \cdots & * & * & 1 \\
1 & * & * & \cdots & * & * & *
\end{pmatrix},
\tag{5.8}
$$

where $*$ denotes the uncertainty in the presence or absence of edge. Under such a numbering the Hamiltonian cycle passes through the vertices in increasing order of numbers. By changing the numbering of vertices Bob can construct from (5.8) various isomorphic matrices. When Alice, replying to Bob's first question, reveals the Hamiltonian cycle, Bob obtains just one of these matrices.

So, Bob does not obtain any additional information from Alice which he could not obtain himself.   □

Consider an example to illustrate all steps and operations of the described protocol.

Consider an example. Take as a basis the graph G shown in Fig. 5.3. Its adjacency matrix is

$$
G =
\begin{array}{c}
\\ 1 \\ 2 \\ 3 \\ 4 \\ 5 \\ 6 \\ 7 \\ 8
\end{array}
\begin{pmatrix}
1 & 2 & 3 & 4 & 5 & 6 & 7 & 8 \\
0 & 0 & 1 & 0 & 0 & 1 & 1 & \boxed{1} \\
0 & 0 & 1 & \boxed{1} & 0 & 0 & 0 & 1 \\
1 & 1 & 0 & 0 & \boxed{1} & 1 & 1 & 0 \\
0 & 1 & 0 & 0 & 0 & \boxed{1} & 0 & 0 \\
0 & 0 & 1 & 0 & 0 & 0 & \boxed{1} & 1 \\
1 & 0 & \boxed{1} & 1 & 0 & 0 & 0 & 0 \\
\boxed{1} & 0 & 1 & 0 & 1 & 0 & 0 & 0 \\
1 & \boxed{1} & 0 & 0 & 1 & 0 & 0 & 0
\end{pmatrix}.
$$

The box $\boxed{\cdot}$ is used to show the Hamiltonian cycle. Let's use the RSA system with public parameters $N = 55$, $d = 3$ for encryption.

At Step 1 of the protocol, Alice chooses a random numbering of vertices, say, 7, 4, 5, 3, 1, 2, 8, 6, and constructs an isomorphic graph

$$
H = \begin{array}{c} \\ 7 \\ 4 \\ 5 \\ 3 \\ 1 \\ 2 \\ 8 \\ 6 \end{array}
\left(
\begin{array}{cccccccc}
7 & 4 & 5 & 3 & 1 & 2 & 8 & 6 \\
0 & 0 & 1 & 1 & \boxed{1} & 0 & 0 & 0 \\
0 & 0 & 0 & 0 & 0 & 1 & 0 & \boxed{1} \\
\boxed{1} & 0 & 0 & 1 & 0 & 0 & 1 & 0 \\
1 & 0 & \boxed{1} & 0 & 1 & 1 & 0 & 1 \\
1 & 0 & 0 & 1 & 0 & 0 & \boxed{1} & 1 \\
0 & \boxed{1} & 0 & 1 & 0 & 0 & 1 & 0 \\
0 & 0 & 1 & 0 & 1 & \boxed{1} & 0 & 0 \\
0 & 1 & 0 & \boxed{1} & 1 & 0 & 0 & 0
\end{array}
\right).
$$

Next, she must encode H by ascribing to the zeros and ones some random numbers. In this particular example let her simply ascribe to the left of each element a randomly chosen digit from the set $\{1, 2, 3, 4, 5\}$:

$$
\tilde{H} =
\begin{pmatrix}
50 & 20 & 11 & 31 & 21 & 40 & 20 & 10 \\
40 & 30 & 50 & 20 & 10 & 41 & 50 & 21 \\
41 & 30 & 50 & 11 & 30 & 20 & 51 & 40 \\
11 & 10 & 41 & 30 & 51 & 41 & 30 & 21 \\
31 & 20 & 40 & 11 & 50 & 10 & 41 & 31 \\
50 & 41 & 20 & 21 & 40 & 10 & 21 & 50 \\
40 & 30 & 31 & 50 & 41 & 21 & 30 & 40 \\
20 & 41 & 10 & 51 & 41 & 20 & 30 & 40
\end{pmatrix}.
$$

Now she encrypts the matrix $\tilde{H}$ by cubing each element modulo 55:

$$
F =
\begin{pmatrix}
40 & 25 & 11 & 36 & 21 & 35 & 25 & 10 \\
35 & 50 & 40 & 25 & 10 & 06 & 40 & 21 \\
06 & 50 & 40 & 11 & 50 & 25 & 46 & 35 \\
11 & 10 & 06 & 50 & 46 & 06 & 50 & 21 \\
36 & 25 & 35 & 11 & 40 & 10 & 06 & 36 \\
40 & 06 & 25 & 21 & 35 & 10 & 21 & 40 \\
35 & 50 & 36 & 40 & 06 & 21 & 50 & 35 \\
25 & 06 & 10 & 46 & 06 & 25 & 50 & 35
\end{pmatrix}.
$$

(It may seem upon attentive examination of matrix F that the cipher used poorly hides the initial matrix H. It is explained by the small value of the modulus $N = 55$ and, as a consequence, the great number of elements in $\tilde{H}$ that are not coprime to the modulus. For any "real" RSA system where N is large this situation is practically impossible.)

At Step 2, Bob receives the matrix F and asks one of the two questions. If he asks Alice to prove the isomorphism of the graphs, Alice simply sends him the encoded matrix $\tilde{H}$ and the numbering used 7, 4, 5, 3, 1, 2, 8, 6 (Step 3). At Step 4, Bob checks the correspondence of $\tilde{H}$ to F, i.e. the equalities $50^3 \bmod 55 = 40$, $20^3 \bmod 55 = 25$ and so on. Next, Bob obtains from $\tilde{H}$ the graph H (by discarding the high-order digits). Then he permutes the vertices of G with respect to the received numbering, as Alice did, and makes sure that H and G are the same graph (up to the numbering of vertices).

If at Step 2 Bob asks Alice to show him the Hamiltonian cycle, Alice sends him the corresponding list of (encoded) edges of graph H: $(1, 5, 21)$, $(5, 7, 41)$, $(7, 6, 21), \ldots, (3, 1, 41)$. Each element contains the vertex numbers and the code of an edge (Step 3). At Step 4, Bob checks the correspondence of the edges in the list to matrix F, for instance, $21^3 \bmod 55 = 21 = F_{1,5}$, $41^3 \bmod 55 = 06 = F_{5,7}$ and so on. Then he makes sure that the path specified by the list passes through all vertices, each vertex being visited only once.

5.4 Digital Cash

Nowadays in many countries people pay for purchases by electronic cards, order plane tickets over the Internet, buy various goods in Internet shops etc. The information about purchases is accumulated in the shops and banks. As a consequence, a new problem has arisen which is sometimes called a "Big Brother problem".

The essence of this problem is that the anonymity of the purchase is lost, i.e. the information about the purchases of any person may be made known to a third party and used against the person. For instance, the information about purchasing train or plane tickets may be of interest to criminals, the information about purchases of alcoholic drinks by a politician can be used against him by his opponents, etc.

Therefore the idea emerged to work out such schemes of electronic payments that would preserve the anonymity of the purchaser to the same extent as payments made by cash. The corresponding protocols have got the name of "digital cash" which emphasizes their main property — to ensure the same degree of anonymity as ordinary cash. The scheme described below was suggested by David Chaum[Chaum (1983); Chaum (1985)], see also [Goldwasser and Bellare (2008)].

For ease of understanding, we first consider two "bad" schemes and then a "good" one.

We begin with a more precise setting of the problem. There are three participants: the Bank, the User (customer), and the Vendor (shop). Both User and Vendor have corresponding accounts in the Bank, and the User wants to buy something from the Vendor. The purchase is done by means of the following three-step process:

(1) the User withdraws a sum, in the form of bank note, from her bank account;
(2) the User pays the Vendor with the note;
(3) the Vendor gives the note to the Bank to credit his account and the User takes her purchase.

We assume that all communications between the participants are carried out over a secured channel which may be created by using the public-key cryptographic methods such as those considered in Chap. 2.

Our goal is to construct an electronic payment scheme that

- makes forgery or fabricating bank notes impossible;
- preserves the customer's anonymity.

We shall user RSA as an underlying cryptographic tool. Let the Bank have the following RSA parameters: secret numbers P, Q, c and public

$$N = PQ,$$
$$d = c^{-1} \bmod (P - 1)(Q - 1). \tag{5.9}$$

We shall first consider the case when a bank note of only one denomination, say, £100 may be used.

Now let's describe the first "bad" scheme. Suppose the User decided to spend £100. Then she must create together with the Bank a digital bank note. To do that the User sends to the Bank a number n which will be the serial number of bank note (it is usually required that n be a random number in the interval $[2, N - 1]$).

The Bank computes

$$s = n^c \bmod N \tag{5.10}$$

and makes a note $\langle n, s \rangle$. The Bank debits the User account with £100 and sends the note back to the User. The parameter s in the note is the Bank's signature. Nobody can forge the signature since the number c is secret.

The User pays (perhaps by sending over the network) the note $\langle n, s \rangle$ to the Vendor in order to buy some goods. The Vendor relays the note to the Bank. First of all, the Bank verifies the signature (it could be done by the Vendor, as well). But, besides, the Bank stores all serial numbers of the notes accepted earlier and now searches for n in that list. If n is found in the list then the payment is rejected (somebody tries to double-spend the note) of which the Bank informs the Vendor. Otherwise, if all tests are successful, the Bank credits £100 to the Vendor account and the Vendor gives the goods to the User.

The drawback of the described scheme is the absence of anonymity. The Bank could have memorized the association between the serial number n and the User and therefore is able to learn who has spent the bank note and where.

Consider the second "bad" scheme which, however, provides anonymity. It is based on the so-called *blind signature*.

Again the User wants to buy some goods. Now she generates a serial number n which will not be sent to the Bank. She generates another random number r, coprime to N, and computes

$$\hat{n} = (n \times r^d) \bmod N \tag{5.11}$$

(recall that the pair N, d is the Bank's public key). The number $\hat{n}$ is sent to the Bank.

The Bank computes

$$\hat{s} = \hat{n}^c \bmod N \tag{5.12}$$

and sends the number $\hat{s}$ back to the User (along with debiting the User account with £100).

The User computes $r^{-1} \bmod N$ and

$$s = (\hat{s} \times r^{-1}) \bmod N. \tag{5.13}$$

Notice that, taking into account the equations (5.12), (5.11), and (5.9), we have

$$s = \hat{n}^c \times r^{-1} = (n \times r^d)^c \times r^{-1} = n^c r^{dc} \times r^{-1} = n^c r^1 r^{-1} = n^c \bmod N,$$

i.e. we obtain the Bank's signature to the number n (see (5.10)) but n is unknown to the Bank (and whatever else). This computation (5.12) is called a *blind signature* since the signer cannot see the real message (n) and cannot ever "extract" it from $\hat{n}$ since r is an unknown random number.

As a result, the User has the number n, which has never been transmitted over communications channels and is unknown to anybody, and the Bank's signature s, which is equal to the one computed by (5.10). The User makes a bank note $\langle n, s \rangle$ and acts the same way as before. But now the note is really anonymous like an ordinary paper note.

The actions of the Vendor and the Bank upon the receipt of the note do not differ from those described in the first scheme.

But why have we called the present scheme bad? It has the following flaw: one can fabricate a new bank note given at least two genuine notes. Let a counterfeiter have two genuine notes $\langle n_1, s_1 \rangle$ and $\langle n_2, s_2 \rangle$. Then he can easily make a fake note $\langle n_3, s_3 \rangle$ by computing

$$n_3 = n_1 n_2 \bmod N,$$

$$s_3 = s_1 s_2 \bmod N.$$

Actually,

$$n_3^c = (n_1 n_2)^c = n_1^c n_2^c = s_1 s_2 = s_3 \bmod N, \tag{5.14}$$

i.e. s_3 is a valid signature on n_3 and the Bank has no reason to reject this fake note (it cannot be differentiated from the genuine ones). Equation (5.14) represents a so-called *multiplicative property* of RSA.

Describe, at last, a "good" scheme free of all drawbacks of the former two. The first variant uses some one-way function

$$f: \{1, \ldots, N\} \to \{1, \ldots, N\},$$

(f can be computed easily but the inverse function f^{-1} is practically uncomputable). Function f is publicly known (i.e. known to the User, Vendor, and Bank).

A bank note is now defined as a pair of numbers $\langle n, s_f \rangle$ where

$$s_f = (f(n))^c \bmod N,$$

i.e. not n is signed but $f(n)$.

The User generates n (keeping it secret), computes $f(n)$, obtains the blind signature of the Bank on $f(n)$ and makes a note $\langle n, s_f \rangle$. This note possesses all the good properties as in the second scheme and, at the same time, cannot be fabricated since it is impossible to compute f^{-1}. For signature verification (i.e. for authentication of the note) one needs to compute $f(n)$ and check that

$$s_f^d \bmod N = f(n).$$

Note that the one-way function must be judiciously chosen. For instance, the function $f(n) = n^2 \bmod N$, which is indeed one-way, does not fit for the protocol in question. The reader may verify that the notes created with this function will still possess the multiplicative property (5.14). In practice, cryptographic hash functions (described in Sec. 8.5) are usually employed.

All the other actions of the Vendor and Bank remain the same as in the schemes described earlier.

The second, simpler, way to overcome the multiplicative property of RSA, is to introduce some redundancy into the message. Suppose the length of the modulus N is 1024 bits. So can be the length of n. Put a (randomly selected) serial number of a note only into the 512 low-order bits of n, and allocate the 512 high-order bits of n to some fixed number. This fixed number may contain some useful information, such as the denomination of a note, the name of a bank, etc. (512 bits are enough to represent a string of 64 ASCII symbols). Now the Bank, upon the receipt of the note, will require a mandatory fixed heading in parameter n and reject the note in case of absence thereof. The probability of the event that after multiplying two numbers modulo N the product will coincide with the factors in 512 bits is negligibly small. Therefore it is impossible to fabricate a note by using the formula (5.14).

Consider an example. Let the private parameters of the Bank be $P = 17$, $Q = 7$, $c = 77$. The corresponding public parameters are $N = 119$, $d = 5$.

To preclude fabricating notes the admissible serial numbers will be those consisting of two identical decimal digits, e.g. 11, 77, 99.

When the User wants to obtain a note she first randomly selects its serial number (from the set of admissible numbers). Suppose the User has selected $n = 33$. Then she selects a random number r coprime to 119. Let $r = 67$, $\gcd(67, 119) = 1$. Then the User computes

$$\hat{n} = (33 \times 67^5) \bmod 119 = (33 \times 16) \bmod 119 = 52.$$

It is the number 52 that she sends to the Bank.

The Bank debits the User account with £100 and sends her back the number

$$\hat{s} = 52^{77} \bmod 119 = 103.$$

The User computes $r^{-1} = 67^{-1} \bmod 119 = 16$, $s = 103 \times 16 \bmod 119 = 101$ and makes a note

$$\langle n, s \rangle = \langle 33, 101 \rangle.$$

She pays this note to the Vendor to obtain some goods.

The Vendor forwards the note to the Bank. The Bank verifies that:

(1) the serial number ($n = 33$) consists of two identical digits (i.e. contains the required redundancy);
(2) a note with this serial number has not been spent before;
(3) the Bank's signature is valid, i.e. $33^5 \bmod 119 = 101$.

All tests being successful, the Bank credits £100 to the Vendor account. The Vendor serves goods to the User.

In the conclusion to this chapter we discuss two more issues regarding the digital cash protocol.

In the presented scheme, independently acting users or even one user who does not remember the numbers of notes produced earlier, can by chance generate two or more notes with equal numbers. Under the conditions of the protocol, only one of these notes (which is submitted first) will be accepted by the Bank. But let's take into account the lengths of the numbers used in the protocol. If the serial number of note is a 512-bit integer and the users generate it randomly then the probability of ever obtaining any equal numbers is negligible.

The second issue is that in the scheme presented, the notes of only one denomination are used, which is, of course, inconvenient for the users. This can be surmounted as follows. The Bank acquires several pairs (c_i, d_i) subject to (5.9) and declares that, say, d_1 corresponds to £1000, d_2 to £500, and so on. When the User asks the Bank for a blind signature she additionally specifies the desired denomination of note. The Bank debits the User account with the specified amount and uses the corresponding secret number c_i to generate the signature. When the Bank receives a signed note afterwards, it uses the numbers d_1, d_2, etc. one after another for signature verification. If the signature is valid for some d_i then the note of ith denomination is accepted. In the variant where the parameter n of the note contains a fixed heading with an indication of the denomination, the Bank directly applies the relevant key d_i.

5.5   Mutual Identification with Key Establishment

In the present section, we consider a cryptographically secure protocol that allows two users A and B to mutually identify each other (i.e. A makes sure that she deals with B, and B makes sure that he deals with A) and to create a common secret key that may be used for further encryption of transmitted messages. In real life A and B may be a user and a computer system, or two computer systems, it does not matter for the protocol described below.

In the course of our study we consider more and more subtle types of attacks and means of protection against them. Thus we have earlier considered (see Sec. 2.1 and 2.2) the approaches to solve the problem of identification and key establishment. But we implicitly assumed then that the adversary can only overhear the information transmitted over open channels. However, in contemporary communications networks, e.g. in the Internet, the user data is transmitted through a number of intermediate nodes (such as routers, gates, mail servers, etc.) that are not controlled by the user. As a result, an adversary settled down on one of such nodes is able not only to overhear the information, i.e. to play just a passive role, but also to perform some active operations, e.g. to alter, install, or delete messages.

Look into a typical attack on the Diffie–Hellman system in a network with an active adversary. Alice chooses her secret number X_A and sends Bob g^{X_A}. Bob chooses his secret number X_B and sends Alice g^{X_B}. But Eve intercepts these numbers and sends Alice and Bob g^{X_E} instead, where X_E is her number. All these numbers look completely random, so neither Alice nor Bob suspects anything. Alice ends up with the key $K_A = g^{X_E X_A}$, and Bob with $K_B = g^{X_E X_B}$. Both these keys can also be computed by Eve. Now when Alice sends Bob a message enciphered with K_A, Eve deciphers it, re-enciphers it with K_B and sends it to Bob. She acts similarly in a case of reverse transmission. Alice and Bob believe that they communicate securely but actually Eve reads all their messages.

Such an attack becomes impossible if Alice and Bob do not transmit their public keys (in the Diffie–Hellman system these are $Y_A = g^{X_A}$ and $Y_B = g^{X_B}$) but take them out of a table or directory obtained earlier from a "reliable" source (as it was assumed in Sec. 2.2).

As a matter of fact, the majority of public key systems require some organizational structure providing for public key certification. Such a structure may look like the following. There is a "trusted" user Trent in the network to which Alice and Bob belong. Trent has no interests of his own but wishes to ensure the reliable and secure functioning of the network (most likely it is not a human but a heavily-guarded computer operating upon a hardcored program). Trent makes use of some reliable cryptosystem (e.g. RSA with a modulus length of about 10000 bits) with corresponding private keys and performs only two tasks:

(1) he adds to his database the information about the public key of a user sent to him as a message encrypted with the use of Trent's public key;
(2) he provides information about the public key of a user supplied with Trent's signature.

Trent's public keys are submitted to all users in some way precluding any interference of Eve, e.g. they are published in the form of an advertisement in a newspaper. Now Alice, having computed her public key, creates a message consisting of her name and key, encrypts it with the use of Trent's public key and sends it to Trent (nobody but Trent can decrypt this message). When Bob needs Alice's public key he sends Trent a request, and Trent answers him with Alice's public key, which he has signed (nobody can forge Trent's signature). Bob verifies the signature using Trent's public key and accepts Alice's key as valid. By implementing this procedure, each user of the network obtains trustworthy information about other users' public keys and Eve cannot interfere in this process.

So, if Alice and Bob use the authentic public keys, the Diffie–Hellman scheme tackles the problem of establishing secret keys. However it provides no explicit identification of the users. Indeed, if Eve tries to act as Alice, then she and Bob will end up with different secret keys but this will become evident only in the future, e.g. when Bob has been unable to decipher a received message or has detected that "Alice" does not understand what he sends her. Often, this scheme requires one to provide explicit identification, i.e. to let the parties know exactly who is who at the end of the protocol.

The Diffie–Hellman scheme has yet another disadvantage: the secret key established by Alice and Bob will always be the same until they change their public keys. But changing keys is a relatively slow process (e.g. it may be necessary to inform all the users in the network about the change of key to let them correct their public key directories). It is desirable to have a protocol which would allow for the instantaneous creation of different, randomly selected secret keys.

The solution is to use some public-key cipher for transporting secret keys. Denote the ciphertext for message x produced with the aid of A's public key by $P_A(x)$. (For example, $P_A(x)$ may be RSA or ElGamal encryption. In the case that RSA encryption has been used, $P_A(x) = x^{d_A} \bmod N_A$ where the pair of numbers d_A and N_A is the public key of user A.) All who know A's public key can compute $P_A(x)$ for message x. At the same time, only A, who knows the corresponding private key, can recover x out of $y = P_A(x)$. Similarly, we shall denote by $P_B(x)$ the ciphertext produced with the aid of B's public key. Let, as before, the symbol $\|$ denote the concatenation of numbers. We shall describe the protocol through a series of improvements so that the reader can better understand the details.

Recall that we are to solve the following problem: Alice and Bob wish to mutually identify each other and establish a common secret key. Consider first the following (flawed) 3-step protocol so that several issues can be discussed.

Step 1 Alice devises a secret key k_1, encrypts it with Bob's public key and sends to Bob:

$$A \longrightarrow B : \quad P_B(k_1). \tag{5.15}$$

Step 2 Bob decrypts k_1, re-encrypts it with Alice's public key and sends to Alice:

$$A \longleftarrow B : \quad P_A(k_1). \tag{5.16}$$

Step 3 Alice decrypts k_1 and compares it to the key she has devised at Step 1.

What do we have as a result of this protocol? First, Alice and Bob have established a common secret key k_1, unknown to Eve (she cannot decrypt either $P_B(k_1)$ or $P_A(k_1)$). Second, Alice has got a cryptographically secure identification of Bob since nobody but him could have decrypted k_1. Obviously, with the present protocol, Bob does not get any identification of Alice (the message (5.15) could be sent by anybody). He could initiate a symmetric protocol:

$$A \longleftarrow B : \quad P_A(k_2), \tag{5.17}$$

$$A \longrightarrow B : \quad P_B(k_2), \tag{5.18}$$

and obtain such identification. However, the issue here is in the logical independence of the two protocols which gives no guarantee that both protocols are conducted by the same participants.

But there is yet a more subtle issue. Alice can use this protocol to break Bob's cryptosystem! This can be done as follows. Suppose Alice has intercepted an encrypted message y intended for Bob, i.e. $y = P_B(x)$. She pretends that she wishes to securely communicate with Bob and initiates the protocol (5.15), (5.16). But instead of $P_B(k_1)$ she sends Bob the message y. Since k_1 is an arbitrary integer, Bob does not suspect anything. He performs his step in the protocol and decrypts x for Alice!

The lesson that should be learned from this is the following: one should not decrypt random numbers. It may impair one's security. The method of circumventing such "dangerous" randomness is to introduce redundancy into messages, e.g. to enclose an element that is known and expected by the recipient. Particularly, in (5.15) Alice could send her name. She could construct a message by allocating 512 bits for random number k_1 and the other 512 bits for her name, her address, a fragment of her public key, or a similar easily verifiable piece of information (denote these all by $\hat{A}$), and send $P_B(k_1\|\hat{A})$ to Bob. In this case Bob would not have sent Alice the message x as above because its corresponding 512 bits had certainly not contained $\hat{A}$.

All the above-stated leads us to the following protocol by Needham and Schroeder[Needham and Schroeder (1978)], see also [Menezes *et al.* (1996)], which completely solves the problem stated in the beginning of the section.

Step 1 Alice devises a number k_1, connects to it her public data $\hat{A}$ and sends to Bob

$$A \longrightarrow B: \quad P_B(k_1\|\hat{A}). \tag{5.19}$$

Step 2 Bob decrypts (5.19) and verifies that the message contains Alice's public data $\hat{A}$. Next he devises a number k_2, connects to it k_1 and sends to Alice

$$A \longleftarrow B: \quad P_A(k_1\|k_2). \tag{5.20}$$

Step 3 Alice decrypts (5.20) and verifies that the message contains k_1. This gives her secure identification of Bob since nobody else could have extracted k_1 from (5.19). Alice sends to Bob

$$A \longrightarrow B: \quad P_B(k_2). \tag{5.21}$$

Step 4 Bob decrypts (5.21) and verifies that it is k_2. This gives him secure identification of Alice since nobody else could have extracted k_2 from (5.20).

Now Alice and Bob can construct from k_1, k_2 a common key, e.g. $k = k_1 \oplus k_2$ where $\oplus$ is bitwise summation modulo 2, or they can use k_1 and k_2 separately for enciphering incoming and outgoing messages.

Consider an example. Let the ElGamal cipher be used in some network with the common public parameters $p = 107$, $g = 2$. Users A and B have public keys $d_A = 58$, $d_B = 28$, to which the private keys $c_A = 33$, $c_B = 45$ correspond. Consider a realization of the Needham–Schroeder protocol for the mutual identification of users A and B and secret key establishment. Due to small value of modulus p in our example, we shall use one decimal digit as the user's identifier. Let $\hat{A} = 1$, $\hat{B} = 2$, and the intended secret key also be one digit.

At the first step of the protocol A devises a secret key, say, $k_1 = 3$, and constructs a message $m = k_1 \| \hat{A} = 31$. This message is encrypted with the ElGamal cipher with B's public key:

$$k = 15, \quad r = g^k \bmod p = 2^{15} \bmod 107 = 26,$$

$$e = m \times d_B{}^k \bmod p = 31 \times 28^{15} \bmod 107 = 47.$$

The pair of numbers $(26, 47)$ is the ciphertext to be sent to B. In the notation of the protocol, $P_B(k_1 \| \hat{A}) = (26, 47)$ and

$$A \longrightarrow B : \quad (26, 47).$$

At the second step B decrypts $(26, 47)$, applying his private key:

$$m' = e \times r^{p-1-c_B} \bmod p = 47 \times 26^{106-45} \bmod p = 31.$$

B verifies that the low-order digit equals the identification number of user A and extracts $k_1 = 3$. Then he selects his secret number, say, $k_2 = 7$, constructs a message $m = k_1 \| k_2 = 37$ and encrypts it using A's public key:

$$k = 77, \quad r = g^k \bmod p = 2^{77} \bmod 107 = 63,$$

$$e = m \times d_A{}^k \bmod p = 37 \times 58^{77} \bmod 107 = 18.$$

The pair of numbers $(63, 18)$ is what he will send to A. That is $P_A(k_1 \| k_2) = (63, 18)$ and

$$A \longleftarrow B : \quad (63, 18).$$

At the third step A decrypts $(63, 18)$:

$$m' = e \times r^{p-1-c_A} \bmod p = 18 \times 63^{106-33} \bmod 107 = 37.$$

A verifies that the high-order digit contains $k_1 = 3$ and extracts $k_2 = 7$. Now A encrypts k_2 for B:

$$k = 41, \quad r = g^k \bmod p = 2^{41} \bmod 107 = 82,$$

$$e = m \times d_B{}^k \bmod p = 7 \times 28^{41} \bmod 107 = 49,$$

and sends to B

$$A \longrightarrow B: \quad (82, 49).$$

At the fourth step B decrypts $(82, 49)$:

$$m' = e \times r^{p-1-c_B} \bmod p = 49 \times 82^{106-45} \bmod 107 = 7.$$

B verifies that he obtains his secret number $k_2 = 7$.

Now A and B can make a common key by a method agreed upon in advance, e.g.

$$k = k_1 \oplus k_2 = 3 \oplus 7 = (011)_2 \oplus (111)_2 = (100)_2 = 4.$$

Problems and Exercises

5.1 For realization of the "Mental poker" protocol the following common parameters are chosen: $p = 23$, $\hat{\alpha} = 5$, $\hat{\beta} = 7$, $\hat{\gamma} = 14$. Besides, there are the following variants for Alice and Bob:

(a) $c_A = 13$, $c_B = 5$, Alice shuffles cards by the rule $(1, 2, 3) \to (3, 2, 1)$, Bob selects the first number and uses the permutation $(1, 2) \to (2, 1)$. Alice selects the second number.

(b) $c_A = 7$, $c_B = 15$, Alice shuffles cards by the rule $(1, 2, 3) \to (1, 3, 2)$, Bob selects the second number and uses the permutation $(1, 2) \to (1, 2)$. Alice selects the first number.

(c) $c_A = 19$, $c_B = 3$, Alice shuffles cards by the rule $(1, 2, 3) \to (2, 1, 3)$, Bob selects the second number and uses the permutation $(1, 2) \to (2, 1)$. Alice selects the second number.

(d) $c_A = 9$, $c_B = 7$, Alice shuffles cards by the rule $(1, 2, 3) \to (3, 2, 1)$, Bob selects the third number and uses the permutation $(1, 2) \to (1, 2)$. Alice selects the second number.

(e) $c_A = 15$, $c_B = 5$, Alice shuffles cards by the rule $(1, 2, 3) \to (1, 2, 3)$, Bob selects the first number and uses the permutation $(1, 2) \to (2, 1)$. Alice selects the first number.

Determine which cards will make up Alice's and Bob's hands. What transmitted numbers will Eve observe?

5.2 In the digital cache system the secret parameters of the Bank are $P = 17, Q = 7, c = 77$, and the corresponding public parameters $N = 119, d = 5$. Make digital bank notes with the following serial numbers:

  (a) $n = 11$ under $r = 5$,
  (b) $n = 99$ under $r = 6$,
  (c) $n = 55$ under $r = 10$,
  (d) $n = 44$ under $r = 15$,
  (e) $n = 77$ under $r = 30$.

Themes for Labs

For all the tasks below, we suggest that the reader select the necessary parameters and cryptographic tools at his/her discretion.

5.3 Make a computer implementation of the "Mental poker" protocol.

5.4 Make a computer implementation of the zero-knowledge protocol based on the graph colouring problem.

5.5 Make a computer implementation of the zero-knowledge protocol based on the Hamiltonian cycle problem.

5.6 Make a computer implementation of the digital cache protocol.

5.7 Make a computer implementation of the Needham–Schroeder mutual identification protocol.

Chapter 6

Elliptic Curve Cryptosystems

6.1 Introduction

In this chapter, we consider one of the important directions of public-key cryptography, elliptic curve systems. Elliptic curves have been studied in mathematics for a long time, but their use in cryptographic applications was first suggested by Victor Miller [Miller (1986)] and Neal Koblitz [Koblitz (1987)]. More than 30 years of active investigations have confirmed the beneficial properties of these systems and led to the invention of efficient implementation methods. Elliptic curves in cryptography are covered by many standards, among which we may mention the US ANSI X9.62 and FIPS 186-2 (2000), the Russian GOST R34.10-2001 (2001) and their improved contemporary versions FIPS-186-4 [FIPS 186-4 (2013)] and GOST R34.10-2012 [RFC 7091 (2013)], respectively.

The main advantage of elliptic curve cryptosystems is that compared to "conventional" systems studied in the previous chapters, they offer a significantly greater level of security within the same computational complexity, or, *vice versa*, significantly lower complexity within the given level of security. This is explained by the fact that for computing inverse functions on elliptic curves, only exponential-time algorithms are known, whereas subexponential algorithms exist in the case of conventional cryptosystems. As a result, the level of security achieved, say, using RSA with a 1024-bit modulus, can be attained using elliptic curve systems with a 160-bit modulus which allows for a simpler hardware and software implementation.

The profound study of elliptic curves requires the knowledge of higher algebra and especially algebraic geometry. We shall however try to set out the matter without resorting to any higher-algebraic concepts. Nevertheless it will be sufficient for understanding construction principles and the functioning of the corresponding cryptosystems. A more detailed treatment of the elliptic curves and their use in cryptography can be found in classical textbooks [Silverman (1986); Menezes (1993); Blake *et al.* (1999)] and more recent publications [Hankerson *et al.* (2004); Washington (2008); Katz and Lindell (2014)].

6.2   Mathematical Foundations

A cubic curve E defined by the equation

$$E: \quad Y^2 = X^3 + aX + b \tag{6.1}$$

is called an *elliptic curve* (in fact, Eq. (6.1) is derived by the transformation of variables from a more general equation which we are not interested in).

Since $Y = \pm\sqrt{X^3 + aX + b}$, the graph of the curve is symmetric with respect to the horizontal axis. To find the points of intersection between the graph and horizontal axis one needs to solve the cubic equation

$$X^3 + aX + b = 0. \tag{6.2}$$

This can be done using the well-known formulas by Cardano. The discriminant of the equation

$$D = \left(\frac{a}{3}\right)^3 + \left(\frac{b}{2}\right)^2. \tag{6.3}$$

If $D < 0$ then (6.2) has three different real roots α, β, γ; if $D = 0$ then (6.2) has three real roots, say, α, β, β, at least two of which are equal; at last, if $D > 0$ then (6.2) has one real root α and two complex conjugate roots. The shape of the curve in all three cases is shown in Figs. 6.1–6.3.

The curve shown in Fig. 6.2 is called *singular*. In its singularity point $(\beta, 0)$, there are two tangents to the curve. We shall exclude singular curves.

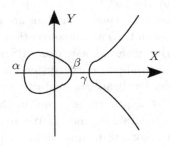

Fig. 6.1   Elliptic curve, $D < 0$.

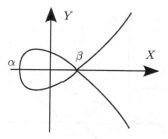

Fig. 6.2   Elliptic curve, $D = 0$.

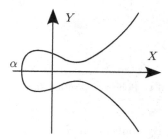

Fig. 6.3   Elliptic curve, $D > 0$.

Therefore, when defining a curve by specifying parameters a and b, we shall require that the condition $D \neq 0$ hold, which is equivalent to

$$4a^3 + 27b^2 \neq 0. \tag{6.4}$$

So, let the elliptic curve E be defined by Eq. (6.1) with the constraint (6.4). Define the operation of point composition on the curve. Take any two points $P = (x_1, y_1)$, $Q = (x_2, y_2) \in E$ and plot a straight line through the points (Fig. 6.4). This line will necessarily intersect the curve at a third point which we denote by R'. (The third point necessarily exists. The fact is that the cubic equation obtained after substitution of the line equation into (6.1) has two real roots corresponding to points P and Q, consequently, the third root corresponding to point R' is also real.) The resultant point $R = (x_3, y_3)$ is obtained by changing the sign of the y-coordinate of point R'. We shall denote the described composition of points by $R = P + Q$.

Let point $P \in E$ have coordinates (x, y). Then the point with coordinates $(x, -y)$ will be denoted by $-P$. We shall assume that the vertical line passing through P and $-P$ intersects the curve at a point at infinity

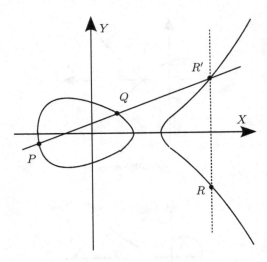

Fig. 6.4   Point composition $R = P + Q$.

$\mathcal{O}$, i.e. $P + (-P) = \mathcal{O}$. By convention, $P + \mathcal{O} = \mathcal{O} + P = P$. As we shall see later, the point at infinity $\mathcal{O}$ plays the role of zero in the elliptic curve arithmetic.

Suppose now that points P and Q (Fig. 6.4) are approaching each other and eventually merge into one point $P = Q = (x_1, y_1)$. Then the composition $R = (x_3, y_3) = P + Q = P + P$ is obtained by plotting the tangent line to the curve at point P and reflecting its second intersection with the curve R' with respect to the horizontal axis (Fig. 6.5). We shall use the following notation: $R = P + P = [2]P$.

Let us derive formulas for determining the coordinates of the resulting point $R = (x_3, y_3)$ on the basis of the coordinates of the initial points $P = (x_1, y_1)$ and $Q = (x_2, y_2)$. First consider the case when $P \neq \pm Q$, $R = P + Q$ (Fig. 6.4). Denote by k the angular coefficient of the line passing through P and Q. It is obvious that

$$k = \frac{y_2 - y_1}{x_2 - x_1}. \tag{6.5}$$

Then the line equation will be $Y - y_1 = k(X - x_1)$, so

$$Y = y_1 + k(X - x_1). \tag{6.6}$$

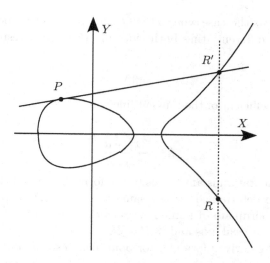

Fig. 6.5   Point doubling $R = P + P = [2]P$.

Substitute the expression for the variable Y into the curve equation (6.1). We obtain

$$(y_1 + k(X - x_1))^2 = X^3 + aX + b.$$

From this by squaring and grouping similar terms we obtain the cubic equation

$$X^3 - k^2 X^2 + \cdots = 0$$

(here $\cdots$ stands for terms not interesting for us). It is known that the sum of the roots of the cubic equation equals the coefficient under X^2, taken with the minus sign (Viète theorem for cubic equations), i.e.

$$x_1 + x_2 + x_3 = k^2,$$

hence

$$x_3 = k^2 - x_1 - x_2. \tag{6.7}$$

Substitute the expression for x_3 into the line equation (6.6) and find the y-coordinate of point R', $y_3' = y_1 + k(x_3 - x_1)$, and by changing the sign, we obtain

$$y_3 = k(x_1 - x_3) - y_1. \tag{6.8}$$

So we have found the coordinates of the point of interest R.

Consider now the case when $P = Q$ and the resulting point $R = [2]P$ (Fig. 6.5). By differentiating both sides of (6.1) with respect to X, we obtain

$$2YY' = 3X^2 + a.$$

The angular coefficient of the tangent line equals the value of the derivative in point P,

$$k = \frac{3x_1^2 + a}{2y_1}. \tag{6.9}$$

Further argumentation is analogous to the former case and the coordinates of point R are determined by the same formulas (6.7) and (6.8). Notice that if the y-coordinate of point P is zero then the tangent line passes in parallel to the vertical axis and $[2]P = \mathcal{O}$.

By using the derived formulas for point composition and accepted conventions to point at infinity, one may verify the following properties of points on elliptic curve:

(1) $P + Q = Q + P$ for all points $P, Q \in E$;
(2) $P + (Q + S) = (P + Q) + S$ for all points $P, Q, S \in E$;
(3) there exists a null element $\mathcal{O}$ (point at infinity) such that $P + \mathcal{O} = \mathcal{O} + P = P$ for all $P \in E$;
(4) for every point $P \in E$ there exists an opposite point $-P \in E$ such that $P + (-P) = \mathcal{O}$.

The listed properties of points match the properties of integer numbers under the summation operation. Therefore point composition is often called *point addition* and operation $[2]P$ *point doubling*.

The analogy with the integers being continued, it is convenient to introduce the following notation. For integer m

$$[m]P = \underbrace{P + P + \cdots + P}_{m},$$

$$[0]P = \mathcal{O},$$

$$[-m]P = -(\underbrace{P + P + \cdots + P}_{m}).$$

Now we are ready to take the first step toward the cryptographic use of elliptic curves. We can see that the computation of point composition (see Eqs. (6.5), (6.9), (6.7), and (6.8)) involves only the operations of addition, subtraction, multiplication, and division of numbers. It means that all the above identities will hold if we operate with integer numbers modulo a prime p. In this case, addition and multiplication are done modulo p, the difference $u - v$ is calculated as $u + (p - v) \bmod p$, and the division u/v is performed by multiplying u by $v^{-1} \bmod p$ (the primality of the modulus guarantees that for any positive integer $v < p$ there exists a number v^{-1} such that $vv^{-1} \bmod p = 1$).

As a result, we obtain a curve

$$E : Y^2 = X^3 + aX + b \quad (\bmod\ p). \tag{6.10}$$

In Eq. (6.10), the variables X, Y and the coefficients a, b take on integer values and all computations are carried out modulo p. In accordance with (6.4), the coefficients a, b are subject to the constraint

$$(4a^3 + 27b^2) \bmod p \neq 0. \tag{6.11}$$

The set $E_p(a, b)$ consists of all points (x, y), $0 \leq x, y < p$, satisfying Eq. (6.10) and the point at infinity $\mathcal{O}$. Denote the number of points in $E_p(a, b)$ by $\#E_p(a, b)$. This quantity is of great importance for cryptographic applications of elliptic curves.

For example, consider the curve

$$E_7(2, 6) : Y^2 = X^3 + 2X + 6 \quad (\bmod\ 7). \tag{6.12}$$

Check condition (6.11):

$$4 \times 2^3 + 27 \times 6^2 = 4 \times 1 + 6 \times 1 = 3 \neq 0 \quad (\bmod\ 7).$$

So this curve is non-singular. Let's find a (random) point in $E_7(2, 6)$. Let $x = 5$. Then

$$Y^2 = 5^3 + 2 \times 5 + 6 = 6 + 3 + 6 = 1 \quad (\bmod\ 7)$$

and $y = 1 \ (\bmod\ 7)$ or $y = -1 = 6 \ (\bmod\ 7)$. We have found two points: $(5, 1)$ and $(5, 6)$. Let's find more points by computing compositions. First find $[2](5, 1)$. Using (6.9), (6.7), and (6.8), we compute

$$k = \frac{3 \times 5^2 + 2}{2 \times 1} = \frac{0}{2} = 0 \quad (\bmod\ 7),$$

$$x_3 = 0 - 2 \times 5 = 4 \quad (\bmod\ 7),$$

$$y_3 = 0 \times (5 - 4) - 1 = 6 \quad (\bmod\ 7).$$

We obtain $[2](5, 1) = (4, 6)$ (one can verify that the point obtained belongs to the curve by substituting its coordinates in Eq. (6.12)). Find a point

$[3](5,1) = (5,1) + (4,6)$. Using (6.5), (6.7), and (6.8), we compute

$$k = \frac{6-1}{4-5} = \frac{5}{6} = 5 \times 6 = 2 \quad (\text{mod } 7),$$

$$x_3 = 2^2 - 5 - 4 = 2 \quad (\text{mod } 7),$$

$$y_3 = 2 \times (5-2) - 1 = 2 \times 3 - 1 = 5 \quad (\text{mod } 7).$$

We obtain $[3](5,1) = (2,5)$. So we have found four points. For the cryptographic use of the curve we must know the total number of points in the set $E_7(2,6)$. We shall find the answer in Sec. 6.6.

Some words about the properties of the set of points $E_p(a,b)$: It is obvious that this set is finite since it consists of only points with integer coordinates $0 \leq x, y < p$. There exists a direct analogy between $E_p(a,b)$ and the set of integer powers reduced modulo p. Thus $E_p(a,b)$ has a generator, i.e. such a point G that the sequence $G, [2]G, [3]G, \ldots, [n]G$, where $n = \#E_p(a,b)$, contains all points from $E_p(a,b)$, $[n]G = \mathcal{O}$ (compare this to the similar property of generator g in Sec. 2.2). The number of points on the elliptic curve given a proper choice of parameters p, a, and b, can be a prime, $\#E_p(a,b) = q$. In this case any point (except $\mathcal{O}$) is a generator of the whole set of points. Such a curve is beneficial in many respects and can always be found for an acceptable time. If for some reason such a curve cannot be found and $\#E_p(a,b) = hq$ where q is again a prime then a subset of $E_p(a,b)$ exists which contains q points with a generator that is any point $G \neq \mathcal{O}$ such that $[q]G = \mathcal{O}$. In the sequel, without lost of generality, we shall assume that we are working with such a subset of cardinality q (and when selecting the curve parameters, we shall strive to obtain $q = \#E_p(a,b)$).

The main cryptographic operation on an elliptic curve is *point multiplication*, i.e. the computation

$$Q = [m]P = \underbrace{P + P + \cdots + P}_{m}. \tag{6.13}$$

This operation may be performed quite efficiently with not more than $2 \log m$ point compositions. The methods of its implementation are completely the same as those of modular exponentiation. For example, to find the point $Q = [21]P$, compute $[2]P, [4]P, [8]P, [16]P$, each time doubling the preceding point, and sum up $P + [4]P + [16]P = Q$ (in total, 4 point doublings and 2 point additions).

The inverse problem, which is traditionally called the *elliptic curve discrete logarithm* problem, is formulated as follows. Given points P and Q

find an integer m such that $[m]P = Q$. This problem is difficult. If the curve parameters are carefully chosen (as described in the next section) then the best algorithms known to date are analogues of the baby-step giant-step algorithm (Sec. 3.2) and require a number of curve operations proportional to $\sqrt{q}$ where q is the cardinality of the set of points generated by Q. All computations on the curve are carried out modulo p, i.e. with numbers of length $t \approx \log p$ bits. For cryptographic applications, $\log q \approx \log p$, so $\sqrt{q} \approx 2^{t/2}$, which means an exponential growth in complexity with the length of numbers increasing.

6.3 Choosing Curve Parameters

In this section, we consider the main recommendations as to the choice of the elliptic curve parameters, namely, coefficients a, b and modulus p, in order to obtain a curve suitable for cryptographic applications. In fact, the criterion of the choice is the impossibility of maintaining some kinds of attacks suggested for elliptic curve cryptosystems. The recommendations below follow the strategy of choosing a *random* curve. This strategy is regarded as the most reliable with respect to the security of the resulting cryptosystem. The alternative approach, not considered here, is to systematically construct the curve with desired properties, which is more efficient from the computational point of view. There are special methods suggested for implementing this approach but the curves obtained are in fact chosen from a relatively small set of curves and are suspected to have some special features which may in the course of time, allow one to invent efficient attacks against them.

Let us describe in steps the process of selecting a good random curve.

(1) Randomly select a prime number p. As will be shown in Sec. 6.6, the number of points on the curve is of the same order as p. So the bitlength of p, $t = \lfloor \log p \rfloor + 1$, must be sufficiently great to prevent the use of general methods for computing discrete logarithms on the curve, which has a complexity proportional to $2^{t/2}$ operations. The value of $t = 128$ bits (4 machine words on 32-bit computers) is not sufficient today because there are reports of people breaking the corresponding curves after several months of intensive distributed computations. But the value of $t = 160$ bits (5 machine words) is still inaccessible by cryptanalysts nowadays and may serve as a starting point. Another consideration when selecting the value of t is based on the demand that the elliptic curve cipher be no less

secure than the block cipher AES (which is now the US standard, see Subsec. 8.2.3). It is believed that the security of AES is provided by the full key length which is 128, 196, or 256 bits. Since the security of the elliptic curve cipher is determined by the value of $t/2$ the length of the modulus must be 256, 392, or 512 bits, respectively.

(2) Select random integers a and b such that $a, b \neq 0$ (mod p) and $4a^3 + 27b^2 \neq 0$ (mod p). Notice, however, that parameter b does not appear anywhere in the formulas for computing compositions. So it is sometimes recommended, for the sake of computational efficiency, to randomly select only b while taking an a equal to a small integer. Thus the US standard FIPS 186-4 assumes the use of curves with $a = -3$ which, as we shall see in Sec. 6.5, slightly simplifies computations.

(3) Determine the number of points on the curve $n = \#E_p(a, b)$ (this is the most complicated step in the described process; its basic algorithm being considered in Sec. 6.6). It is important that n have a large prime divisor q, or better, that it be itself prime, $n = q$. If n has only small factors then many small subsets with their own generators exist in $E_p(a, b)$, and the Pohlig–Hellman algorithm [Pohlig and Hellman (1978); Menezes *et al.* (1996)] can quickly find the general logarithm through the logarithms in these small subsets. If the search for the curve with $n = q$ takes up too much time, then one may admit $n = hq$ where h is a small integer. Recall that the security of the elliptic curve cryptosystem is determined not by modulus p but by the number of points in the working subset q. If h is small, then q is of the same order as p. If the number of points on the curve does not satisfy the requirements, revert to Step 2.

(4) Verify whether the inequalities $p^k - 1 \bmod q \neq 0$ hold for all k, $0 < k < 32$. If not, revert to Step 2. This check prevents the MOV-attack [Menezes (1993)] (named after its inventors Menezes, Okamoto, and Vanstone) and, as well, excludes the so-called supersingular curves and the curves with $\#E_p(a, b) = p - 1$. The MOV-attack and the special types of curves mentioned allow one to reduce the elliptic curve discrete logarithm problem to simpler problems.

(5) Verify whether the inequality $q \neq p$ holds. If not, revert to Step 2. The matter is that for the curves with $q = p$ which are called anomalous, efficient methods of computing discrete logarithms are suggested.

(6) At this step a suitable curve for cryptographic applications has been obtained. We have parameters p, a, b, the number of points n, and the

cardinality of the working subset q. It is usually required that one finds a point G, the generator of the working subset. If $q = n$, then any point (except $\mathcal{O}$) is the generator. If $q < n$, then select random points G' until $G = [n/q]G' \neq \mathcal{O}$ is obtained. To find a random point on the curve take a random number $x < p$, compute $e = (x^3 + ax + b) \bmod p$ and try to extract the square root $y = \sqrt{e} \bmod p$. If the square root exists, we obtain the point (x, y), otherwise try another number x. The algorithms for computing square roots modulo a prime can be found, e.g. in [Menezes *et al.* (1996), Chap. 3].

6.4 Constructing Cryptosystems

Any cryptosystem based on discrete logarithms can be easily extended to elliptic curves. The basic principle is to replace the operation $y = g^x \bmod p$ with $Y = [x]G \bmod p$ (the indication of the modulus here is not generally accepted, but, in fact, all computations are carried out modulo p). One should, however, remember that in the case of an elliptic curve with the cardinality of working subset q, the values of x effectively lie in the interval $0 < x < q$. This is because $[q]G = \mathcal{O}$ and hence the integer factors in point multiplication are reduced modulo q. Another difference is that y is a number but Y is a point and one is usually required to convert a point into an integer. The simplest way to do that is to use the x-coordinate of the point.

It is also possible to construct an analogue of the RSA on elliptic curves. In this case the curve is defined modulo a composite N. But we do not gain any advantage here since the length of the modulus remains the same in order to make its factorization intractable.

We demonstrate the technique of using elliptic curves with the examples of the ElGamal cipher and the DSA signature.

6.4.1 *Elliptic Curve ElGamal Encryption*

For the community of users of a network, an elliptic curve $E_p(a, b)$ is chosen and a point G thereon such that G, $[2]G$, $[3]G$, ..., $[q]G$ are different points and $[q]G = \mathcal{O}$ for some prime q.

Every user U selects a number c_U, $0 < c_U < q$ to be his/her private key and computes the point $D_U = [c_U]G$ which is the corresponding public key. The common parameters and public keys are submitted to all users.

Suppose user A wants to send a message to user B. Assume that the message is represented as a number $m < p$. A does the following:

1 selects a random integer k, $0 < k < q$;
2 computes $R = [k]G$, $P = [k]D_B = (x, y)$;
3 encrypts $e = m\,x \bmod p$;
4 sends B the ciphertext (R, e).

User B, upon receiving (R, e),

5 computes $Q = [c_B]R = (x, y)$;
6 decrypts $m' = ex^{-1} \bmod p$.

Let's give a justification of the protocol. Using the definitions of point Q at Step 5 and point R at Step 2 we can write

$$Q = [c_B]R = [c_B]([k]G) = [k]([c_B]G).$$

The public key of user B, by definition, is $D_B = [c_B]G$. So we can see that $Q = [k]D_B$, i.e. Q is the same point as P at Step 2. Hence the coordinate x at Step 3 equals that at Step 6. Therefore $m' = m$.

The coordinate x of point Q remains secret for the adversary because she does not know the secret number k. The adversary may try to recover k from R but to do that she must solve the elliptic curve discrete logarithm problem which is believed to be impossible.

In the most likely use of the presented protocol, the message m will be the secret key for some block or stream cipher. In this case it makes sense to choose the curve parameters so that $\log q$ is about twice the length of the cipher key.

·6.4.2 *Elliptic Curve Digital Signature Algorithm*

The algorithm ECDSA presented here underlies the US digital signature standard FIPS-186-4 [FIPS 186-4 (2013)] and is quite analogous to the digital signature algorithm (DSA) described in Sec. 4.3 except that exponentiations are replaced by point multiplications on the curve. As in the preceding subsection, for the community of users, an elliptic curve $E_p(a, b)$ is chosen and a point G thereon such that G, $[2]G$, $[3]G$, $\ldots$, $[q]G$ are different points and $[q]G = \mathcal{O}$ for some prime q (the bitlength of p and q is 160 bits).

Every user U selects a number x_U, $0 < x_U < q$ to be his/her private key and computes the point $Y_U = [x_U]G$ which is the corresponding public key. The common parameters and public keys are submitted to all users. (Note that FIPS-186-4 also allows one to use curves over so-called binary fields, not considered in our book.)

To sign a message $\bar{m}$ user A does the following:

1 computes hash function $h = h(\bar{m})$ (various implementations of ECDSA may use various hash functions);
2 selects a random integer k, $0 < k < q$;
3 computes $P = [k]G = (x, y)$;
4 computes $r = x \bmod q$ (if $r = 0$, revert to Step 2);
5 computes $s = k^{-1}(h + rx_A) \bmod q$ (if $s = 0$, revert to Step 2);
6 signs on the message with the pair of numbers (r, s).

For verification of the signed message $(\bar{m}; r, s)$, any user who knows the public key Y_A does the following:

7 computes $h = h(\bar{m})$;
8 verifies that $0 < r, s < q$;
9 computes $u_1 = h \times s^{-1} \bmod q$ and $u_2 = r \times s^{-1} \bmod q$;
10 computes the composition of points $P = [u_1]G + [u_2]Y_A = (x, y)$;
11 verifies that $P \neq \mathcal{O}$ and $x \bmod q = r$.

The user rejects the signature if at least one test at Step 8 or 11 fails. Otherwise, the user accepts the signature as authentic.

The proof of correctness for this protocol can be done in the same way as in Sec. 4.3.

The current Russian standard GOST R 34.10-2012 digital signature [RFC 7091 (2013)] differs from ECDSA in the following items when signing a message:

1 the Streebog algorithm (GOST R 34.11-2012 [RFC 6986 (2013)]) is used as a hash function;
5 the signature component s is computed as $s = (kh + rx_A) \bmod q$.

Correspondingly, when verifying the signature, the computation of u_1 and u_2 changes:

9 $u_1 = s \times h^{-1} \bmod q$ and $u_2 = -r \times h^{-1} \bmod q$.

So all the differences are the same as the ones earlier considered in Sec. 4.3.

6.5   Efficient Implementation of Operations

In this section, we consider the main approaches to making efficient computations on elliptic curves. As we have already discussed, the point multiplication by m, i.e. computing $[m]P$ where m is a large integer and P is a point on the curve, can be performed using the same methods as for exponentiation (upon replacement of ordinary modular multiplication by point addition). Here, for the sake of concreteness, we explicitly describe one of the simplest methods — left-to-right point multiplication (cf. Algorithm 2.4). There are other more efficient methods for exponentiation which may be successfully applied to elliptic curve point multiplication. But the gain is usually not so great (about 25%) and these methods go beyond the scope of our book (see their description in, e.g. [Menezes *et al.* (1996); Blake *et al.* (1999)]).

Algorithm 6.1   Point multiplication (from left to right)

INPUT: Point P, integer $m = (m_t m_{t-1} \ldots m_1)_2$.
OUTPUT: Point $Q = [m]P$.

1. $Q \leftarrow \mathcal{O}$;
2.   FOR $i = t, t-1, \ldots, 1$ DO
3. $Q \leftarrow [2]Q$,
4.   IF $m_i = 1$ THEN $Q \leftarrow Q + P$;
5.   RETURN Q.

This algorithm requires not more than t point additions and t point doublings (on average, t doublings and $t/2$ additions).

Let's demonstrate the work of the algorithm by computation of $[21]P$. Here $21 = (10101)_2 = m_1 m_2 m_3 m_4 m_5$, $t = 5$. We show what happens on each iteration.

$$[i = 5 \; m_5 = 1] : Q \leftarrow \mathcal{O}, \qquad\qquad Q \leftarrow Q + P = P;$$
$$[i = 4 \; m_4 = 0] : Q \leftarrow [2]Q = [2]P;$$
$$[i = 3 \; m_3 = 1] : Q \leftarrow [2]Q = [4]P, \quad Q \leftarrow Q + P = [5]P;$$
$$[i = 2 \; m_2 = 0] : Q \leftarrow [2]Q = [10]P;$$
$$[i = 1 \; m_1 = 1] : Q \leftarrow [2]Q = [20]P, \quad Q \leftarrow Q + P = [21]P.$$

For ease of exposition, reproduce here the formulas for point addition and doubling derived in Sec. 6.2. Denote the points participating in these operations by $P_1 = (x_1, y_1)$, $P_2 = (x_2, y_2)$, and $P_3 = (x_3, y_3)$. The point addition $P_3 = P_1 + P_2$ where $P_1, P_2 \neq \mathcal{O}$ and $P_1 \neq \pm P_2$ is computed by the formulas

$$k = \frac{y_2 - y_1}{x_2 - x_1},$$
$$x_3 = k^2 - x_1 - x_2, \qquad\qquad (6.14)$$
$$y_3 = k(x_1 - x_3) - y_1 \qquad (\bmod\ p).$$

If $P_1 = \mathcal{O}$ then $P_3 = \mathcal{O} + P_2 = P_2$, and similarly with $P_2 = \mathcal{O}$. If $P_1 = -P_2$ then $P_3 = \mathcal{O}$. Finally, if $P_1 = P_2$ then we must perform doubling.

The point doubling $P_3 = [2]P_1$ where $P_1 \neq \mathcal{O}$ and $y_1 \neq 0$ is computed by the formulas

$$k = \frac{3x_1^2 + a}{2y_1},$$
$$x_3 = k^2 - 2x_1, \qquad\qquad (6.15)$$
$$y_3 = k(x_1 - x_3) - y_1 \qquad (\bmod\ p).$$

If $P_1 = \mathcal{O}$ or $y_1 = 0$ then $P_3 = \mathcal{O}$.

Computations by (6.14) and (6.15) have been considered in the example on page 89.

One speaks that in computations by (6.14) and (6.15) the *affine* representation of points is used, i.e. a point P is represented by its two coordinates $P = (x, y)$. A point at infinity $\mathcal{O}$ has no such representation because its coordinates must be ∞. But recall that it plays the role of zero in point operations. So, technically, in Algorithm 6.1 $\mathcal{O}$ is simply a flag indicating that one should omit the operations $Q \leftarrow [2]Q$ until the first addition $Q \leftarrow Q + P$ which is performed as an assignment $Q \leftarrow P$.

The formulas (6.14) and (6.15) are used to perform computations at Lines 3 and 4 of Algorithm 6.1 with obvious substitutions. Notice that if computations on the curve are carried out in a subset of points of cardinality q and q is prime (as we always assume) and factor m lies in the interval $0 < m < q$ then the conditions for point addition formulas (i.e. $P_1, P_2 \neq \mathcal{O}$ and $P_1 \neq \pm P_2$) and point doubling formulas ($P_1 \neq \mathcal{O}$ and $y_1 \neq 0$) are automatically fulfilled at Lines 3 and 4 of Algorithm 6.1 and need not be checked (provided the first doublings are omitted and the first addition is replaced by assignment, as discussed above).

Now let's consider some issues surrounding the computational efficiency of point operations. Denote by M and I, respectively, the cost (time) of multiplication and inversion modulo p. Then it follows from (6.14) and (6.15) that under the affine point representation, the cost of point addition equals $1I + 3M$ and the cost of doubling is $1I + 4M$ (operations of addition with and multiplication by small integers are of no noticeable effect to the cost).

The relation between the costs of multiplication and inversion may differ depending on implementation, but I is always greater than M. If multiplication is implemented by summations and shifts, it will be but a little faster than inversion (by a factor of 2–3). In this case the use of affine representation is appropriate. But if the processor that performs computations is supplied with an embedded parallel multiplier (such as, e.g., x86 processors) then inversion may be significantly slower than multiplication. We can roughly estimate the costs of corresponding computations. If t is the bitlength of numbers then multiplication requires at most on the order of $(t/32)^2 = t^2/1024$ machine operations (the word size is 32 bits). On the other hand, the number of iterations in the extended Euclidean algorithm which computes inversion, is proportional to t by its nature. Even if we manage on each iteration to implement linearity in t computations with 32-bit numbers (which is possible) then we obtain the total complexity on the order of $t(t/32) = t^2/32$ machine operations, i.e. one inversion will correspond to 32 multiplications. In reality, each iteration of the Euclidean algorithm involves several operations and multiplication can be done with faster methods, so $I > 32M$.

Consider another approach to implementing point operations. We can get rid of inversions at each step of Algorithm 6.1 if operating with coordinates as rational numbers, making computations separately with the numerator and denominator. The following transformation of the variables is the most beneficial:

$$x \to \frac{X}{Z^2}, \quad y \to \frac{Y}{Z^3}. \qquad (6.16)$$

A point on the curve is represented by a triplet (X, Y, Z) and one speaks of the transition to a *weighted projective* representation (for simplicity, we shall omit the word "weighted"). The conversion from affine to projective coordinates is quite simple:

$$(x, y) \to (x, y, 1). \qquad (6.17)$$

After that all computations are carried out in projective coordinates (without computing inversions). The reverse conversion from projective to affine coordinates is done as follows:

$$(X, Y, Z) \rightarrow (X/Z^2, Y/Z^3), \tag{6.18}$$

and costs $1I + 4M$ (one computation of Z^{-1}, two multiplications for obtaining Z^{-2} and Z^{-3} and, finally, the two multiplications XZ^{-2} and YZ^{-3}).

Derive the formulas for point addition in projective representation. First in Eq. (6.14) for x_3, transform variables according to (6.16). After reducing to a common denominator and cancelling we obtain

$$x_3 = \frac{X_3}{Z_3^2} = \frac{(Y_2Z_1^3 - Y_1Z_2^3)^2 - (X_1Z_2^2 + X_2Z_1^2)(X_2Z_1^2 - X_1Z_2^2)^2}{Z_1^2Z_2^2(X_2Z_1^2 - X_1Z_2^2)^2}. \tag{6.19}$$

From this we find the expressions for X_3 and Z_3 taking, respectively, the numerator and the square root from the denominator of the right side of (6.19). To obtain an expression for Y_3, resort to a trick that allows one to save one multiplication. Notice that $P_1 + P_2 = P_2 + P_1$ and hence

$$y_3 = \left((x_1 - x_3)\frac{y_2 - y_1}{x_2 - x_1} - y_1 + (x_2 - x_3)\frac{y_2 - y_1}{x_2 - x_1} - y_2 \right) \Big/ 2.$$

Transform variables according to (6.16) and, instead of Z_3, use its representation from (6.19). After reducing to a common denominator, cancelling, and reducing the similar terms we obtain

$$\begin{aligned} y_3 = \frac{Y_3}{Z_3^3} &= \frac{((X_1Z_2^2 + X_2Z_1^2)(X_2Z_1^2 - X_1Z_2^2)^2 - 2X_3)(Y_2Z_1^3 - Y_1Z_2^3)}{2Z_1^3Z_2^3(X_2Z_1^2 - X_1Z_2^2)^3} \\ &\quad - \frac{(Y_1Z_2^3 + Y_2Z_1^3)(X_2Z_1^2 - X_1Z_2^2)^3}{2Z_1^3Z_2^3(X_2Z_1^2 - X_1Z_2^2)^3}. \end{aligned} \tag{6.20}$$

Based on Eqs. (6.19) and (6.20), write Algorithm 6.2.

Algorithm 6.2 ADDITION IN PROJECTIVE REPRESENTATION

INPUT: $P_1 = (X_1, Y_1, Z_1)$, $P_2 = (X_2, Y_2, Z_2)$,
$\quad\quad\quad P_1, P_2 \neq \mathcal{O}$, $P_1 \neq \pm P_2$
OUTPUT: $P_3 = (X_3, Y_3, Z_3) = P_1 + P_2$
$\quad\quad\quad$ (all computations are modulo p)

$$\lambda_1 = X_1 Z_2^2 \qquad\qquad 2M$$
$$\lambda_2 = X_2 Z_1^2 \qquad\qquad 2M$$
$$\lambda_3 = \lambda_2 - \lambda_1$$
$$\lambda_4 = Y_1 Z_2^3 \qquad\qquad 2M$$
$$\lambda_5 = Y_2 Z_1^3 \qquad\qquad 2M$$
$$\lambda_6 = \lambda_5 - \lambda_4$$
$$\lambda_7 = \lambda_1 + \lambda_2$$
$$\lambda_8 = \lambda_4 + \lambda_5$$
$$Z_3 = Z_1 Z_2 \lambda_3 \qquad\qquad 2M$$
$$X_3 = \lambda_6^2 - \lambda_7 \lambda_3^2 \qquad\qquad 3M$$
$$\lambda_9 = \lambda_7 \lambda_3^2 - 2X_3$$
$$Y_3 = (\lambda_9 \lambda_6 - \lambda_8 \lambda_3^3)/2 \qquad \underline{\quad 3M\quad}$$
$$16M$$

As follows from the algorithm's description, the cost of addition in projective coordinates equals $16M$. We do not count the simple operations of addition, subtraction, and multiplication and division by 2 (to explain how to compute $v/2 \bmod p$ notice that if v is even then $v/2 \bmod p = v/2$ (right shift per 1 bit); if v is odd then $v/2 \bmod p = (v+p)/2 \bmod p$, where $v+p$ is even, so $v/2 \bmod p = (v+p)/2$).

If one of the points, say, P_2, is given in affine coordinates, i.e. $Z_2 = 1$ then the cost of addition decreases to $11M$. This is called *mixed* addition. Algorithm 6.1 is constructed so that mixed additions can always be used, i.e. the cost of the computations at Line 4 equals $11M$.

Consider an example. Compute the sum $(5,1)+(4,6)$ in projective coordinates for the curve of the example on page 89 (all operations are modulo 7).

$$P_1 = (5, 1, 1), \quad P_2 = (4, 6, 1).$$

$$\lambda_1 = 5 \times 1 = 5,$$

$$\lambda_2 = 4 \times 1 = 4,$$

$$\lambda_3 = 4 - 5 = 6, \ \lambda_4 = 1 \times 1 = 1,$$

$$\lambda_5 = 6 \times 1 = 6,$$

$$\lambda_6 = 6 - 1 = 5,$$

$$\lambda_7 = 5 + 4 = 2,$$

$$\lambda_8 = 1 + 6 = 0,$$

$$Z_3 = 1 \times 1 \times 6 = 6,$$

$$X_3 = 5^2 - 2 \times 6^2 = 2,$$

$$\lambda_9 = 2 \times 6^2 - 2 \times 2 = 2 - 4 = 5,$$

$$Y_3 = (5 \times 5 - 0 \times 6^3)/2 = 25/2 = (25 + 7)/2 = 16 = 2;$$

$$P_3 = (2, 2, 6).$$

To check the result convert point P_3 to affine representation. For that purpose compute

$$6^{-1} = 6, \quad 6^{-2} = 6 \times 6 = 1, \quad 6^{-3} = 1 \times 6 = 6.$$

We finally obtain

$$P_3 = (2 \times 1, 2 \times 6) = (2, 5)$$

which coincides with the result of the example on page 89.

Note that condition $P_1, P_2 \neq \mathcal{O}$ is equivalent to $Z_1, Z_2 \neq 0$ and condition $P_1 \neq \pm P_2$ is equivalent to $X_1 \neq X_2$.

To derive the formulas for doubling a point in projective representation substitute (6.16) into (6.15):

$$x_3 = \frac{X_3}{Z_3^2} = \frac{(3X_1^2 + aZ_1^4)^2 - 8X_1Y_1^2}{(2Z_1Y_1)^2}, \tag{6.21}$$

$$y_3 = \frac{Y_3}{Z_3^3} = \frac{(4X_1Y_1^2 - X_3)(3X_1^2 + aZ_1^4)Z_1^2 - 8Y_1^4}{(2Z_1Y_1)^3}, \tag{6.22}$$

which leads to the following Algorithm 6.3.

Algorithm 6.3 Doubling in projective representation

INPUT: $P_1 = (X_1, Y_1, Z_1), P_1 \neq \mathcal{O}$

OUTPUT: $P_3 = (X_3, Y_3, Z_3) = [2]P_1$

$$
\begin{array}{lll}
\lambda_1 & = 3X_1^2 + aZ_1^4 & 4M \\
\lambda_2 & = 4X_1Y_1^2 & 2M \\
Z_3 & = 2Y_1Z_1 & 1M \\
X_3 & = \lambda_1^2 - 2\lambda_2 & 1M \\
\lambda_3 & = 8Y_1^4 & 1M \\
Y_3 & = \lambda_1(\lambda_2 - X_3) - \lambda_3 & \underline{1M} \\
& & 10M
\end{array}
$$

We can see that the cost of doubling in projective coordinates equals $10M$. But if the curve parameter $a = -3$ then $\lambda_1 = 3(X_1 - Z_1^2)(X_1 + Z_1^2)$ and the cost of doubling decreases to $8M$.

Notice once again that in all the above algorithms computations are performed modulo p. Therefore much depends on the efficiency of modular arithmetic. For randomly selected moduli, the best approach to date is the use of Montgomery representation for integers [Montgomery (1985)], see also [Menezes *et al.* (1996)]. In Montgomery representation, multiplication modulo p is equivalent to two ordinary multiplications.

6.6   Counting Points on an Elliptic Curve

In this section, we consider the algorithm by René Schoof suggested in [Schoof (1995)] for finding $\#E_p(a, b)$, i.e. the number of points whose coordinates satisfy the curve equation (6.10) and are positive integers less than p (plus point at infinity $\mathcal{O}$). Schoof's algorithm was the first polynomial-time algorithm for counting points; its complexity is estimated as $O(\log^6 p)$ modular operations. This algorithm forms a basis for all modern methods used for random curves.

We begin with the theorem proved by Helmut Hasse in 1933 (proofs for all theorems may be found in [Silverman (1986)]).

Theorem 6.1. (Hasse) $\#E_p(a, b)$ *satisfies the inequalities*

$$p + 1 - 2\sqrt{p} \le \#E_p(a, b) \le p + 1 + 2\sqrt{p}.$$

It is useful to represent $\#E_p(a, b)$ in the form

$$\#E_p(a, b) = p + 1 - t. \tag{6.23}$$

Parameter t in (6.23) can be zero, a positive integer, or a negative integer and is called the *trace of Frobenius* for $E_p(a, b)$. If we could find t, we would be able to obtain the number of points on the curve using Eq. (6.23).

Up to now we were only interested in curve points with positive integer coordinates less than p. But for the rest of the section we shall consider all solutions of the curve equation (6.10). The trace of Frobenius is remarkably related to the modulus p.

Theorem 6.2. *For all x and y satisfying the curve equation* (6.10) *the identity holds*

$$(x^{p^2}, y^{p^2}) + [p](x, y) = [t](x^p, y^p) \tag{6.24}$$

(*addition in the formula means composition of points*).

Now our task is to solve Eq. (6.24) with respect to the unknown t. Notice that the point composition of the form $Q = [m]P$ can be expressed through the coordinates of point P. For instance,

$$[2](x,y) = \left(x' = \left(\frac{3x^2 + a}{2y} \right)^2 - 2x, \quad y' = \frac{3x^2 + a}{2y}(x - x') - y \right)$$

$$= \left(\frac{x^4 - 2ax^2 - 8bx + a^2}{4y^2}, \right.$$

$$\left. \frac{x^6 + 5ax^4 + 20bx^3 - 5a^2x^2 - 4abx - 8b^2 - a^3}{8y^3} \right).$$

The point $[3](x,y)$ can be obtained as $[2](x,y) + (x,y)$ by substituting the obtained coordinates for the point $[2](x,y)$ into Eqs. (6.5), (6.7), (6.8) (the interested reader may do that). The process of obtaining expressions for subsequent points seems much too complicated, nevertheless, it can be described by the following simple recurrence scheme:

$$\psi_0 = 0,$$

$$\psi_1 = 1,$$

$$\psi_2 = 2y,$$

$$\psi_3 = 3x^4 + 6ax^2 + 12bx - a^2,$$

$$\psi_4 = 4y(x^6 + 5ax^4 + 20bx^3 - 5a^2x^2 - 4abx - 8b^2 - a^3),$$

$$\psi_{2m+1} = \psi_{m+2}\psi_m^3 - \psi_{m-1}\psi_{m+1}^3, \quad m \geq 2,$$

$$\psi_{2m} = (\psi_{m+2}\psi_{m-1}^2 - \psi_{m-2}\psi_{m+1}^2)\psi_m/2y, \quad m > 2.$$

For $m \geq 2$ and $P = (x,y)$

$$[m]P = \left(\frac{\psi_m^2 x - \psi_{m-1}\psi_{m+1}}{\psi_m^2}, \frac{\psi_{m+2}\psi_{m-1}^2 - \psi_{m-2}\psi_{m+1}^2}{4y\psi_m^3} \right). \tag{6.25}$$

Polynomial $\psi_m(x,y)$ is called the *division polynomial* of order m. As we consider the curve reduced modulo p, the coefficients of all polynomials ψ are also reduced modulo p. With the aid of the above scheme the division polynomial of order m can be computed for $O(\log m)$ steps (the reader not familiar with polynomial arithmetic may consult [Knuth (1981)]). Notice that under an odd m, polynomials ψ_m depend on only one variable x since the other variable y is used only in even powers and y^2 is replaced by the right side of the curve equation (6.10). Notice also that the polynomials of the "second layer" (ψ_{2m}, ψ_{2m+1}) include the products of 4 polynomials of the "first layer" (from ψ_{m-2} to ψ_{m+2}), therefore, the degree of polynomial ψ_m grows as $O(m^2)$.

A complex point P on curve E is called the *torsion point* of order m if $[m]P = \mathcal{O}$. Due to (6.25) it is quite obvious that a point $P = (x, y)$ is a torsion point of order m if and only if $\psi_m(x, y) = 0$.

The idea of Schoof's algorithm is to search for solutions of Eq. (6.24) (with respect to t) over the sets of torsion points of small orders with subsequent determination of the general solution. For a torsion point of order m the factors are reduced modulo m and polynomials reduced modulo ψ_m, so Eq. (6.24) takes the form

$$(x^{p^2}, y^{p^2})_m + [p_m](x, y) = [t_m](x^p, y^p)_m \tag{6.26}$$

where $p_m = p \bmod m$, $t_m = t \bmod m$, $(x^k, y^k)_m = (x^k \bmod \psi_m, y^k \bmod \psi_m)$, besides, x and y are linked by the curve equation $y^2 = x^3 + ax + b$. According to the Hasse theorem

$$|t| \le 2\sqrt{p}. \tag{6.27}$$

Let us take for the values of m prime numbers up to $m_{\max}$ such that

$$\prod_{\substack{m \text{ prime} \\ 2 \le m \le m_{\max}}} m > 4\sqrt{p}. \tag{6.28}$$

Then having obtained t_m we shall uniquely determine the trace of Frobenius t satisfying (6.27) by using the Chinese Remainder Theorem (see [Knuth (1981); Menezes *et al.* (1996)]).

Consider briefly the method of solving Eq. (6.26) for $m > 2$. First compute the polynomial ψ_m. Since m is odd, $\psi_m = \psi_m(x)$. (Further on, all operations with polynomials are carried out modulo ψ_m, the power of y is reduced to 1 by the curve equation, and coefficients are computed modulo p.) Compute the polynomials x^p, y^p, x^{p^2}, y^{p^2} using the same exponentiation algorithm as for integers. By (6.25) compute $Q = [p_m](x, y)$ and using the point addition formulas find in symbolic form the composition $R = (x^{p^2}, y^{p^2})_m + Q$. If $R = \mathcal{O}$ then $t_m = 0$. Otherwise, in order to find t_m, compute the x-coordinates of points $P = [\tau](x^p, y^p)_m$ for all τ, $0 < \tau < m$. For each τ we must verify the equality between x_R and x_P. To do that we represent the difference of the x-coordinates in the form $x_R - x_P = u(x) - yv(x) = 0$. Take from this $y = u(x)/v(x)$, substitute it into the curve equation and obtain some polynomial $h_x(x) = 0$.

If h_x mod $\psi_m \neq 0$ then x_R and x_P are different and we must try another value of τ. Otherwise, if $x_R = x_P$ then compute the y-coordinate of point P and, by similar techniques, transform the difference $y_R - y_P$ into a polynomial $h_y(x) = 0$. If h_y mod $\psi_m = 0$ then $t_m = \tau$, otherwise $t_m = -\tau$ mod m.

When $m = 2$, $\psi_2 = y$ and the difficulty arises with the computation of x^p mod y. But here one simple observation helps. Since we exclude singular curves, our curve may have either one or three intersections with the horizontal axis. All other points appear in pairs (x, y), $(x, -y)$ and there is one point at infinity $\mathcal{O}$. So the number of points on the curve is even or odd depending on whether $X^3 + aX + b$ can be factored modulo p or not. A simple criterion is known for making such a decision (see, e.g. [Menezes *et al.* (1996); Gallager (1968)]).

Theorem 6.3. *A third-degree polynomial $F(X)$ cannot be factored modulo p if and only if*

$$\gcd(F(X), X^p - X) = 1.$$

As a result we have $t_2 = 1$ if $\gcd(X^3 + aX + b, X^p - X) = 1$, and $t_2 = 0$ otherwise.

Let us estimate the complexity of Schoof's algorithm. First, give the following well-known property of prime numbers (see [Rosen (1992); Menezes *et al.* (1996)]).

Proposition 6.1. *The number of primes less than n is approximately $n/\ln n$.*

It follows from Proposition 6.1 that $m_{\max} = O(\log p)$ and the number of moduli for which the computations are performed is $O(\log p)$. The most time-consuming step in the algorithm is the computation of x^{p^2} and the similar polynomials. If a fast exponentiation method is used, this step requires $O(\log p)$ multiplications with polynomials of degree $O(m^2) = O(\log^2 p)$. Each multiplication requires $O(\log^4 p)$ numerical multiplications modulo p, i.e. there is a total of $O(\log^5 p)$ multiplications modulo p. One multiplication modulo p requires $O(\log^2 p)$ bit operations. So the computation of x^{p^2} requires $O(\log^7 p)$ bit operations. Taking into account the number of moduli we obtain the overall complexity $O(\log^8 p)$ bit operations.

Consider an example. Determine the number of points on the curve used in the example on page 89:

$$Y^2 = X^3 + 2X + 6 \quad (\text{mod } 7) \quad (a = 2, b = 6).$$

First apply the exponential-time algorithm: for all values of X from 0 to 6 find corresponding values of Y (if any). We shall need a list of squares modulo 7:

$$0^2 = 0,$$
$$1^2 = 1,$$
$$2^2 = 4,$$
$$3^2 = 9 = 2,$$
$$4^2 = 2,$$
$$5^2 = 4,$$
$$6^2 = 1 \quad (\text{mod } 7).$$

With the use of this list find the set of points $E_7(2,6)$:

$$\begin{aligned}
&x = 0,\ y^2 = 6, &&y \text{ does not exist,}\\
&x = 1,\ y^2 = 1+2+6 = 9 = 2, &&y = 3 \text{ and } y = -3 = 4,\\
&x = 2,\ y^2 = 8+4+6 = 4, &&y = 2 \text{ and } y = -2 = 5,\\
&x = 3,\ y^2 = 27+6+6 = 4, &&y = 2 \text{ and } y = -2 = 5,\\
&x = 4,\ y^2 = 64+8+6 = 1, &&y = 1 \text{ and } y = -1 = 6,\\
&x = 5,\ y^2 = 125+10+6 = 1, &&y = 1 \text{ and } y = -1 = 6,\\
&x = 6,\ y^2 = 216+12+6 = 3, &&y \text{ does not exist.}
\end{aligned}$$

Counting the number of points found and adding the point at infinity we obtain

$$\#E_7(2,6) = 11.$$

It is clear that this method cannot be applied if p is large, but we shall use the result for checking.

Begin the execution of Schoof's algorithm. Three moduli $m = 2, 3, 5$ will suffice since $2 \times 3 \times 5 = 30 > 4\sqrt{7} = 10.58$ (in fact, two moduli $m = 3, 5$ would be enough but we shall use also $m = 2$ for the sake of exposition).

For ease of designation, we shall write polynomials as decimal numbers (the size of the modulus allows us to do that). Thus, for instance,

$$x^4 + 5x^2 + 2 = 1x^4 + 0x^3 + 5x^2 + 0x + 2 = 10502,$$
$$x^4 + x = 1x^4 + 0x^3 + 0x^2 + 1x + 0 = 10010.$$

All operations with coefficients will be performed modulo 7. Compute the necessary division polynomials:

$$\psi_0 = 0,$$

$$\psi_1 = 1,$$

$$\psi_2 = 2y,$$

$$\psi_3 = 30523,$$

$$\psi_4 = 4y \times 1031115 = 4054446y,$$

$$\psi_5 = \psi_4\psi_2^3 - \psi_1\psi_3^3 = 4054446 \times 1026^2 - 6025554626356$$

$$= 5055036550230.$$

Now we are to solve Eq. (6.26) for $m = 3$. Compute modulo ψ_3:

$$x^7 = 1363,$$

$$y^7 = (y^2)^3 y = 1026^3 y = 1360y,$$

$$x^{49} = 10 = x,$$

$$y^{49} = 1026^{24}y = 6y,$$

$$p_3 = 7 \bmod 3 = 1.$$

The left side of (6.26) converts to

$$R = (x, 6y) + (x, y) = \mathcal{O}.$$

Hence, $t_3 = 0$.

Now solve Eq. (6.26) for $m = 5$. Compute modulo ψ_5:

$$x^7 = 10000000,$$

$$y^7 = 1064524266y,$$

$$x^{49} = 531353334500,$$

$$y^{49} = 650465522521y,$$

$$p_5 = 2.$$

Let's find a point $Q = [2](x, y)$. In the general case, it is done by using Eq. (6.25):

$$Q = \left(\frac{4y^2x - \psi_3}{4y^2}, \frac{\psi_4}{4y^4}\right) = \left(\frac{10314}{4013}, \frac{1031115y}{1045431}\right).$$

We can see that $x_Q \neq x^{49}$, so we shall look for $\tau > 0$. Find a point $R = (x^{49}, y^{49}) + Q$ by Eqs. (6.5), (6.7), (6.8):

$$k = \frac{\dfrac{1031115y}{1045431} - 650465522521y}{\dfrac{10314}{4013} - 531353334500}$$

$$= \frac{(1031115 - 650465522521 \times 1045431)4013y}{1045431(10314 - 531353334500 \times 4013}$$

$$= \frac{541024434205y}{115461562234},$$

$$x_R = \frac{541024434205^2 y^2}{115461562234^2} - 531353334500 - \frac{10314}{4013}$$

$$= \frac{552631612401}{533030166456},$$

$$y_R = \left(531353334500 - \frac{552631612401}{533030166456}\right) \times \frac{541024434205y}{115461562234}$$

$$-650465522521y = \frac{515441613166y}{115165441243}.$$

Let's try $\tau = 1$, $P = (x^7, y^7)$. Verify the hypothesis $x_R - x_P = 0$:

$$h_x = 552631612401 - 533030166456 \times 10000000$$

$$= 61115566241 \neq 0 \bmod \psi_5.$$

Try $\tau = 2$. Compute $P = [2](x^7, y^7)$. Here it is convenient to use point addition since we add the point (x^7, y^7) to the previous point P. We obtain

$$k = \frac{3 \times 10000000^2 + 2}{2 \times 1064524266y} = \frac{434232361462}{2051341455y},$$

$$x_P = \frac{434232361462^2}{2051341455^2 y^2} - 2 \times 10000000 = \frac{213203662514}{220445441503}.$$

Verify the hypothesis $x_R - x_P = 0$:

$$h_x = 552631612401 \times 220445441503 - 213203662514 \times 533030166456$$

$$= 0 \bmod \psi_5.$$

Hence, $x_R = x_P$. Now we need to compare y_R and y_P. We have

$$y_P = \left(10000000 - \frac{213203662514}{220445441503}\right) \times \frac{434232361462}{2051341455y} - 1064524266y$$

$$= \frac{510334350655}{221015611231y}.$$

Verify whether $y_R - y_P = 0$:

$$h_y = 515441613166y \times 221015611231y - 510334350655 \times 115165441243$$

$$= 0 \bmod \psi_5.$$

Hence, $t_5 = 2$.

Finally, determine t_2. We must find the greatest common divisor for $x^3 + ax + b$ and $x^p - x$. Apply the Euclidean algorithm for polynomials. Notice that under the large p used in cryptography, we cannot store in memory and operate with the polynomial $x^p - x$. But at the first step of the Euclidean algorithm the remainder is computed as $(x^p - x) \bmod (x^3 + ax + b)$, therefore it suffices to set as the input not the polynomial $x^p - x$ but the remainder. So we compute $x^p \bmod (x^3 + ax + b)$ using a fast exponentiation algorithm and subtract x. After that preparation we run the Euclidean algorithm. In our example,

$$x^7 = 304 \bmod 1026,$$

$$x^7 - x = 364,$$

$$\gcd(1026, 364) = 1.$$

Hence, $t_2 = 1$.

Now apply the Chinese Remainder Theorem [Knuth (1981); Menezes *et al.* (1996)]. We have

$$t = 1 \bmod 2,$$

$$t = 0 \bmod 3,$$

$$t = 2 \bmod 5,$$

$$N = 2 \times 3 \times 5 = 30.$$

The solution $t' = t \bmod N$ is found by the formula

$$t' = \sum_{i=1}^{3} a_i N_i M_i \bmod N$$

where

$$a_1 = 1, \ N_1 = 30/2 = 15, \ M_1 = 15^{-1} \bmod 2 = 1,$$
$$a_2 = 0, \ N_2 = 30/3 = 10, \ M_2 = 10^{-1} \bmod 3 = 1,$$
$$a_3 = 2, \ N_3 = 30/5 = 6, \ \ M_3 = 6^{-1} \bmod 5 = 1.$$

Substituting the numbers we obtain

$$t' = 1 \times 15 \times 1 + 0 \times 10 \times 1 + 2 \times 6 \times 1 = 27.$$

To make the solution satisfy the inequality (6.27) subtract the modulus:

$$t = t' - N = -3.$$

Using Eq. (6.23), we eventually find

$$\#E_7(2,6) = 7 + 1 - (-3) = 11.$$

We see that the determination of the number of points on the curve is not a simple problem. Solving it requires high-performance computers. In practice, improved versions of Schoof's algorithm are used that involve subtle higher-algebraic constructions. The main feature of these methods is the reduction of the degree of division polynomials from $O(m^2)$ down to $O(m)$. As a result, the complexity is reduced to $O(\log^6 p)$ and may be further decreased down to $O(\log^{4+\epsilon} p)$ owing to the use of asymptotically faster methods of multiplication and division.

6.7 Using Standard Curves

In view of the fact that generating random curves according to the guidelines of Sec. 6.3, especially performing the step of point counting, appears quite difficult, it is enough in practice to use the curves suggested by various standards and other sources. For instance, the US standard FIPS 186-4 [FIPS 186-4 (2013)] suggests specific elliptic curves for several lengths of moduli. Generally speaking, there are no restrictions that prevent one well-chosen elliptic curve from being used by all the users all over the world. However, such a curve, being widely used, will attract the considerable forces of cryptanalysts and adversaries. One cannot rule out the possibility that, in the course of time, some attacks on that specific curve will be invented by utilizing its hidden properties that have not been taken into account earlier. But this is only a possibility which is considered highly improbable by many specialists.

Let us give an example of a real curve suggested by FIPS 186-4 (Curve P-256). By a backslash\we denote the continuation of a number at the next line. It is assumed that the curve is defined by the equation $Y^2 = X^3 + aX + b \bmod p$, that the number of points on the curve $\#E_p(a, b) = n$, and that the point $G = (x_G, y_G)$ is a generator of the working subset of points of cardinality q where q is prime.

$$p = 2^{256} - 2^{224} + 2^{192} + 2^{96} - 1$$

$$= 115792\ 089210356\ 248762697\ 446949407\ 573530086\backslash$$

$$143415290\ 314195533\ 631308867\ 097853951$$

$$a = -3$$

$$b = \text{0x } \text{5ac635d8 aa3a93e7 b3ebbd55 769886bc 651d06b0}\backslash$$

$$\text{cc53b0f6 3bce3c3e 27d2604b}$$

$$n = 115792\ 089210356\ 248762697\ 446949407\ 573529996\backslash$$

$$955224135\ 760342422\ 259061068\ 512044369$$

(prime number)

$$q = n$$

$$x_G = \text{0x } \text{6b17d1f2 e12c4247 f8bce6e5 63a440f2 77037d81}\backslash$$

$$\text{2deb33a0 f4a13945 d898c296}$$

$$y_G = \text{0x } \text{4fe342e2 fe1a7f9b 8ee7eb4a 7c0f9e16 2bce3357}\backslash$$

$$\text{6b315ece cbb64068 37bf51f5}$$

We can see that parameters p and a are scarcely conceived as random, and that all the "randomness" of the curve is determined by the random choice of parameter b.

The first question that arises when we are given a curve such as the one above is: are there no errors in the record of parameters? Three basic tests can be performed to ascertain this.

(1) Verify that p is prime.
(2) Verify that the point $G = (x_G, y_G)$ lies on the curve (satisfies the curve equation).
(3) Verify that n is indeed the number of points on the curve. Note that this check makes sense also if we ourselves compute n, e.g. by the use of Schoof's algorithm. In the general case, $n = hq$ where h is a small integer and q prime. First of all, by trial division and testing primality,

one should make certain that n complies with the specified form. Then randomly select a point P on the curve (one may take $P = [k]G$ where k is a random integer). The number n is guaranteed to be the number of points if simultaneously $[n]P = \mathcal{O}$ and $[h]P \neq \mathcal{O}$. This condition being unsatisfied, two variants are possible: If $[n]P \neq \mathcal{O}$ then n is not a number of points; but if $[h]P = \mathcal{O}$ (which is extremely unlikely) then one needs to take another point P.

In addition to the proposed tests one may verify all other requirements described in Sec. 6.3.

The second question that arises when we are given a "cooked" curve, is whether it actually was generated randomly? This question is also important for many other cryptographic schemes. Maybe, the curve suggested possesses some rare property allowing one to break the resulting cryptosystem, and the one who has manufactured the curve will be able later on to access the secret information encrypted with the aid of this curve. To prove that the curve was indeed randomly generated, we must prove that its parameters were chosen randomly but not at will. For instance, for the curve recommended above, we must prove that parameter b was selected at random. But how can one prove that some number is random? Actually, what we need is to prove that it was not systematically constructed. This problem is solved as follows. Let $h(x)$ be a cryptographically secure hash function. To generate a number b we select a number s, compute $b = h(s)$ and suggest both b and s. If the hash function satisfies all security requirements (see Sec. 8.5) then b cannot have any prescribed properties and we can rely on it, as it is truly random. The number s is the "certificate" which proves the "purity" of number b (everyone can verify that $b = h(s)$). The elliptic curve described above has such a certificate, based on the hash function SHA-1 [FIPS 180-1 (1995)], and the standard specifies the procedure of its usage. Therefore we may be sure that the curve is actually random.

Problems and Exercises

6.1 The elliptic curve is defined by the parameters $p = 11$, $a = 4$, $b = 7$. Determine whether the following points are on the curve: $(1,1)$, $(1,2)$, $(2,1)$, $(2,2)$, $(5,8)$.

6.2 For the elliptic curve with parameters $p = 7$, $a = 2$, $b = 6$ compute the following point compositions: $[2](2,2)$, $[2](4,6)$, $(1,3) + (1,4)$, $(2,2) + (3,2)$, $(3,5) + (5,1)$.

Themes for Labs

In labs, it is recommended to use the elliptic curve with the following parameters:

$$p = 31991, \quad a = -3 = 31988, \quad b = 1000.$$

The number of points on this curve

$$n = 32089 \quad \text{(prime number)}.$$

As a generator, one may take the point

$$G = (0, 5585).$$

It is convenient to represent the point at infinity $\mathcal{O}$ as a point with coordinates (0,0).

6.3 Write the set of programs (program functions) for the computation of elliptic curve point addition, doubling, and multiplication. We propose several equalities for program testing:

$$(51, 7858) + (91, 5500) = (7252, 18353),$$

$$(7777, 10935) + (16000, 20400) = (12395, 26268),$$

$$(12405, 28624) + (2963, 16300) = (14905, 2313),$$

$$(8020, 1740) + (8020, 30251) = \mathcal{O},$$

$$[2](0, 5585) = (8, 19435),$$

$$[2](23161, 17992) = (26775, 10831),$$

$$[2](110, 13171) = (26948, 16087),$$

$$[10000](31122, 9) = (31180, 29596),$$

$$[12345](13140, 5033) = (9362, 27046),$$

$$[11111](11007, 23704) = (850, 6718).$$

6.4 Make a program implementation of the ElGamal cipher on an elliptic curve. When debugging and testing the program one may use the following example of the cipher:

$$c = 5103, \quad D = (12507, 2027);$$

$$m = 10000, \quad k = 523;$$

$$R = (9767, 11500), \quad P = (25482, 16638);$$

$$e = 11685.$$

The obtained ciphertext $((9767, 11500), 11685)$ must decrypt to the message 10000 under the secret key 5103.

6.5 Make a program implementation of the algorithms of elliptic curve signature generation and verification. As usual, assume that $h(m) = m$. As the parameter q, take $n = 32089$ (the number of points on the curve). The signed message

$$(1000; 4615, 5944)$$

must be declared valid for the signer whose public key is $Y = (12224, 7207)$.

Chapter 7

Theoretical Security of Cryptosystems

7.1 Introduction

One of the first open works on cryptography was published in 1949 by Claude Shannon [Shannon (1949)]. Shannon considered the classical secret-key cryptosystem shown schematically in Fig. 1.1 (p. 3). In this system, we have a secure channel for transmitting secret keys. However notice that in our day we may replace the secure channel with a *secured* channel which is virtually created when the secret key is computed by means of public-key cryptographic methods, e.g. the Diffie–Hellman key agreement or the Needham–Schroeder protocol. In this chapter, we shall consider only the classical scheme with the secret key, but many of the results may be extended to the case of generating secret keys by public-key methods.

We may roughly divide all cipher schemes into two big classes:

(1) the schemes which are unbreakable in principle, which can be strictly proved;
(2) the schemes whose security is based on the impossibility of searching through a large number of keys (although, in principle, they can be broken).

In this chapter, we shall study the systems from the first class. The second class will be the topic of the next chapter. To expose the matter of this chapter we need some elementary notions and facts from probability theory. We shall use these without giving strict definitions and proofs which may be found in almost any textbook on probability theory, see, e.g. [Feller (1968)]. Many of the results discussed in the following sections are due to [Shannon (1948)] and [Shannon (1949)].

7.2   Theory of Perfect Secrecy

Let $M = \{M_1, M_2, M_3, \ldots, M_m\}$ be the set of all admissible messages (e.g. the set of all texts in English of the length of no more than 1000 letters), $K = \{K_1, K_2, K_3, \ldots, K_n\}$ be the set of all possible keys, and $E = \{E_1, E_2, \ldots, E_k\}$ be the set of all cryptograms (i.e. enciphered messages). The cryptograms are the functions of the source message and the key, i.e. $E_j = f(M_i, K_l)$.

Assume that the set of messages M obeys a probability distribution P, i.e. a probability $P(M_i)$ is defined for all $i = 1, 2, \ldots, m$. This is an *a priori* distribution which is also known to an adversary. Notation $P(A|B)$ will be used, as usual, for the conditional probability of event A given event B (i.e. $P(A|B)$ is the probability of occurrence of event A provided that event B has occurred).

Definition 7.1. A cryptosystem is said to be *perfectly secure* (or to provide *perfect secrecy*) if the equality

$$P(M_i|E_j) = P(M_i) \tag{7.1}$$

holds for all M_i, K_l, and $E_j = f(M_i, K_l)$.

Let's give some explanations. Suppose that Eve overhears the cryptogram E_j. If Eq. (7.1) holds for all admissible messages then Eve does not obtain any information about the message transmitted, i.e. the knowledge of E_j is of no use for her.

Consider a schematic example. Let M be the set of all 6-letter words in English. Let it be known *a priori* that

$$P(\text{message} = \text{``dollar''}) = 0.000150,$$
$$P(\text{message} = \text{``bottle''}) = 0.000012, \text{ etc.} \tag{7.2}$$

Suppose we have a non-perfect system and Eve upon interception and computation obtains the following data:

$$P(\text{message} = \text{``dollar''}) = 10^{-20},$$
$$P(\text{message} = \text{``bottle''}) = 0.9999.$$

It means that Eve has, in fact, deciphered the message: she is almost sure that the word "bottle" was transmitted because the probability of anything else does not exceed 0.0001.

Suppose now that we have a perfect system. In this case, for any intercepted cryptogram E_j, Eve obtains

$$P(\text{message} = \text{"dollar"}|E_j) = 0.000150,$$

$$P(\text{message} = \text{"bottle"}|E_j) = 0.000012, \text{ etc.}$$

i.e. her *a posteriori* distribution completely coincides with the *a priori* distribution (7.2). It means that she might pay no attention to the intercepted cryptogram but might still guess the message based on the source probabilities. We can see that Eq. (7.1) is actually a reasonable definition of perfect secrecy.

Explore the properties of perfect secrecy systems.

Theorem 7.1. *If a system is perfectly secure (Eq. (7.1) holds) then the equality*

$$P\left(E_j|M_i\right) = P\left(E_j\right) \tag{7.3}$$

is valid for all i and j. The converse is also true: if (7.3) holds then the system is perfectly secure.

Proof. By definition of conditional probability

$$P\left(A|B\right) = \frac{P(AB)}{P(B)}$$

under $P(B) \neq 0$. Therefore given $P(E_j) \neq 0$ we can write

$$P(M_i|E_j) = \frac{P(M_iE_j)}{P(E_j)} = \frac{P(M_i)P(E_j|M_i)}{P(E_j)}.$$

Taking into account Eq. (7.1) we obtain

$$P\left(M_i|E_j\right) = \frac{P(M_i|E_j)P(E_j|M_i)}{P(E_j)},$$

i.e.

$$\frac{P(E_j|M_i)}{P(E_j)} = 1.$$

So Eq. (7.3) is proved. The converse proposition can be proved by the reverse chain of the presented equalities, see [Shannon (1949)]. □

7.3　The One-Time Pad Cipher

This cipher was first described by Frank Miller, see [Bellovin (2011)], and then reinvented by Gilbert Vernam [Vernam (1926)] The cipher was used in practice but the proof of its security was given much later in [Shannon (1949)]. This cipher is mainly called a *one-time pad*. We shall describe it for the case of the binary alphabet.

Let the set of messages M consist of binary words of length n, i.e. there are no more than 2^n messages. In the one-time pad cipher, the set of keys consists of the words of the same length n and each key is used with probability $1/2^n$. In other words, all keys are equiprobable.

Let the message be $\bar{m} = m_1 m_2 \ldots m_n$ and the key $\bar{k} = k_1 k_2 \ldots k_n$. Then the ciphertext $\bar{e} = e_1 e_2 \ldots e_n$ is produced by the rule:

$$e_i = m_i \oplus k_i, \quad i = 1, 2, \ldots, n, \tag{7.4}$$

where $\oplus$ denotes addition modulo 2. In other words, the message is enciphered by the scheme

$$\oplus \frac{\begin{array}{cccc} m_1 & m_2 & \ldots & m_n \\ k_1 & k_2 & \ldots & k_n \end{array}}{e_1 \; e_2 \ldots e_n}.$$

Since addition and subtraction modulo 2 are the same, deciphering is done by the rule

$$m_i = e_i \oplus k_i. \tag{7.5}$$

Let $\bar{m} = 01001$, $\bar{k} = 11010$. Then we obtain $\bar{e} = 10011$. Summing up $\bar{e}$ with $\bar{k}$ we recover $\bar{m} = 01001$.

Theorem 7.2. *The one-time pad cipher is perfectly secure.*

Proof. According to Theorem 7.1, it is sufficient to prove that (7.3) holds. We have

$$\begin{aligned} P(E_j|M_i) &= P(\bar{e}|\bar{m}) \\ &= P(k_1 = e_1 \oplus m_1, k_2 = e_2 \oplus m_2, \ldots, k_n = e_n \oplus m_n) \\ &= P(\bar{k} = k_1 \ldots k_n) = 2^{-n} \end{aligned}$$

(in the last equality we used the assumption that all keys are equiprobable). Find $P(E_j)$. Provided that events M_i are pairwise mutually exclusive, one can use the total probability formula

$$P(E_j) = \sum_{i=1}^{2^n} P(M_i)P(E_j|M_i).$$

Taking into account that $P(E_j|M_i) = 2^{-n}$ we obtain

$$P(E_j) = 2^{-n} \sum_{i=1}^{2^n} P(M_i).$$

Since the sum of probabilities of all messages equals 1 we obtain

$$P(E_j) = 2^{-n}.$$

So, $P(E_j|M_i) = P(E_j) = 2^{-n}$, i.e. Eq. (7.3) holds. $\square$

It is known that the one-time pad cipher was used for securing governmental communications, e.g. on the so-called "Moscow–Washington" hotline [Menezes *et al.* (1996)]. The key was delivered by a trusted courier.

There is a point of view that the one-time pad cipher is very expensive because the length of the key must be equal to the message length. On the other hand, the cipher can be used in many practical situations. For example, students Alice and Bob can agree to use this cipher for securing their e-mail messages when they part for the holidays (we advise the reader to work out the scheme and write the program assuming that the length of the letters they will exchange does not exceed the size of a standard flash drive).

An important question that arises when using the one-time pad in practice is how to ensure the equal probabilities of the keys. It is equivalent to the claim that all bits of the key be independent and equiprobable. We need special generators that would meet this requirement. But in reality the generators may deviate from the ideal. For instance, the bits may be emitted with probabilities close but not equal to $1/2$ (say, $P(0) = 0.501$, $P(1) = 0.499$). Will the cipher be secure in this case? The answer will be given in Sec. 7.5 but here we just remark that the one-time pad cipher is resistant to small deviations from randomness and the independence of the key symbols.

7.4 Elements of Information Theory

We have proved that the one-time pad cipher is perfectly secure but it requires the key to be as long as the message. Shannon showed that in any perfect secrecy system the key length must be no less than the message entropy (the notion we shall define below), i.e. proportional to the message length. However in many practical systems, we have to use short keys (say, of a few hundred or a few thousand bits) for encrypting long messages (of hundreds of kilobytes and more). In this case, we may construct the so-called *ideal* cryptosystems described firstly by Shannon. For constructing ideal systems and studying their properties Shannon suggested that one use the notions and results of information theory. In this section, we shall define and briefly illustrate these. A sufficiently complete and strict study can be found in many textbooks, e.g. [Gallager (1968); McEliece (1984); Blahut (1987); Welsh (1988); Cover and Thomas (2006)]. It is also useful to consult the pioneering work [Shannon (1948)]. The reader may refer to any of these books for strict definitions and proofs.

We begin with a definition of the main notion, the Shannon entropy. Let a discrete random variable ξ be given, taking on the values $a_1, a_2, \ldots, a_r$ with the probabilities $P_1, P_2, \ldots, P_r$, respectively.

Definition 7.2. The *entropy* of random variable ξ is defined as

$$H(\xi) = -\sum_{i=1}^{r} P_i \log P_i \qquad (7.6)$$

assuming $0 \log 0 = 0$.

If one uses binary logarithms (i.e. to the base 2) then the entropy is measured in bits, which is generally accepted in cryptography, information theory, and computer science. In the case of natural logarithms, the unity of measure is nat, in the case of decimal logarithms — dit.

If $r = 2$, Eq. (7.6) can be written differently with the following notation: $P_1 = p$, $P_2 = 1 - p$. Then

$$H = -(p \log p + (1 - p) \log(1 - p)). \qquad (7.7)$$

The graph of the entropy for this case is shown in Fig. 7.1.

Consider the simplest properties of entropy.

Proposition 7.1.
(1) $H\left(\xi\right) \geq 0$;
(2) $H\left(\xi\right) \leq \log r$;
(3) $H\left(\xi\right) = \log r$ *if* $P_i = 1/r$, $i = 1, 2, \ldots, r$.

Proof. The first property is quite obvious (see (7.6)). We prove the second property only for $r = 2$ since the general case is similar. Explore the graph

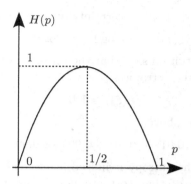

Fig. 7.1   The graph of binary entropy.

of entropy. We need to find the maximum of the function (7.7). For that, we find the first and second derivatives of $H(p)$ assuming for simplicity that the logarithms are natural.

$$H'(p) = - \left(\ln p + p \cdot \frac{1}{p} - \ln(1-p) - \frac{1-p}{1-p} \right) = -\ln p + \ln(1-p).$$

Hence $H'(p) = 0$ if $p = 1/2$. Find the second derivative

$$H''(p) = -\frac{1}{p} - \frac{1}{1-p}.$$

We can see that $H''(p) < 0$ when $p \in (0; 1)$. It means that the function $H(p)$ attains the maximum when $p = 1/2$ and is convex in the interval $(0; 1)$. So the graph depicted in Fig. 7.1 is justified. It is plain that under any other base of the logarithm the graph will be analogous.

The third property follows directly from the definition of entropy (7.6):

$$H(\xi) = -\sum_{i=1}^{r} \frac{1}{r} \log \frac{1}{r} = -r \cdot \frac{1}{r} \log \frac{1}{r} = \log r. \qquad \square$$

The physical sense of the entropy is the quantitative measure of uncertainty. Consider, for instance, the three different random variables ξ_1, ξ_2 and ξ_3 taking on the values a_1 and $a_2(r = 2)$:

$$\xi_1 : P(a_1) = 1, \qquad P(a_2) = 0;$$
$$\xi_2 : P(a_1) = 0.5, \qquad P(a_2) = 0.5;$$
$$\xi_3 : P(a_1) = 0.01, \qquad P(a_2) = 0.99.$$

Intuition suggests that the uncertainty of ξ_1 is zero. Actually,

$$H(\xi_1) = -(1 \cdot \log 1 + 0 \cdot \log 0) = 0.$$

Look at ξ_2 and ξ_3. Intuition says that the uncertainty of ξ_2 is higher than that of ξ_3. Compute the entropies:

$$H(\xi_2) = 1 \text{ bit}$$

As has been computed above,

$$H(\xi_3) = -(0.01 \cdot \log 0.01 + 0.99 \cdot \log 0.99) \approx 0.08 \text{ bit.}$$

We can see that the entropy is indeed a reasonable measure of uncertainty. But examples of that sort are not those that interest us. The entropy plays a key role in many problems of telecommunications and information sciences. In particular, the entropy characterizes the maximum attainable degree of data compression. More exactly, if a source with the limit entropy h (defined below) generates a (sufficiently long) message of n symbols, this message can be compressed up to nh bits on average. For example, if $h = 1/2$, the message can be compressed to half of its size. It should be pointed out that we speak of so-called lossless compression when the source message can be recovered without distortion.

Consider now a two-dimensional random variable defined by the following distribution

$$P_{ij} = P(\xi_1 = a_i, \ \xi_2 = b_j), \quad 1 \le i \le r, 1 \le j \le s. \tag{7.8}$$

Introduce the following notation:

$$P_{i\cdot} = P(\xi_1 = a_i) = \sum_{j=1}^{s} P_{ij},$$

$$P_{\cdot j} = P(\xi_2 = b_j) = \sum_{i=1}^{r} P_{ij}.$$

By analogy with (7.6) define the entropy of the two-dimensional random variable

$$H(\xi_1, \xi_2) = -\sum_{i=1}^{r} \sum_{j=1}^{s} P_{ij} \log P_{ij}. \tag{7.9}$$

Similarly, for a three-dimensional random variable (ξ_1, ξ_2, ξ_3) and probability distribution P_{ijk}, define

$$H(\xi_1, \xi_2, \xi_3) = -\sum_{i} \sum_{j} \sum_{k} P_{ijk} \log P_{ijk}. \tag{7.10}$$

The entropy of an n-dimensional random variable is defined in the same way.

Suppose now that the value of ξ_1 is known but the value of ξ_2 is not. Then it is natural to define the conditional entropy

$$H(\xi_2|\xi_1) = -\sum_{i=1}^{r} P_{i\cdot} \sum_{j=1}^{s} \frac{P_{ij}}{P_{i\cdot}} \log \frac{P_{ij}}{P_{i\cdot}}. \tag{7.11}$$

This is the mean conditional entropy of the random variable ξ_2 under the condition that the value of ξ_1 is known.

Proposition 7.2. *Properties of two-dimensional entropy*

$$H(\xi_1, \xi_2) = H(\xi_1) + H(\xi_2|\xi_1), \tag{7.12}$$

in particular, for independent random variables ξ_1 and ξ_2,

$$H(\xi_2|\xi_1) = H(\xi_2),$$
$$H(\xi_1, \xi_2) = H(\xi_1) + H(\xi_2). \tag{7.13}$$

Recall from probability theory that ξ_1 and ξ_2 are independent if $P_{ij} = P_i P_j$ for all i and j. The proof of the proposition is quite simple and can be found in the literature. We confine ourselves only to its interpretation. In the first experiment, let ξ_1 be observed, in the second experiment ξ_2. Then the total uncertainty must be equal to the uncertainty of the first experiment summed up with the conditional uncertainty of the second. In case of the independent ξ_1 and ξ_2, the knowledge of one variable does not offer any information about the value of the other, which corresponds to (7.13).

Let an n-dimensional random variable $(\xi_1, \xi_2, \ldots, \xi_n)$ be given. Then the following equation holds:

$$H(\xi_1, \ldots, \xi_n) = H(\xi_1) + H(\xi_2|\xi_1) + H(\xi_3|\xi_1, \xi_2)$$
$$+ \cdots + H(\xi_n|\xi_1, \ldots, \xi_{n-1}). \tag{7.14}$$

For independent random variables,

$$H(\xi_1, \ldots, \xi_n) = \sum_{i=1}^{n} H(\xi_i) \tag{7.15}$$

(observe that (7.12), (7.13) are special cases of (7.14), (7.15)).

In the general case,

$$H(\xi_k|\xi_1, \ldots, \xi_{k-1}) \le H(\xi_k). \tag{7.16}$$

Consider a sequence of random variables $\xi_1, \xi_2, \xi_3, \ldots$ (ξ_i takes on values in A), which may be interpreted as a random process with discrete time.

We shall assume that this process is stationary, i.e. informally, probabilities for $(\xi_1, \ldots, \xi_n)$ are the same as for $(\xi_{\Delta+1}, \ldots, \xi_{\Delta+n})$ for all positive integers n and Δ.

Let $H(\xi_1, \ldots, \xi_n)$ be the entropy of an n-dimensional random variable $(\xi_1, \ldots, \xi_n)$. Denote by

$$h_n^+ = \frac{1}{n} H(\xi_1, \ldots, \xi_n)$$

the entropy rate of the nth order and define

$$h_n^- = H(\xi_n | \xi_1, \ldots, \xi_{n-1}).$$

Note the following properties:

$$h_n^+ \leq h_{n-1}^+, \quad n > 1, \tag{7.17}$$

$$h_n^- \leq h_n^+, \tag{7.18}$$

$$h_n^- \leq h_{n-1}^-, \quad n > 1. \tag{7.19}$$

For independent $\xi_1, \xi_2, \ldots, \xi_n$ the equalities

$$h_n^+ = h_n^- = h$$

hold. (The process generating independent random variables is said to be the memoryless process.)

Theorem 7.3. *For a stationary process, the limits* $\lim_{n \to \infty} h_n^+$ *and* $\lim_{n \to \infty} h_n^-$ *exist and are equal.*

Denote the common value of these limits by h_∞,

$$h_\infty = \lim_{n \to \infty} h_n^+ = \lim_{n \to \infty} h_n^-. \tag{7.20}$$

Let the alphabet $A = \{a_1, a_2, \ldots a_r\}$ be given. We know that

$$\max H(\xi_1) = \log r$$

for memoryless processes, therefore, taking into account (7.19) and (7.20), we obtain $\max h_\infty = \log r$, the maximum being reached for the memoryless processes with equal probabilities of letters $1/r$. It is natural to introduce the quantity

$$R = \log r - h_\infty \tag{7.21}$$

called *redundancy* (per source letter). Informally, this is, so to speak, the "unused" portion of the alphabet. Redundancy is a quantitative measure of the mutual dependence and non-uniformity of the letters. Note that in the second example with the Caesar cipher (p. 5), the redundancy of the encrypted message equals zero since all letters (decimal digits) are equiprobable and independent, i.e. $h_\infty = \log 10$ and $R = 0$. And this caused the simple Caesar cipher to become unbreakable.

7.5 Robustness of the One-Time Pad Under Small Deviations of the Key from Randomness

Consider a generalization of the one-time pad to the case in which the plaintext $m_1 \ldots m_n$, key sequence $k_1 \ldots k_n$ and ciphertext $e_1 \ldots e_n$ belong to the alphabet $A = \{0, 1, \ldots, r - 1\}$, $r \geq 2$. Encryption and decryption are determined by the equalities

$$e_i = (m_i + k_i) \bmod r, \quad m_i = (e_i - k_i) \bmod r. \tag{7.22}$$

In the case $r = 2$ Eqs. (7.22) may be represented in a more familiar way

$$e_i = m_i \oplus k_i, \quad m_i = e_i \oplus k_i, \tag{7.23}$$

where $a \oplus b = (a + b) \bmod 2$.

We know that for the cipher to be perfectly secure, it is required that the symbols of the key sequence be equiprobable and independent, i.e. for every word $k_1 \ldots k_n$, $k_i \in A$, $P(\text{key} = k_1 \ldots k_n) = r^{-n}$. By using the introduced notion of the Shannon entropy the property of perfect secrecy may be represented as $H(M|E) = H(M)$, where, as earlier, M is the set of all messages and E the set of intercepted ciphertexts.

If the message is generated by a stationary and ergodic source, then the perfect secrecy of the one-time pad has a simple interpretation elucidating the purport of the notion. As follows from the well-known Shannon–McMillan–Breiman theorem [Gallager (1968); Cover and Thomas (2006)], the set of all messages $m_1 \ldots m_n$, under large n, can be split into two parts: the $2^{H(m_1 \ldots m_n)}$ messages whose probabilities are almost equal and sum up to almost 1, and the remaining messages whose combined probability is close to 0. Eve knows that, almost surely, the encrypted message belongs to the first set but all messages in this set are almost equiprobable, the number of such messages growing exponentially as 2^{hn}, where $h = h_\infty$ is the limiting entropy of the source (in what follows we shall call it simply the entropy for brevity). This is the reason why Eve is unable to determine the proper message.

But what will happen to the cipher (7.22) when the key sequence is generated by a stationary ergodic source and slightly deviates from the sequence of equiprobable and independent symbols? The answer to the question has been given in [Ryabko (2015)]. It was shown in this paper that the properties of the resulting cipher remain, in a certain sense, close to the one-time pad. More specifically, the set of messages with almost equal probabilities with the combined probability close to 1 grows as $2^{n(h-R_K)}$, where h is the source entropy and R_K is the redundancy of the key source, $R_K = \log r - h(K)$, where r is the number of letters in the alphabet and $h(K)$ is the entropy of the key source. If the redundancy R_K tends to zero, the number of elements in the high-probability set approaches 2^{hn}, which is the case of the one-time pad. It is this property that permits one to claim that the one-time pad cipher is robust to small deviations.

It is interesting to note that C. Shannon in his seminal paper [Shannon (1948)] has remarked that the problem of theoretical secrecy "is closely related to questions of communication in the presence of noise". So, mathematically, the problems of decrypting messages and filtering stochastic processes are quite similar. The approach we adhere to is close to the methods of [Ryabko and Ryabko (2011a)] where the problem of stationary process filtering is considered.

Let us proceed to a more formal justification of the propositions stated above. To begin, let us formulate the already mentioned Shannon–McMillan–Breiman theorem:

Theorem 7.4. *Let $U = U_1 U_2 U_3 \ldots$ be a stationary ergodic process. Then for all positive ε, δ, for almost all $U_1 U_2 U_3 \ldots$ there exists n' such that for $n > n'$*

$$P\left\{\left|-\frac{1}{n}\log P(U_1\cdots U_n) - h(U)\right| < \epsilon\right\} \geq 1 - \delta. \qquad (7.24)$$

Recall that we are examining the case when the plaintext $m_1, m_2, \ldots$ and the key sequence $k_1, k_2, \ldots$ are independently generated by stationary ergodic processes over the same finite alphabet $A = \{0, 1, \ldots, r-1\}$, $r \geq 2$, and the ciphertext $e_1, e_2, \ldots$ is determined by (7.22). The Shannon entropy of order n and the limiting entropy are given by

$$h_n(M) = -\frac{1}{n}\sum_{u \in A^n} P_M(u)\log P_M(u), \quad h(M) = \lim_{n\to\infty} h_n(M), \qquad (7.25)$$

where $P_M(u)$ is the probability of $m_1 m_2 \ldots m_n = u$. Define also the conditional entropy:

$$h_n(M|E) = h_n(M,E) - h_n(E), \quad h(M|E) = \lim_{n\to\infty} h_n(M|E). \qquad (7.26)$$

The main statement of this section is

Theorem 7.5. *Let the message $M = m_1 m_2 \ldots$ and the secret key $K = k_1 k_2 \ldots$ be independent stochastic processes over the alphabet $A = \{0, 1, \ldots, r - 1\}$, such that $(M, K) = (m_1, k_1), (m_2, k_2), \ldots$ is a stationary ergodic process and $E = e_1 e_2 \ldots$ is determined by (7.22). Then with probability 1 for every $\varepsilon > 0$ and $\delta > 0$ there exists an integer n' such that for every $n > n'$ and $E_1^n = e_1 e_2 \ldots e_n$ there is a set of possible decryptions $\Psi(E_1^n)$ for which:*

(1) $P(\Psi(E_1^n)) > 1 - \delta$;

(2) *for every $M^1 = m_1^1 \ldots m_n^1$, $M^2 = m_1^2 \ldots m_n^2$ from $\Psi(E_1^n)$*

$$\frac{1}{n} \left| \log P(M^1 | E_1^n) - \log P(M^2 | E_1^n) \right| < \varepsilon;$$

(3) $\liminf_{n \to \infty} (1/n) \log |\Psi(E_1^n)| \geq h(M|E)$.

Proof. Since the process (M, E) is a deterministic function of (M, K), the ergodicity and stationarity of (M, K) implies the ergodicity and stationarity of (M, E).

Proceed to constructing the set $\Psi(E_1^n)$. We are to apply Theorem 7.4 but first notice that $h(M|E) = h(M, E) - h(E)$ and $\log P(m_1 \ldots m_n | e_1 \ldots e_n) = \log P(m_1 \ldots m_n; e_1 \ldots e_n) - \log P(e_1 \ldots e_n)$. Theorem 7.4 may be rewritten as follows: for any positive ε, δ and for almost all (M_1, E_1), $(M_2, E_2), \ldots$ there exists n' such that for $n > n'$

$$P \left\{ \left| -\frac{1}{n} \log P(m_1 \ldots m_n | e_1 \ldots e_n) - h(M|E) \right| < \varepsilon/2 \right\} \geq 1 - \delta. \quad (7.27)$$

Define $\Psi(E_1^n)$ as a set of all messages that satisfy (7.27) and obtain the first statement of the theorem.

To prove the second statement of the theorem notice that for $M^1 = m_1^1 \ldots m_n^1$, $M^2 = m_1^2 \ldots m_n^2$ belonging to $\Psi(E_1^n)$ from (7.27)

$$\frac{1}{n} \left| \log P(M^1 | E_1^n) - \log P(M^2 | E_1^n) \right|$$

$$\leq \frac{1}{n} \left| \log P(M^1 | E_1^n) - h(M|E) \right| + \frac{1}{n} \left| \log P(M^2 | E_1^n) - h(M|E) \right|$$

$$< \varepsilon/2 + \varepsilon/2 = \varepsilon.$$

From the definition of $\Psi(E_1^n)$ and the first statement we obtain $|\Psi(E_1^n)| > (1 - \delta) 2^{n(h(M|E) - \varepsilon)}$. By observing that this is true for any $\varepsilon > 0$, $\delta > 0$ and $n > n'$ we obtain the third statement of the theorem. $\square$

So the set of possible variants of decryption $\Psi(E_1^n)$ grows exponentially, its combined probability is close to 1 and the probabilities of messages in this set are close to each other.

Theorem 7.5 enables us to estimate the cipher characteristics with the aid of conditional entropy $h(M|E)$. The following estimates do not require one to compute conditional entropy and are based on easier to find values.

Corollary 7.1. *For almost all $e_1e_2\ldots$*

$$\liminf_{n\to\infty}\frac{1}{n}\log|\Psi(E_1^n)|\geq h(M)+h(K)-\log r, \qquad (7.28)$$

$$h(M|E)\geq h(M)+h(K)-\log r. \qquad (7.29)$$

Proof. From the equality $h(M,E)=h(M)+h(E|M)$ observed in the previous section, we obtain:

$$h(M|E)=h(M,E)-h(E)=h(E|M)+h(M)-h(E).$$

By taking into account that $\max h(E)=\log r$, where r is the number of letters in the alphabet, we obtain $h(M|E)\geq h(E|M)+h(M)-\log r$. From the independence of M and K and the definition of the cipher (7.29) it is plain that $h(E|M)=h(K)$. This and the preceding inequality give (7.29). In its turn, (7.29) and the third statement of Theorem 7.5 give (7.28). $\square$

Using the notion of redundancy introduced earlier we can express the growth rate of the set $\Psi(E_1^n)$ in the following way:

$$\liminf_{n\to\infty}\frac{1}{n}\log|\Psi(E_1^n)|\geq h(M)-R_K,$$

$$\liminf_{n\to\infty}\frac{1}{n}\log|\Psi(E_1^n)|\geq h(K)-R_M, \qquad (7.30)$$

$$\liminf_{n\to\infty}\frac{1}{n}\log|\Psi(E_1^n)|\geq \log r-(R_M+R_K),$$

where $R_K=\log r-h(K)$ and $R_M=\log r-h(M)$ are the redundancies. Besides, from the definition of redundancy and (7.29) we obtain the inequality

$$h(M|E)\geq h(K)-R_M.$$

These inequalities allow one to quantify the impact of redundancy on the strength of the cipher and confirm the fact that decreasing redundancy increases the reliability (security) of cipher.

Let us go back to the question about the influence of deviations from randomness in the one-time pad key sequence. Let there be given a message to be encrypted $m_1 m_2 \ldots$, $m_i \in \{0,1\}$, and let the sequence of key symbols $k_1 k_2 \ldots \ldots$, $k_i \in \{0,1\}$, be generated by a source that differs from the memoryless source with $P(0) = P(1) = 0.5$ (for instance, the key $k_1 k_2 \ldots$ is generated by the memoryless source with symbol probabilities $P(0) = 0.5 - \tau$, $P(1) = 0.5 + \tau$, where τ is a small number). From (7.30) we can see that the size of the set of highly-probable decryptions $\Psi(E_1^n)$ grows exponentially with the exponent not less than $h(M) - R_K$, where $R_K = 1 - h(K)$ is the redundancy of the key. It is obvious that if R_K tends to zero, the size of the set of high-probable decryptions approaches the size of the corresponding set in the one-time pad. Indeed, in this case $h(K) = 1$ and hence the redundancy $R_K = 0$ as in the one-time pad. Informally, we can say that the one-time pad cipher is robust to small deviations of the key from randomness.

7.6 Running-Key Ciphers

In the preceding section, we have considered the cipher determined by Eq. (7.22). We have shown that this cipher remains unbreakable even if the key sequence is generated with small deviations from randomness. However, in the epoch when computers had not yet existed and there were no easy-to-use random number generators, the cipher (7.22) was applied in such a way that a certain text (as a rule, of the same nature as the text to be encrypted) played the role of the key. For example, a text in English was encrypted with the aid of another text in English and the secret was the information about the place where the second text might be taken from (it might be from a certain book present in the libraries of both sender and receiver with indication of a particular page, line, etc.). Under such usage the cipher (7.22) is called a "running-key cipher".

The results presented in the previous sections allow us to make a conclusion about the security of the running-key cipher. We show this with the texts in English.

According to the research presented in such papers as [Shannon (1951); Takahira *et al.* (2016)], the entropy of English language $h(M) \approx 1$ bit per symbol, the size of the alphabet being $r = 26$ letters (this estimate is obtained by taking into account strong dependences between the text symbols whereby the text is perceived not as a random sequence but rather as something having meaning). If an English text is used as the key, as well, then $h(K) \approx 1$. Based on (7.29) we have

$$h(M|E) \geq 1 + 1 - \log 26 = 2 - 4.7 = -2.7.$$

Such an estimate of the entropy does not ensure the security of the cipher. And indeed, there are methods (see [Menezes *et al.* (1996)]) that enable us to recover both the message and the key from the ciphertext (this, in particular, means that $h(M|E) = 0$ which does fit the estimate obtained). Therefore, the "classical" running-key cipher is completely insecure.

However back in 1949 C. Shannon suggested two methods of improving the running-key cipher [Shannon (1949)], which we shall consider in detail. Rigorous mathematical analysis of these methods was carried out in [Ryabko (2017)].

The first method is based on increasing the entropy of the text that is used as the key by eliminating inter-symbol dependences. This can be done if we take from the text, say, every 10th letter. At the distance of 10 letters any remnants of dependences are in fact lost.

Consider, for instance, a sequence of letters obtained from the opening paragraph of one of the most important US historical documents:

$$CMTCOOHLHCTNAW\,AAUTLRU\,IECNKESAEEEN$$

(spaces and punctuation marks have preliminarily been deleted, the letters converted to upper case). In this way we obtain a sequence of independent symbols but the frequencies of occurrence, typical for English, are preserved. The entropy of such a text, according to Shannon [Shannon (1951)], is estimated as 4.14 bits per symbol which is noticeably greater than 1 bit per symbol in the original text. Let us estimate the security of the running-key cipher under this choice of the key sequence applying the inequality (7.29):

$$h(M|E) \geq 1 + 4.14 - 4.7 = 0.44.$$

The positive uncertainty means the impossibility of unique message decryption (without knowledge of the secret key). For example, given the length of the encrypted message $n = 1000$ symbols, the size of the set of almost equiprobable decryptions (i.e. the number of plausible texts in English), by Theorem 7.5 is,

$$\left|\left(E_1^{1000}\right)\right| \geq 2^{1000 h(M|E)} = 2^{440}.$$

Such a cipher cannot be broken in principle.

The second method of strengthening running-key ciphers consists in summing up several texts to produce a key sequence. In this cipher construction we have a message $M = m_1 m_2 \ldots$ and d texts used as the keys: $K^1 = k_1^1 k_2^1 \ldots$, $K^d = k_1^d k_2^d \ldots$. For simplicity, assume that the message as well as the keys are generated by the same stationary ergodic source over the alphabet of r letters $A = \{0, 1, \ldots, r-1\}$. It means in practice that the message and keys are texts in same language, e.g. English. The symbols of the ciphertext $E = e_1 e_2 \ldots$ are computed by the formula

$$e_i = (m_i + k_i^1 + \cdots + k_i^d) \bmod r. \tag{7.31}$$

The formula for decryption is obvious.

The following theorem gives an estimate of the security of this cipher:

Theorem 7.6. *If a running-key cipher is constructed from d keys according to (7.31), and the message M and all the keys are generated by the same stationary ergodic source, then the uncertainty of a message symbol given a ciphertext E, $h(M|E)$, satisfies the following inequality:*

$$h(M|E) \geq \frac{1}{d}((d+1)h(M) - \log r), \tag{7.32}$$

where $h(M)$ is the source entropy.

Proof. The message and the keys are independent, so according to (7.15)

$$h(M) + h(K^1) + \cdots + h(K^d) = h(M, K^1, \ldots, K^d).$$

The ciphertext E is uniquely determined by $M, K^1, \ldots, K^d$. Hence

$$h(M, K^1, \ldots, K^d) = h(E, M, K^1, \ldots, K^d).$$

Applying (7.14) we have

$$h(E, M, K^1, \ldots, K^d)$$
$$= h(E) + h(M|E) + h(K^1|E, M) + \cdots + h(K^{d-1}|E, M, K^1, \ldots, K^{d-2})$$
$$+ h(K^d|E, M, K^1, \ldots, K^{d-1}). \tag{7.33}$$

Observe that the last term in (7.33) equals zero since K^d is uniquely determined from (7.31) if we know $E, M, K^1, \ldots, K^{d-1}$. Observe also that due to the independence of the message and the keys all conditional entropies in (7.33) are conditioned by the ciphertext E alone. This allows us to write the resulting equality:

$$h(M) + h(K^1) + \cdots + h(K^d)$$
$$= h(E) + h(M|E) + h(K^1|E) + \cdots + h(K^{d-1}|E). \quad (7.34)$$

As the message and the keys are generated by the same source

$$h(M) = h(K^1) = \cdots = h(K^d).$$

Moreover, as the message and the keys participate in (7.31) with completely equal "rights"

$$h(M|E) = h(K^1|E) = \cdots = h(K^{d-1}|E).$$

This allows us to represent (7.34) as

$$(d+1)h(M) = h(E) + dh(M|E),$$

wherefrom

$$h(M|E) = \frac{(d+1)h(M) - h(E)}{d}.$$

Taking into account that $h(E) \leq \log r$ we obtain (7.32). $\qquad \square$

Consider an example. Let the message and the keys be texts in English with an entropy of 1 bit per symbol. We shall use 4 keys. Then according to (7.32)

$$h(M|E) \geq \frac{1}{4}((4+1) \times 1 - 4.7) = 0.075.$$

Given that the length of the encrypted message $n = 1000$ symbols, the size of the set of almost equiprobable decryptions

$$|(E_1^{1000})| \geq 2^{75}.$$

This means that the cipher cannot be broken.

If we had used only 3 keys, we would have obtained $h(M|E) \geq -0.23$. There are no information-theoretic guarantees of the cipher security in that case. It only remains to find an algorithm that will recover the message and the keys from the ciphertext.

7.7 Unicity Distance for Secret Key Cipher

In the previous sections we got acquainted with the constructions that allow us to produce unbreakable ciphers. But to implement these constructions we need long one-time keys which are not always easily established between a sender and receiver of messages. Many practical cryptographic schemes are built upon short (say, 128–256 bits) long-term (reusable) keys. In the rest of the chapter we study information-theoretic properties of ciphers with short long-term keys and discuss what guarantees of security may be ensured in that case.

Consider the secret-key cryptosystem shown in Fig. 1.1 (p. 3). Let the source generate the message $\bar{m} = m_1 m_2 \dots m_n$. Alice and Bob have the secret key k, known only to them. Let $\bar{e} = e_1 e_2 \dots e_n$ be the ciphertext produced under that key.

Let us clarify the problem through an example. Let the memoryless source generate letters over the alphabet $A = \{a, b, c\}$ with probabilities $P(a) = 0.8$, $P(b) = 0.15$, $P(c) = 0.05$. Let the cipher substitute the letters in the message with other letters according to some fixed permutation depending on the key k:

$$(a, b, c)\, k = 1,$$
$$(a, c, b)\, k = 2,$$
$$(b, a, c)\, k = 3,$$
$$(b, c, a)\, k = 4,$$
$$(c, a, b)\, k = 5,$$
$$(c, b, a)\, k = 6.$$

That is, there are 6 possible keys (from 1 to 6) and if e.g. $k = 5$, the following substitution is made in the message: $a \to c$, $b \to a$, $c \to b$.

Let it be that Eve has eavesdropped the ciphertext

$$\bar{e} = cccbc$$

and wishes to determine the value of the key. Try to do it with her. Compute the *a posteriori* probabilities of the keys used. We can do that using the Bayes formula

$$P(K_i|E) = \frac{P(K_i)P(E|K_i)}{\sum_{j=1}^{t} P(K_j)P(E|K_j)}$$

where $K_1, \ldots, K_t$ are mutually exclusive events and $E \subset \sum_{i=1}^{t} K_i$. In our case, event E is the receipt of the ciphertext $\bar{e} = cccbc$, $t = 6$ and K_i means that the key $k = i$ was chosen.

We assume that all keys are equally likely, i.e.

$$P(K_1) = P(K_2) = P(K_3) = P(K_4) = P(K_5) = P(K_6) = 1/6.$$

Then

$$P(E|K_1) = P(\bar{m} = cccbc) = 0.05^4 \cdot 0.15 \approx 0.000001,$$

$$P(E|K_2) = P(\bar{m} = bbbcb) = 0.15^4 \cdot 0.05 \approx 0.000025,$$

$$P(E|K_3) = P(\bar{m} = cccac) = 0.8 \cdot 0.05^4 \approx 0.000005,$$

$$P(E|K_4) = P(\bar{m} = bbbab) = 0.8 \cdot 0.15^4 \approx 0.000405,$$

$$P(E|K_5) = P(\bar{m} = aaaca) = 0.8^4 \cdot 0.05 \approx 0.020480,$$

$$P(E|K_6) = P(\bar{m} = aaaba) = 0.8^4 \cdot 0.15 \approx 0.061440.$$

From this we easily find

$$\sum_{j=1}^{6} P(K_j) P(E|K_j) \approx 0.013726$$

and obtain using the Bayes formula the *a posteriori* probability that the key $k = 1$ was used given the ciphertext $\bar{e} = cccbc$ is received:

$$P(K_1|E) = P(\bar{m} = cccbc|\bar{e} = cccbc) \approx \frac{(1/6) \cdot 0.000001}{0.013726} \approx 0.000011.$$

Continuing similarly, find the *a posteriori* probabilities of the other keys:

$$P(K_2|E) = P(\bar{m} = bbbcb|\bar{e} = cccbc) \approx 0.000304,$$

$$P(K_3|E) = P(\bar{m} = cccac|\bar{e} = cccbc) \approx 0.000061,$$

$$P(K_4|E) = P(\bar{m} = bbbab|\bar{e} = cccbc) \approx 0.004918,$$

$$P(K_5|E) = P(\bar{m} = aaaca|\bar{e} = cccbc) \approx 0.25,$$

$$P(K_6|E) = P(\bar{m} = aaaba|\bar{e} = cccbc) \approx 0.75.$$

We can see that the most probable keys are $k = 5$ and $k = 6$, the probabilities of all other keys being less than 0.01.

We can see that having eavesdropped only 5 letters Eve is almost certainly able to determine the key. So, from this example and from the example with the Caesar cipher (Chap. 1), we can conclude that, evidently, there exists some critical length of ciphertext, n, after which the key can be determined with a probability close to 1. More formally, it can be written

$$H\left(K|e_1,\ldots,e_n\right) \approx 0. \tag{7.35}$$

This means that, on average, it suffices to intercept n symbols of ciphertext to determine the key used with near certainty. The number n satisfying Eq. (7.35) is called the *unicity distance* of a cipher. The following result from [Shannon (1949)] relates unicity distance with message redundancy and secret key entropy.

Proposition 7.3. *Let the secret-key cryptosystem be considered and let $H(K)$ be the entropy of the key and R the message redundancy. Then for the unicity distance n, the inequality*

$$n \geq \frac{H(K)}{R} \tag{7.36}$$

holds.

Let's give some notes on this proposition before discussing the proof.

(1) We can see that if the message redundancy $R = 0$ then the key will never be determined since $n = \infty$. That is, the cipher cannot be broken (we have demonstrated this in the example with the combination lock (p. 5).
(2) The redundancy can be decreased by means of data compression. The point is that lossless compression preserves the entropy while decreasing the length of the data. Consequently, in the compressed data, the entropy per symbol (entropy rate) is higher and the redundancy per symbol (redundancy rate) is lower, see (7.21). Therefore after the compression, the unicity distance of a cipher increases.
(3) In practice, it is better to use the systems in which the key changes long before the unicity distance is reached.

Proof. We present only the main idea of the proof. Let it be that the adversary intercepting the ciphertext $\bar{e} = e_1 e_2 \ldots e_n$ has uniquely determined the key and, therefore, the message. It means that her uncertainty is decreased by $H\left(K\right) + H\left(m_1,\ldots,m_n\right)$ since she has learned both the key and the message. With that she obtains n letters over an r-letter alphabet $\{a_1,\ldots,a_r\}$. We know that the maximum value of the entropy $h_\infty = \log r$, which means that the adversary's uncertainty can be decreased at most by $n \log r$. Hence

$$n \log r \geq H\left(K\right) + H\left(m_1,\ldots,m_n\right),$$

consequently,

$$n \left(\log r - H\left(m_1, \ldots, m_n\right)/n\right) \geq H\left(K\right),$$

from which we obtain that

$$n \geq \frac{H(K)}{\log r - H\left(m_1, \ldots, m_n\right)/n} = \frac{H(K)}{R}$$

(here we used the convergence $H\left(m_1, \ldots, m_n\right)/n \to h_\infty$ and the definition of redundancy in (7.21)).   □

Consider an example. Let's estimate the unicity distance for the cipher from the example on page 133. We have $H(K) = \log 6 \approx 2.58$, $\log r = \log 3 \approx 1.58$ and the entropy per source letter

$$H = -(0.8 \log 0.8 + 0.15 \log 0.15 + 0.05 \log 0.05) \approx 0.88.$$

So

$$n \geq \frac{2.58}{1.58 - 0.88} \approx 3.7.$$

We could see that 5 letters were enough to determine the key almost surely and that the inequality (7.36) corresponds well with our example.

Let's show with one more example how the mutual dependence of letters increases redundancy and thereby decreases the unicity distance.

Consider an example. Let a Markov source be given, i.e. a source with a memory in which each next letter probability may depend on the preceding letter. The source is defined by the following transition matrix:

	a	b	c
a	0	0.9	0.1
b	0	0.1	0.9
c	0.4	0.3	0.3

and the initial probabilities $P(a) = 0.19$, $P(b) = 0.34$, $P(c) = 0.47$. This means that the first letter is generated with its initial probability, and each next letter is generated with probability given by the row of the transition matrix corresponding to the preceding letter, e.g. after the letter a the letters b and c may occur with probabilities 0.9 and 0.1, respectively.

Let, as in the previous example, the cipher with 6 possible keys be used and the intercepted ciphertext be

$$\bar{e} = bbacbac.$$

We can see from the transition matrix that the combination aa is impossible (the probability of the occurrence of a after the preceding a is zero) and the combination bb unlikely (the probability of b after b equals 0.1). Consequently, the first pair of letters in the message is most likely cc, i.e. the substitution $c \rightarrow b$ was used in encryption. Then ac in the ciphertext corresponds to either ab or ba in the message. From the transition matrix, the combination ba is impossible and only ab remains. Therefore we may conclude that, with high probability, the key is 2, i.e. the second permutation was used:

$$k = 2 \quad (a \rightarrow a,\ b \rightarrow c,\ c \rightarrow b).$$

Now compute the exact *a posteriori* probabilities of the keys as we did in the example on page 133. Note that the probability of a particular source message equals to the product of the probability of the first letter and the probabilities of transitions from one letter to another.

$$P(E|K_1) = P(\bar{m} = bbacbac) = 0.34 \cdot 0.1 \cdot 0 = 0,$$

$$P(E|K_2) = P(\bar{m} = ccabcab) = 0.47 \cdot 0.3 \cdot 0.4 \cdot 0.9 \cdot 0.9 \cdot 0.4 \cdot 0.9$$

$$= 0.016446,$$

$$P(E|K_3) = P(\bar{m} = aabcabc) = 0.19 \cdot 0 = 0,$$

$$P(E|K_4) = P(\bar{m} = aacbacb) = 0.19 \cdot 0 = 0,$$

$$P(E|K_5) = P(\bar{m} = ccbacba) = 0.47 \cdot 0.3 \cdot 0.3 \cdot 0 = 0,$$

$$P(E|K_6) = P(\bar{m} = bbcabca) = 0.34 \cdot 0.1 \cdot 0.9 \cdot 0.4 \cdot 0.9 \cdot 0.9 \cdot 0.4$$

$$= 0.003966.$$

From this we find

$$\sum_{j=1}^{6} P(K_j)\, P(E|K_j) \approx 0.003402$$

and obtain what we need using the Bayes formula, i.e. the *a posteriori* probabilities of keys under the condition that the ciphertext is $\bar{e} = bbacbac$:

$$P(K_1|E) = 0,$$

$$P(K_2|E) = P(\bar{m} = ccabcab|\bar{e} = bbacbac) \approx 0.8,$$

$$P(K_3|E) = 0,$$

$$P(K_4|E) = 0,$$

$$P(K_5|E) = 0,$$

$$P(K_6|E) = P(\bar{m} = bbcabca|\bar{e} = bbacbac) \approx 0.2.$$

These computations confirm the correctness of the above informal observation.

The unicity distance estimation can be used in constructing cryptosystems. For instance, it seems reasonable to change the key as the total length of the encrypted messages approaches the unicity distance.

New approaches to constructing theoretically secure cryptosystems connected with the use of special coding methods were suggested in the works [Ryabko and Fionov (1997); Ryabko and Fionov (1999b); Ryabko and Fionov (1999c); Ryabko (2000)]. The suggested methods are complicated to describe but efficient from the computational point of view and allow for the construction of unbreakable secret-key ciphers. The main idea of these methods is to ensure, by means of special coding, the zero redundancy of the message to be encrypted. One of these methods will be considered in the next section.

7.8 Ideal Cryptosystems

In Sec. 7.2, the notion of perfect secrecy was introduced and it was shown then that the one-time pad cipher is perfectly secure. We could see that in this cipher the key length equals the message length and the key is used only once. If we want to use a short long-term key (which is demanded by the majority of practical applications) then what security level can we attain at best? In the notes to Proposition 7.3, it was pointed out that under the null redundancy of the message the unicity distance is infinite. It means that even a short (or, equivalently, applied many times) key used for encrypting a very long message cannot be disclosed. In its turn this means that an adversary who tries to recover the message will face an uncertainty equal to that of the key. Evidently, this is the best that can be done under the said conditions (it is helpful to recall here again the example with the combination lock from Chap. 1). These observations lead us to the notion of the strongly ideal cipher introduced in [Shannon (1949)].

Let the message $m_1 m_2 \ldots m_t$ be encrypted under the secret key $\bar{k} = k_1 k_2 \ldots k_s$ and let the ciphertext $\bar{e} = e_1 e_2 \ldots e_t$ be produced. Denote by $H(m_1 m_2 \ldots m_t)$ the entropy of the message, and by $H(\bar{e})$ and $H(\bar{k})$ the entropies of the ciphertext and the key, respectively. Then $H(m_1 m_2 \ldots m_t | \bar{e})$ is the uncertainty of the message and $H(\bar{k} | \bar{e})$ the uncertainty of the key given the ciphertext $\bar{e}$.

Definition 7.3. The cipher is called *strongly ideal* if

$$H(m_1 m_2 \ldots m_t | \bar{e}) = H(\bar{k} | \bar{e}) = \min\{H(m_1 m_2 \ldots m_t), H(\bar{k})\}. \qquad (7.37)$$

Let's first consider the case when $\min\{H(m_1 m_2 \ldots m_t), H(\bar{k})\} = H(m_1 m_2 \ldots m_t)$. In this case the system provides perfect secrecy. Indeed, Eq. (7.37) converts to $H(m_1 m_2 \ldots m_t | \bar{e}) = H(m_1 m_2 \ldots m_t)$ which means perfect secrecy by definition, see Eq. (7.1).

In the other case, when the entropy of the key is less than the entropy of the message, Eq. (7.37) is reduced to

$$H(m_1 m_2 \ldots m_t | \bar{e}) = H(\bar{k} | \bar{e}) = H(\bar{k}) \qquad (7.38)$$

for all sufficiently large t. Since we shall deal mainly with the case when the message length t is large (or even infinite) we shall use Eq. (7.38) as the definition of a strongly ideal cipher.

Informally, the strong ideality of the cipher means that the number of solutions of a cryptogram equals the number of possible keys, all the solutions being equiprobable (as in the example with the combination lock).

In this section, we shall consider the construction of the ideal system suggested in [Ryabko (2000)] but confine ourselves to the description of the main idea only as applied to the case of a binary source with unknown statistics, i.e. to the case when the message consists of letters of the alphabet $A = \{a_1, a_2\}$, the letters being independent but their probabilities unknown.

Let the source generate potentially unbounded messages $m_1 m_2 \ldots m_t$, $t \to \infty$, and let there be a fixed-length key $\bar{k} = k_1 k_2 \ldots k_s$, $s \geq 1$. (As we mentioned above, the per-letter source entropy is assumed to be non-zero since, otherwise, there is no necessity to transmit anything.) We shall split the message into blocks of n letters where $n > 1$ is a parameter of the method. Denote one of such blocks by $\bar{m}$. Describe the transformations carried out on each n-letter block.

First determine the number of the individual letters a_1 and a_2 in $\bar{m}$. Let there be, say, n_1 letters a_1 and $n_2 = n - n_1$ letters a_2. Define $u(\bar{m})$ as a word of length $\lceil \log(n+1) \rceil$ bits which encodes n_1.

Now consider the set S of all sequences which consists of n_1 letters a_1 and n_2 letters a_2. There are

$$|S| = \binom{n}{n_1} = \frac{n!}{n_1!(n - n_1)!}$$

elements in this set. Despite the fact that the probabilities of the sequences from S are unknown, one thing may be stated — they are equal to each other (because of the independence of the individual letters). Set a lexicographic order on S (assuming that $a_1 < a_2$) and compute the ordinal number of $\bar{m}$ within S (the efficient algorithm in [Ryabko (1998)] can be used for this computation, but its description goes beyond the scope of the book). Denote the computed ordinal by $\omega(\bar{m})$.

Split the set S into the non-overlapping subsets $S_0, S_1, \ldots, S_\nu$ with the numbers of elements equal to the powers of 2 (e.g. if $|S| = 21$ then three subsets may result with cardinalities 16, 4, and 1). Using $\omega(\bar{m})$, determine to what subset $\bar{m}$ belongs (denote the ordinal number of this subset by $v(\bar{m})$) and find the ordinal of $\bar{m}$ within this subset (denote this ordinal by $w(\bar{m})$).

Look attentively at the ordinal of the message within the subset $w(\bar{m})$. What is remarkable is that the $w(\bar{m})$ is a completely random sequence of zeroes and ones (i.e. all bits are equiprobable and independent). Indeed, $w(\bar{m})$ is the ordinal of one of the equiprobable sequences of letters in a set of 2^b elements (for some b). The ordinals of all such sequences are all possible combinations of b binary digits. But if all the combinations of b bits are equiprobable, then the individual bits are equiprobable and independent.

So, by processing consecutive blocks of the message in the described way we represent the message in the form

$$u(\bar{m}_1)v(\bar{m}_1)w(\bar{m}_1)u(\bar{m}_2)v(\bar{m}_2)w(\bar{m}_2)\ldots.$$

Now describe the procedure of encrypting the transformed message. It may seem strange at first sight, but the words $u(\cdot)$ and $v(\cdot)$ are not encrypted at all! Only the words $w(\cdot)$ are encrypted under the secret key $\bar{k}$. As one of the possibilities, we may use as the cipher the bitwise sum modulo 2 with a periodically continued key. To describe such a cipher enumerate sequentially the symbols of all words $w(\cdot)$ and denote these by $w_1 w_2 w_3 \ldots$. Then the encryption is performed according to the formula

$$z_i = w_i \oplus k_{i \bmod s}.$$

As a result, we have encrypted the source message in the following way:

$$m_1 m_2 \ldots m_t \longrightarrow \bar{e} = u(\bar{m}_1)v(\bar{m}_1)z(\bar{m}_1)u(\bar{m}_2)v(\bar{m}_2)z(\bar{m}_2)\ldots. \qquad (7.39)$$

By the algorithm's construction, it is clear that the message can be recovered from the right side of (7.39) if we know the secret key $\bar{k}$. First we need to decrypt the symbols of the words $w(\cdot)$ with the formula

$$w_i = z_i \oplus k_{i \bmod s}, \qquad (7.40)$$

and then the consecutive blocks of the message can be recovered from the words $u(\cdot)v(\cdot)w(\cdot)$.

Table 7.1 The set of equiprobable messages; $n_1 = 1, n_2 = 4$.

Message	Ordinal in S	S_v	w
$a_1 a_2 a_2 a_2 a_2$	000		00
$a_2 a_1 a_2 a_2 a_2$	001		01
$a_2 a_2 a_1 a_2 a_2$	010	S_0	10
$a_2 a_2 a_2 a_1 a_2$	011		11
$a_2 a_2 a_2 a_2 a_1$	100	S_1	—

Table 7.2 The set of equiprobable messages; $n_1 = 2, n_2 = 3$.

Message	Ordinal in S	S_v	w
$a_1 a_1 a_2 a_2 a_2$	0000		000
$a_1 a_2 a_1 a_2 a_2$	0001		001
$a_1 a_2 a_2 a_1 a_2$	0010		010
$a_1 a_2 a_2 a_2 a_1$	0011	S_0	011
$a_2 a_1 a_1 a_2 a_2$	0100		100
$a_2 a_1 a_2 a_1 a_2$	0101		101
$a_2 a_1 a_2 a_2 a_1$	0110		110
$a_2 a_2 a_1 a_1 a_2$	0111		111
$a_2 a_2 a_1 a_2 a_1$	1000	S_1	0
$a_2 a_2 a_2 a_1 a_1$	1001		1

Let it be required to encrypt the message

$$a_2 a_2 a_1 a_2 a_2 a_2 a_1 a_2 a_2 a_1$$

under the 3-bit key $\bar{k} = 011$. Split the message into two blocks of 5 symbols, $n = 5$.

Perform the transformation for the first block $\bar{m}_1 = a_2 a_2 a_1 a_2 a_2$. For this block, $n_1 = 1$ and $u(\bar{m}_1) = (001)_2$. Consider now the ordered set of all messages consisting of 1 letter a_1 and 4 letters a_2 (see Table 7.1). There are $\frac{5!}{1!4!} = 5$ such messages, so we have two subsets S_0 and S_1 with the numbers of elements 4 and 1, respectively.

We can see that $\bar{m}_1$ enters S_0 under the ordinal $2 = (10)_2$. So we obtain the following two words: $v(\bar{m}_1) = 0$, $w(\bar{m}_1) = (10)_2$.

Now perform the transformation for the second block of the message. $\bar{m}_2 = a_2 a_1 a_2 a_2 a_1$. For this block, $n_1 = 2$ and $u(\bar{m}_2) = (010)_2$. Consider the ordered set of all messages consisting of 2 letters a_1 and 3 letters a_2 (see Table 7.2). There are $\frac{5!}{2!3!} = 10$ such messages, so we have two subsets S_0 and S_1 with the number of elements 8 and 2, respectively.

We can see that $\bar{m}_2$ enters S_0 under the ordinal $6 = (110)_2$. So we obtain $v(\bar{m}_2) = 0$, $w(\bar{m}_2) = (110)_2$.

To that point, we have obtained the following binary code of the transformed message:

$$001\ 0\ 10\ 010\ 0\ 110$$

(blank spaces here are only for ease of perception; they are not needed for unique decoding).

Now encrypt the transformed message. The periodically continued key looks like $\bar{k} = 011011\ldots..$ The bitwise summation modulo 2 of the words $w(\cdot)$ with that key gives

$$\oplus\ \frac{\begin{array}{c}1\ 0\ 1\ 1\ 0\\0\ 1\ 1\ 0\ 1\end{array}}{1\ 1\ 0\ 1\ 1}.$$

The ciphertext looks like this:

$$\bar{e} = 001\ 0\ 11\ 010\ 0\ 011.$$

Discuss now the main properties of the described method.

Proposition 7.4. *The cipher constructed is strongly ideal.*

Proof. Without much rigour, the idea of the proof is the following. As we have already noted in the method description, the word $w(\bar{m})$ for each block $\bar{m}$ consists of the equiprobable and independent symbols 0 and 1 (is completely random, in short). Since the blocks of the message are independent, the sequence $w(\bar{m}_1)w(\bar{m}_2)\ldots = w_1 w_2 w_3 \ldots$ in the transformed message is also completely random. But any sequence $w_1 w_2 w_3 \ldots$ corresponds to some message and all such messages are equiprobable. Therefore, under substitution of any key in deciphering Eq. (7.40), we obtain some solution, all the solutions being equiprobable. As a result, having only the ciphertext, we cannot say anything about the key used, i.e.

$$H(\bar{k}|\bar{e}) = H(\bar{k}).$$

Further, each individual message $m_1 m_2 \ldots m_t$ converts to one and only one sequence $w_1 w_2 w_3 \ldots$ and, under a sufficiently large t, namely, such that the length of the sequence $w_1 w_2 w_3 \ldots$ is no less than the key length, each different key, being used in (7.40), will produce different equiprobable messages. Therefore

$$H(m_1 m_2 \ldots m_t|\bar{e}) = H(\bar{k}).$$

Non-zero source entropy guarantees that the required sufficiently large t always exists.

So, we can see that (7.38) holds. $\square$

The peculiarity of the described method is that not all of the transformed message is encrypted but only a part of it. In the example provided, it may even seem that too much information remains "open". What portion of information is concealed by the cipher? The following proposition answers this question.

Proposition 7.5. *Let the message be generated by a memoryless source with the entropy h per letter. Then for every block $\bar{m}$ of n symbols, the expected length of the encrypted word $w(\bar{m})$ satisfies the inequality*

$$E(|w(\bar{m})|) > nh - 2\log(n+1) \tag{7.41}$$

(here $E(\cdot)$ denotes expectation and $|\cdot|$ the length).

Proof. The code component $u(\bar{m})$ can take on any value from 0 to n, therefore its maximal entropy is $\log(n+1)$.

The word $v(\bar{m})$ can take on any value from 0 to ν which is related with splitting the set S into the subsets $S_0, S_1, \ldots, S_\nu$. It is obvious that $\nu \leq \lfloor \log |S| \rfloor$. From the well-known inequality $|S| = \binom{n}{n_1} < 2^n$ we obtain $\log |S| < n$ and, hence, $\nu \leq \log |S| < n$. Therefore the maximal entropy of the word $v(\bar{m})$ is less than $\log(n+1)$.

The entropy of the block $H(\bar{m}) = nh$ (since the letters are generated by a memoryless source). The transformation of the block does not change the entropy. Therefore for the entropy of the word $w(\bar{m})$ we have

$$H(w(\bar{m})) > nh - 2\log(n+1)$$

(we subtract from the block entropy the upper bounds for the entropies of $u(\bar{m})$ and $v(\bar{m})$). But as the word $w(\bar{m})$ consists of equiprobable and independent symbols 0 and 1, its average length equals the entropy which completes the proof. $\square$

Informally, Proposition 7.5 says that "almost all" the information in the message is contained in the encrypted codeword w if the blocklength n is sufficiently large. In other words, the presented cipher conceals "almost all" the information and even an exhaustive search through the whole set of keys does not allow us to break the cipher.

Problems and Exercises

7.1   Encrypt the message $\bar{m}$ with the one-time pad cipher under the key $\bar{k}$:

    (a) $\bar{m} = 1001101011$, $\bar{k} = 0110100101$,

    (b) $\bar{m} = 0011101001$, $\bar{k} = 1100011100$,

    (c) $\bar{m} = 1000011100$, $\bar{k} = 1001011010$,

    (d) $\bar{m} = 0011100010$, $\bar{k} = 0110111001$,

    (e) $\bar{m} = 1001101011$, $\bar{k} = 1000111010$.

7.2   Let a memoryless source generate letters over the alphabet $A = \{a, b, c\}$ with probabilities $P(a)$, $P(b)$, $P(c)$. The encrypter substitutes the letters using one of the six possible permutations, as in the example on page 133. Determine the *a posteriori* probabilities of keys given the ciphertext $\bar{e}$:

    (a) $P(a) = 0.1$, $P(b) = 0.7$, $P(c) = 0.2$, $\bar{e} = abaacac$,

    (b) $P(a) = 0.9$, $P(b) = 0.09$, $P(c) = 0.01$, $\bar{e} = cbaccca$,

    (c) $P(a) = 0.14$, $P(b) = 0.06$, $P(c) = 0.8$, $\bar{e} = bbabbcab$,

    (d) $P(a) = 0.7$, $P(b) = 0.05$, $P(c) = 0.25$, $\bar{e} = cccacbbc$,

    (e) $P(a) = 0.1$, $P(b) = 0.7$, $P(c) = 0.2$, $\bar{e} = abbbbab$.

7.3   For the cipher and sources of Problem 7.2, compute the entropy and unicity distance.

7.4   Given the ciphertext $\bar{e}$, find the *a posteriori* probabilities of the keys and their corresponding messages if it is known that the cipher from the example on page 133 was used and the messages are generated by the Markov source described in the example on page 136:

    (a) $\bar{e} = bcacbcacc$,

    (b) $\bar{e} = caaabaaba$,

    (c) $\bar{e} = aacabcaac$,

    (d) $\bar{e} = bcaaaacaa$,

    (e) $\bar{e} = aaacaaaca$.

Chapter 8

Modern Secret Key Ciphers and Hash Functions

8.1 Introduction

In this chapter, we shall consider computationally secure secret-key ciphers which can be broken theoretically but breaking them will require a huge amount of computations, e.g. 10^{20} years of computations on a supercomputer, before they can be broken. The main advantage of these ciphers is their fast operation — they encrypt and decrypt data much faster than public-key and theoretically secure ciphers. In the subsequent sections we shall describe the most prominent ciphers, but before that, in order to explain the principles of their construction, we continue using the example of the Caesar cipher from Chap. 1.

In Chap. 1 we have considered the ciphertext-only attack on the Caesar cipher. It was shown that in the case of redundant messages, this cipher can be easily broken by the exhaustive key search. Let's look for a means of increasing the security of the Caesar cipher. Maybe, the first thing that comes to mind is to increase the number of possible keys. In this case, Eve will spend more time in searching for a correct key.

The natural way to increase the number of possible keys for the Caesar cipher is to use different keys for different symbols of the message. For instance, we may encrypt every odd letter with the key k_1 and every even letter with the key k_2. Then the secret key $k = (k_1, k_2)$ will consist of two integers and the number of possible keys will be $26^2 = 676$. Let's encrypt the same message as in Chap. 1 with the key $k = (3, 5)$:

$$\text{SEQUENCE} \xrightarrow{3,5} \text{VJTZHSFJ.} \tag{8.1}$$

This scheme can easily be extended to an arbitrary secret key length $k = (k_1, k_2, \ldots, k_t)_{26}$. With a t of about 10 or more the exhaustive key search becomes infeasible.

Nevertheless, this cipher is easily disclosed by using the so-called *frequency analysis*. This analysis is based on the statistics of the language in which the message is written. The key search begins with the keys corresponding to the most frequent letters or combinations. For instance, it is known that in a typical text in English, the letter E occurs more frequently than the other letters. Look at VJTZHSFJ in (8.1) and determine what letters are more frequent at odd and even positions. At even positions, this is the letter J. Make an assumption that it substitutes for the letter E and hence that $k_2 = $ J − E = 5. At odd positions, all the letters are different (just because the message used in the example is too small). Try to find k_1, as before, with an exhaustive search. After several trials we find $k_1 = 3$. So, in this particular example, to recover the message from the ciphertext we had to check only 4 keys out of 676 (specifically, we have checked $(0, 5), (1, 5), (2, 5), (3, 5)$).

Let's try to slightly improve the cipher in order to complicate the frequency analysis. We need somehow to intermingle the letters, to make them affect each other in order to hide the individual frequencies of occurrence. As before, we shall use the key $k = (k_1, k_2)$ and encrypt the message in two-letter blocks m_i, m_{i+1}. One of the simplest variants of the cipher may look like this:

$$\tilde{m}_i = m_i + m_{i+1},$$

$$\tilde{m}_{i+1} = m_{i+1} + \tilde{m}_i,$$

$$c_i = \tilde{m}_i + k_1, \tag{8.2}$$

$$c_{i+1} = \tilde{m}_{i+1} + k_2 \pmod{26}$$

(all operations are modulo 26). Here m_i is an odd letter of the message, m_{i+1} is an even letter, k_1, k_2 are the key digits, and c_i, c_{i+1} the resulting symbols of ciphertext. For instance, the pair of symbols SE is encrypted under the key $k = (3, 5)$ in the following way:

$$\tilde{m}_i = \text{S} + \text{E} = \text{W},$$

$$\tilde{m}_{i+1} = \text{E} + \text{W} = \text{A},$$

$$c_i = \text{W} + 3 = \text{Z},$$

$$c_{i+1} = \text{A} + 5 = \text{F},$$

i.e. SE converts to ZF.

Note that this cipher is decipherable. The decryption algorithm usually called the *inverse cipher* is written as follows:

$$\tilde{m}_{i+1} = c_{i+1} - k_2,$$
$$\tilde{m}_i = c_i - k_1,$$
$$m_{i+1} = \tilde{m}_{i+1} - \tilde{m}_i,$$
$$m_i = \tilde{m}_i - m_{i+1} \qquad (\text{mod } 26).$$

(8.3)

Applying the cipher (8.2) to our message under the key $(3, 5)$ we obtain

$$\text{SEQUENCE} \longrightarrow \text{WAKEREGK} \xrightarrow{3,5} \text{ZFNJUJJP}.$$

Here, for clarity, after the first arrow, the intermediate result obtained after the first two operations in (8.2) is shown (this is an "intermingled" but not yet encrypted text). We can see that this cipher hides the frequencies of letters, which complicates the frequency analysis. Of course, the frequencies of the pairs (digrams) are preserved but we can conceal them too if we encrypt the message in blocks of 3 letters, etc.

So, we have considered two ways of improving the cipher: increasing the length of the key and combining symbols into blocks with mixing transformations. Both methods are widely used in real modern ciphers. Now we shall consider one more trick which is also used in practice. For the sake of simplicity, we proceed with the same example.

The cipher (8.2) is more complicated to Eve compared to the cipher (8.1) and gives us the opportunity to consider another scenario of attack. Up to this point we considered only the ciphertext-only attacks. But what will happen if Eve somehow procures the plaintext corresponding to a ciphertext transmitted earlier? Here we have a situation where the known-plaintext attack (see Chap. 1, p. 5) is being used. For instance, Eve has the pair (SEQUENCE, VJTZHSFJ) for the cipher (8.1). Then she immediately computes the secret key $k_1 = V - S = 3$, $k_2 = J - E = 5$ and is able to decrypt all further messages from Alice to Bob. When the cipher (8.2) is used, the pair (SEQUENCE, ZFNJUJJP) does not allow for such an obvious solution, although breaking the cipher (8.2) is simple too. Eve performs the first two operations from (8.2), which do not require the secret key, for the word SEQUENCE, obtains the intermediate word WAKEREGK and using the pair (WAKEREGK, ZFNJUJJP), as in the previous case, finds the key $k = 3, 5$.

How one can hamper Eve's actions? The idea is simple. In encryption, we shall use the cipher (8.2) twice. So we obtain:

$$\text{SEQUENCE} \xrightarrow{3,5} \text{ZFNJUJJP} \xrightarrow{3,5} \text{HOZKGRBS}. \qquad (8.4)$$

Now, having the pair (SEQUENCE, HOZKGRBS), Eve cannot derive the key, at least, her algorithm is not obvious (she cannot obtain the intermediate word ZFNJUJJP since it was constructed with the use of a secret key unknown to her).

In the scheme (8.4), the single realization of the algorithm (8.2) is called a cipher *round*.

We have illustrated the relation between the security of the cipher and such parameters as the length of key, the block size, and the number of rounds. We have also shown the necessity of "intermingling" transformations. The real ciphers employ the same techniques, though enhanced, to withstand the advanced methods of cryptanalysis, such as differential and linear cryptanalysis (the reader may consult [Schneier (2000)] as a guide to basic cryptanalytic methods).

8.2   Block Ciphers

The *block cipher* can be defined as a transformation of a word (or a block) X of length n bits dependent on the key K. We shall denote the transformed word by Y. For all ciphers considered in this section, the length of word Y is equal to the length of word X.

In other words, the block cipher is an invertible function E (i.e. a function for which an inverse function exists). The specific look E_K of this function is determined by the key K,

$$Y = E_K(X),$$

$$X = E_K^{-1}(Y) \quad \text{for all } X.$$

Here E_K^{-1} denotes the deciphering transformation and is often called the *inverse cipher*.

For cryptographic applications, a block cipher must meet a number of requirements depending on the situation in which it is used. In most cases it is enough to claim that the cipher be secure with respect to the chosen-plaintext attack. This automatically assumes its security with respect to the known-plaintext and ciphertext-only attacks. One should notice that in the chosen-plaintext attack, the cipher can always be broken by the exhaustive key search. Therefore the requirement for the cipher to be secure may be re-formulated as follows.

The cipher is secure (under the chosen-plaintext attack) if there exist no algorithms for breaking it which are essentially more efficient than the exhaustive key search.

We shall content ourselves with this loose definition of security. In fact, compliance to this definition is not proved for any cipher which is in use today. To be more realistic we should rephrase the definition as the following.

The cipher is believed to be secure (under the chosen-plaintext attack) if there are no algorithms known for breaking it which are essentially faster than the exhaustive key search.

In the rest of the section we consider some modern block ciphers. Our task is not just to give the description of the algorithms as it may be found in the literature but also to explain the basic principles of construction of the block ciphers. Besides, our discussion will be helpful for a better understanding of the matters set forth in the official documents (standards). Then we shall study the techniques of using block ciphers to solve various cryptographic problems.

Until recently, no book on cryptography could do without a description of the cipher DES (Data Encryption Standard). This cipher was adopted as a standard in the USA in 1977. Its main parameters are: a block size of 64 bits, a key length of 56 bits, and 16 rounds. This cipher was intensively used for more than 20 years and even today can be found in many working systems. Despite numerous attacks on the DES, it has not been broken. However, the high level of computer performance today enables one to break the DES by exhaustive key search. For instance, in 1993 a technical description was published of a system which cost 1 million dollars and allowed us to disclose the DES key in 7 hours. As a result, the DES is not recommended for use in newly created cryptosystems. So we do not describe the DES. In 2001, after a special competition, a new block cipher standard was adopted in the USA, called the AES (Advanced Encryption Standard), which is based on the Rijndael block cipher developed by Belgian specialists Vincent Rijmen and Joan Daemen.

The majority of modern block ciphers are constructed in significantly different ways from the DES. Nevertheless, there is (at least) one active cipher built on the same principles as the DES. This is the Russian standard block cipher, known by the code name "Magma", which was first introduced in 1989 and then revised in 2015. Due to its extremely simple design and for historical reasons it will be convenient to begin with this cipher.

8.2.1   *The Magma Cipher*

The Magma cipher was first suggested in GOST 28147-89 [RFC 5830 (2010)] and, as follows from its designation, was adopted as a standard in 1989 in the USSR (the word GOST is an acronym of GOvernmental STandard). In 2015 it was revised and together with a new cipher called "Kuznyechik" (described later on) became a part of a new GOST R 34.12-2015.

The main parameters of the Magma cipher are: a key length of 256 bits, a block size of 64 bits, 32 rounds. Magma is more convenient for program implementation than the DES; the gains made by using Magma are 1.5 times the gains made by using the DES. Unlike the DES, Magma was seemingly not as much of a subject of thorough analysis by the world "open" cryptographic community. Nevertheless, as the specialists conclude, the conservative design and the size of the main parameters (the key length, the block size, and the number of rounds) made us believe that the cipher could not be weak (see [Schneier (1996)]). No effective attacks against Magma have been published.

Magma, as well as the DES, is based on the so-called *Feistel structure* [Feistel (1973)]. The block is split into two equal parts, the right R and the left L. The right half is combined with the key element and a certain algorithm encrypts the left half. Before the next round the parts are replaced with each other. Such a structure allows one to use the same algorithm for decryption as for encryption. It is of special importance in the case of hardware implementation because both the direct and the inverse ciphers are produced by one and the same device (only the order in which the key elements are fed in differs).

Proceed to the description of the Magma cipher. Introduce the necessary notation and definitions. The sequence of 32 bits is called a word. The plaintext block X (64 bits), as well as the ciphertext block Y, consists of two words, the left L and the right R, L being the high-order word and R the low-order one. The secret key K (256 bits) is considered to consist of 8 words $K = K_0 K_1 \cdots K_7$. It provides the basis for the construction of the so-called *round key* $W = W_0 W_1 \cdots W_{31}$ that contains 32 words (the method of constructing the round key will be given further on).

There are 8 tables needed for the cipher operation $S_0, S_1, \ldots, S_7$ (also called S-boxes). Each table contains 16 4-bit elements, numbered from 0 to 15. Denote by $S_i[j]$ the jth element of the ith table. The revision of 2015 enforces the following content of the tables:

$$S_0 = (12, 4, 6, 2, 10, 5, 11, 9, 14, 8, 13, 7, 0, 3, 15, 1)$$

$$S_1 = (6, 8, 2, 3, 9, 10, 5, 12, 1, 14, 4, 7, 11, 13, 0, 15);$$

$$S_2 = (11, 3, 5, 8, 2, 15, 10, 13, 14, 1, 7, 4, 12, 9, 6, 0);$$

$$S_3 = (12, 8, 2, 1, 13, 4, 15, 6, 7, 0, 10, 5, 3, 14, 9, 11);$$

$$S_4 = (7, 15, 5, 10, 8, 1, 6, 13, 0, 9, 3, 14, 11, 4, 2, 12);$$

$$S_5 = (5, 13, 15, 6, 9, 2, 12, 10, 11, 7, 8, 1, 4, 3, 14, 0);$$

$$S_6 = (8, 14, 2, 5, 6, 9, 1, 12, 15, 4, 11, 0, 13, 10, 3, 7);$$

$$S_7 = (1, 7, 14, 13, 0, 5, 8, 3, 4, 15, 10, 6, 9, 12, 11, 2).$$

The following operations are used in the cipher:

$+$ addition modulo 2^{32};

$\hookleftarrow$ cyclic shift to the left by the specified number of bits;

$\oplus$ bitwise "exclusive or" of two words, i.e. bitwise addition modulo 2.

Algorithm 8.1 BASIC CYCLE OF THE MAGMA CIPHER

INPUT: Block L, R, round key W.
OUTPUT: Transformed block L, R.
1.   FOR $i = 0, 1, \ldots, 31$ DO
2. $k \leftarrow R + W_i, \quad k = (k_7 \cdots k_0)_{16}$;
3.   FOR $j = 0, 1, \ldots, 7$ DO
4. $k_j \leftarrow S_j[k_j]$;
5. $L \leftarrow L \oplus (k \hookleftarrow 11)$;
6. $L \longleftrightarrow R$;
7.   RETURN L, R.

(At Step 4 of the algorithm distinct 4-bit elements of the variable k are used.)

The described "basic cycle" is used for encryption and decryption. To encrypt a block X, construct the round key

$$W = K_0 K_1 K_2 K_3 K_4 K_5 K_6 K_7 K_0 K_1 K_2 K_3 K_4 K_5 K_6 K_7$$

$$K_0 K_1 K_2 K_3 K_4 K_5 K_6 K_7 K_7 K_6 K_5 K_4 K_3 K_2 K_1 K_0, \qquad (8.5)$$

use X and W as the inputs and obtain the encrypted block Y as the output.

To decrypt a block, construct the round key

$$W = K_0K_1K_2K_3K_4K_5K_6K_7K_7K_6K_5K_4K_3K_2K_1K_0$$

$$K_7K_6K_5K_4K_3K_2K_1K_0K_7K_6K_5K_4K_3K_2K_1K_0,$$

i.e. (8.5) in the reverse order, input W, Y and obtain X as the output.

A program implementation usually requires us to rework the loop beginning at Step 3 of Algorithm 8.1 since operating with half-bytes is inefficient. It is clear that the same transformation can be performed with the use of 4 tables of 256 bytes each, or two tables of 65536 half-words each. For instance, when working with bytes, we have $k = (k_3 \cdots k_0)_{256}$ and Steps 3–4 of Algorithm 8.1 are rewritten as follows:

3.   FOR $j = 0, 1, 2, 3$ DO
4. $k_j \leftarrow T_j[k_j]$.

The tables T_j, $j = 0, 1, 2, 3$, are computed beforehand from S-boxes:

FOR $i = 0, 1, \ldots, 255$ DO
$T_j[i] \leftarrow S_{2j}[i \bmod 16] + 16S_{2j+1}[i \text{ div } 16].$

8.2.2 The RC6 Cipher

The RC6 cipher was designed by Ron Rivest in 1998. RC6 took part in the competition for the new US block cipher standard carried out in the years 1999–2001. It had advanced to the finals but lost the first place to another cipher (Rijndael). Nevertheless, intensive investigations of RC6 undertaken during the course of the competition do not reveal any weakness in it and this cipher is highly esteemed by the specialists.

In RC6, the user specifies the word size w (16, 32, or 64 bits), the number of rounds r, and the key length l in bytes (from 0 to 255). The block consists of 4 words and the round key W of $2r+4$ words. A particular variant of the cipher is denoted by the template RC6-$w/r/l$. For example, RC6-32/20/16 is the variant with a block size and key length of 128 bits, and with 20 rounds (this variant had been proposed as a candidate for the US standard).

The cipher uses the following operations (all on the w-bit words):

$+, -$ addition and subtraction modulo 2^w;
  $\oplus$ bitwise "exclusive or" of two words (the sum modulo 2);
$\hookleftarrow, \hookrightarrow$ cyclic left and right shifts by a specified number of bits (note that given the word size of w bits the number of shift positions is reduced

modulo w, such a reduction being usually done automatically at machine level — the processor uses only the low-order $\log w$ bits of the number defining the shift amount);

* multiplication modulo 2^w.

The encryption and decryption algorithms are shown below.

Algorithm 8.2 RC6: ENCRYPTION

INPUT: Four-word block (a, b, c, d), round key W.
OUTPUT: Encrypted block (a, b, c, d).
1. $b \leftarrow b + W_0, \ d \leftarrow d + W_1$;
2.   FOR $i = 1, 2, \ldots, r$ DO
3. $t \leftarrow (b * (2b + 1)) \hookleftarrow \log w$,
4. $u \leftarrow (d * (2d + 1)) \hookleftarrow \log w$,
5. $a \leftarrow ((a \oplus t) \hookleftarrow u) + W_{2i}$,
6. $c \leftarrow ((c \oplus u) \hookleftarrow t) + W_{2i+1}$,
7. $(a, b, c, d) \leftarrow (b, c, d, a)$;
8. $a \leftarrow a + W_{2r+2}, \ c \leftarrow c + W_{2r+3}$;
9.   RETURN (a, b, c, d).

To decrypt the block all operations are performed in reverse order.

Algorithm 8.3 RC6: DECRYPTION

INPUT: Four-word block (a, b, c, d), round key W.
OUTPUT: Decrypted block (a, b, c, d).
1. $c \leftarrow c - W_{2r+3}, \ a \leftarrow a - W_{2r+2}$;
2.   FOR $i = r, r - 1, \ldots, 1$ DO
3. $(a, b, c, d) \leftarrow (d, a, b, c)$,
4. $t \leftarrow (b * (2b + 1)) \hookleftarrow \log w$,
5. $u \leftarrow (d * (2d + 1)) \hookleftarrow \log w$,
6. $a \leftarrow ((a - W_{2i}) \hookrightarrow u) \oplus t$,
7. $c \leftarrow ((c - W_{2i+1}) \hookrightarrow t) \oplus u$;
8. $d \leftarrow d - W_1, \ b \leftarrow b - W_0$;
9.   RETURN (a, b, c, d).

The process of round key formation (the round key schedule) is more complicated in RC6 than in Magma, which is typical for most modern

Table 8.1   "Magic" numbers for RC6.

w	16	32	64	
P_w	b7e1	b7e15163	b7e15162	8aed2a6b
Q_w	9e37	9e3779b9	9e3779b9	7f4a7c15

ciphers. In fact, the secret key K is expanded to a longer pseudo-random sequence W in order to make the cryptanalysis of a cipher harder. Denote by c the number of words in the key, $c = 8l/w$. With the round key schedule algorithm the secret key K is expanded to the round key W:

$$K_0 K_1 \cdots K_{c-1} \longrightarrow W_0 W_1 \cdots W_{2r+3}.$$

In the algorithm of the round key schedule the following "magic" numbers are used: P_w, the first w bits of the binary expansion for $e - 2$ where $e = 2.718281828\ldots$ is the base of natural logarithm, and Q_w, the first w bits of the binary expansion for $\phi - 1$ where $\phi = (\sqrt{5} - 1)/2$ is the golden section. In Table 8.1 the values of P_w and Q_w are given in the hexadecimal system for various word lengths.

With all this in mind, the algorithm of the round key formation for RC6 is written down as follows.

Algorithm 8.4   RC6: ROUND KEY SCHEDULE

INPUT: Secret key K.
OUTPUT: Round key W.
1. $W_0 \leftarrow P_w$;
2.   FOR $i = 1, 2, \ldots, 2r + 3$ DO $W_i \leftarrow W_{i-1} + Q_w$;
3. $a \leftarrow 0, b \leftarrow 0, i \leftarrow 0, j \leftarrow 0$;
4. $k \leftarrow 3 \max(c, 2r + 4)$;
5.   DO k times
6. $W_i \leftarrow (W_i + a + b) \hookleftarrow 3, \quad a \leftarrow W_i$,
7. $K_j \leftarrow (K_j + a + b) \hookleftarrow (a + b), \quad b \leftarrow K_j$,
8. $i \leftarrow i + 1 \bmod 2r + 4, \quad j \leftarrow j + 1 \bmod c$;
9.   RETURN W.

Discuss briefly the main ideas behind the construction of RC6. First of all, note that similarly to the DES and Magma, in each round of RC6, one half of the block is used for encrypting the other. Indeed, the values of the variables t and u (Lines 3–4 of Algorithm 8.2) are determined only by the words b and d, respectively. Then these variables are used to modify the words a and c prior to summation with the elements of the key (Lines 5–6). Therefore, a dependence upon b and d is introduced in a and c. In the next round, the pairs a, c and b, d exchange roles and b and d are transposed (Line 7). Owing to such a structure the number of rounds has to be even.

The function $f(x) = (2x^2 + x) \bmod 2^w$, chosen for the computation of t and u, is known to manifest a strong dependence of the high-order bits of its value upon all the bits of the argument. These are the high-order bits of f that must determine the shift amount in Lines 5–6 of the algorithm. So these bits are put in the low-order bits of t and u by means of rotation $\hookleftarrow \log w$. The use of the "exclusive or" for the modification of a and c is quite traditional but the use of data-dependent rotations is a characteristic feature of RC6.

Lines 1 and 8 are intended to hide the words unmodified in the first and last rounds.

The recommended number of rounds $r = 20$ is connected with the results of investigating the cipher's security with respect to differential and linear cryptanalysis.

In the course of studying the security of RC6 no weak keys were found, i.e. any key, even all - zero keys, ensures the declared security of the cipher. It is believed that for RC6-32/20/16 there exist no attacks more efficient than the brute force attack.

8.2.3   The Rijndael (AES) Cipher

This cipher is designed by Belgian specialists Vincent Rijmen and Joan Daemen and has won in the AES competition as was mentioned before. In 2001, Rijndael was adopted as the new US standard (also known as the AES). Perhaps it will play as important a role in practical cryptography as was played by the DES for decades. Rijndael is noticeably more complicated than RC6 and Magma although its computer implementation is very fast. We shall describe only the main ideas behind the construction of the cipher. Details and implementation examples may be found in [Daemen and Rijmen (2002); Daemen and Rijmen (2003); FIPS 197 (2001)].

The Rijndael/AES cipher is characterized by a block size of 128 bits, a key length of 128, 192, or 256 bits, and 10, 12, or 14 rounds depending on the key length.

Let's agree on notation. A word (32 bits) is a sequence of 4 bytes. The bytes in a word are numbered from 0 (the least significant byte) to 3 (the most significant byte). A data block consists of 4 words that are also numbered from 0 to 3. For ease of designation, we shall assume that the ordinal numbers of bytes in a word and the words in a block are always reduced modulo 4, without explicit indication. A data block is a matrix of 4×4 bytes, the words corresponding not to the rows (as is usual) but to the columns. For instance, $X_{2,3}$ denotes the 2nd byte of the 3rd word of block X. Nevertheless, an item with only one subscript denotes a word, e.g. X_3 is the 3rd word of the block. We shall follow this agreement in order not to change the terminology used by Rijndael.

For making transformations in a block, the round key W is used it is derived from the secret key K. The length of the secret key l implicates the number of rounds r:

$$l = 128 \Rightarrow r = 10,$$

$$l = 192 \Rightarrow r = 12,$$

$$l = 256 \Rightarrow r = 14.$$

The round key consists of blocks (per 128 bits), the number of blocks being equal to the number of rounds plus 1,

$$W = W_0, W_1, \ldots, W_r.$$

We first describe the encryption algorithm and then give necessary explanations.

Algorithm 8.5 RIJNDAEL: ENCRYPTION

INPUT: Block X, round key W.
OUTPUT: Block Y.
1. $Y \leftarrow X \oplus W_0$;
2.   FOR $i = 1, 2, \ldots, r - 1$ DO
3. $Y \leftarrow \text{SubBytes}(Y)$,
4. $Y \leftarrow \text{ShiftRows}(Y)$,
5. $Y \leftarrow \text{MixColumns}(Y)$,
6. $Y \leftarrow Y \oplus W_i$;
7. $Y \leftarrow \text{SubBytes}(Y)$,
8. $Y \leftarrow \text{ShiftRows}(Y)$,
9. $Y \leftarrow Y \oplus W_r$;
10.   RETURN Y.

Three criteria formed the basis for Rijndael's design: security with respect to all known attacks, speed and compactness of code, and simplicity and clearness of design. As distinct from the previous ciphers considered, Rijndael does not use any analogue of the Feistel structure. Each round consists of three different invertible transformations called layers:

(1) the linear mixing layer guarantees high diffusion between bytes over multiple rounds for masking statistical relations;
(2) the non-linear layer implemented with S-boxes having optimum non-linearity properties precludes the application of the linear the differential method and other methods of cryptanalysis;
(3) the key addition layer performs the encryption.

Encryption begins and ends with the operation of adding the key. This allows us to conceal the input of the first round from the known-plaintext attack and to make the result of the last round cryptographically meaningful.

The SubBytes procedure (byte substitution) implements the non-linear layer. The other procedures, ShiftRows and MixColumns, present the linear mixing layer. The key addition layer is realized by means of bitwise "exclusive or" $\oplus$.

Notice that there is no MixColumns transformation in the last round. This seems at first sight to worsen the structure of the cipher. But it is not so. Denote the steps 3–6 of the algorithm by B, R, C, and K, respectively, and write the sequence of operations in the form of a linear chain:

$$\text{KBRCKBRCK} \cdots \text{BRCKBRK.} \qquad (8.6)$$

To decrypt a block one has to perform all the operations in the reverse order using the inverse functions. As will be shown below, the transformations B and R can be swapped without affecting the result. The transformations C and K can also be swapped provided some changes are made to the round key. Under such an alteration the sequence (8.6) is rewritten as

$$\text{KRBKCRBKC} \cdots \text{RBKCRBK.} \qquad (8.7)$$

The sequence (8.7), read from right to left, matches the sequence (8.6) exactly. This means that we can decrypt the block using the same sequence of operations as in encryption. It is important that the sequence of operations BRCK (as will be shown below) can be efficiently implemented by table lookups, the tables being constantly defined, i.e. independent of either the key or the data.

Now we proceed immediately to the description of the transformations BRC. In order to understand the Rijndael transformations one has to learn polynomial arithmetic (see, e.g. [Knuth (1981)]). However, if the reader is interested mainly in the computer implementation of the cipher, he/she may jump immediately to p. 163 where efficient tabular algorithms are presented.

In Rijndael, as well as in many other modern ciphers, polynomial arithmetic is used. We consider several basic operations in this arithmetic but refer the reader to the literature (e.g., [Knuth (1981)]) for more thorough study.

Each data byte in Rijndael (and any binary sequence in general) is considered as a polynomial with binary coefficients 0 and 1 and all operations with coefficients are performed modulo 2. If a is a binary number, then $a(x)$ is an associated polynomial. For example,

$$a = 10010011 \quad \Rightarrow \quad a(x) = x^7 + x^4 + x + 1,$$

i.e. the degree of x equals the bit number in a (bits are numbered from right to left starting with 0) and the x coefficient is the bit value (the terms with zero coefficients are not written). Sometimes, for brevity, the number a may be represented in other systems, e.g., the decimal system, but the associated polynomial remains the same:

$$a = 147 \quad \Rightarrow \quad a(x) = x^7 + x^4 + x + 1.$$

The first important operation is the polynomial addition. It is implemented simply by bitwise xor (sum modulo 2) of the corresponding numbers:

$$a(x) + b(x) \equiv a \oplus b.$$

Notice that modulo 2 sum determines that the polynomial subtraction is the same xor operation.

Polynomial multiplication by x is implemented by shifting the corresponding binary number one position left, and division by x (with the remainder discarded) by shifting it one position right:

$$a(x) \cdot x \equiv a \ll 1, \quad a(x)/x \equiv a \gg 1.$$

The second important operation is the modular multiplication of polynomials. In particular in Rijndael, it is required to multiply byte-polynomials modulo $m(x) = x^8 + x^4 + x^3 + x + 1$. As in the case of the integer numbers, the result being a remainder, all intermediate operations may be performed with remainders. To multiply polynomial $a(x)$ by $b(x)$ we need to repeatedly multiply $a(x)$ by x and add the result to the product if $b(x)$ has 1 in the corresponding position. After each multiplication by x we reduce the result modulo $m(x)$. Since the degrees of the multiplied polynomials are always less than the degree of $m(x)$, the degree of $a(x) \cdot x$ can remain less than or become equal to the degree of $m(x)$. In the former case, no modular reduction is needed. In the latter case, it suffices to do a single subtraction of $m(x)$. These observations lead us to the following algorithm.

Algorithm 8.6 MODULAR MULTIPLICATION OF POLYNOMIALS

INPUT: Polynomials $a(x)$, $b(x)$ of degree less than n,
         polynomial $m(x)$ of degree n.
OUTPUT: Polynomial $c(x) = a(x) \cdot b(x) \bmod m(x)$.
1. $c \leftarrow 0$.
2.   WHILE $b \neq 0$ DO
3.   IF $b_0 = 1$ THEN $c \leftarrow c \oplus a$;
4. $a \leftarrow a \ll 1$;
5.   IF $a_n = 1$ THEN $a \leftarrow a \oplus m$;
6. $b \leftarrow b \gg 1$.
7.   RETURN c.

The selected polynomial $m(x) = x^8 + x^4 + x^3 + x + 1$ has the following important property: it cannot be represented as the product of other polynomials with binary coefficients (this is an analogue of a prime number in binary polynomial arithmetic). As a result, any polynomial $a(x) \neq 0$ has the inverse, i.e. the polynomial $a^{-1}(x)$ such that $a(x) \cdot a^{-1}(x) \bmod m(x) = 1$ (the inverse is computed by the extended Euclidean algorithm in which all numbers are replaced by polynomials). In terms of the theory of groups, one says that byte-polynomials constitute a field $\mathbb{F}_{2^8}$.

Each word of data, i.e. a sequence of 4 bytes, in Rijndael is represented as a polynomial with coefficients in $\mathbb{F}_{2^8}$, i.e. each byte-coefficient is considered as a binary polynomial reduced modulo $m(x)$. For example, the word 7500a302, written in the hexadecimal system, consists of 4 bytes (from most to least significant): 75, 00, a3, and 02, and can be represented as the polynomial

$$7500a302 = (75)y^3 + (a3)y + 2$$

(here we use the indeterminate y just to avoid confusion between word-polynomials and the byte-polynomials defined above). The arithmetic of these word-polynomials is more complicated but we need not go into details. Now we are ready to describe the Rijndael transformations.

The transformation SubBytes(Y) is applied independently to each byte b in block Y:

$$b(x) \leftarrow b^{-1}(x) \bmod m(x) \quad (0 \leftarrow 0),$$

$$b(x) \leftarrow \left((x^7 + x^6 + x^5 + x^4 + 1)b(x) + (x^7 + x^6 + x^2 + x)\right) \bmod (x^8 + 1).$$

The results of this transformation are computed for each byte from 0 to 255 beforehand, and are stored in the table S (this is an S-box). Then the transformation SubBytes(Y) is reduced to performing for each byte b in Y the operation

$$b \leftarrow S[b].$$

The content of table S is explicitly given in [Daemen and Rijmen (2003)].

The transformation ShiftRows(Y) acts upon each row r_i in block Y, i.e. upon the sequence of the ith bytes of the block words ($i = 0, 1, 2, 3$). The operation involved is the cyclic shift left by a specified number of bytes, denoted by $\hookleftarrow$. The rule of the transformation is

$$r_i \leftarrow (r_i \hookleftarrow i), \quad i = 0, 1, 2, 3.$$

For example, show the contents of the block before and after the ShiftRows transformation:

	Y				ShiftRows(Y)		
03	02	01	00	03	02	01	00
13	12	11	10	12	11	10	13
23	22	21	20	21	20	23	22
33	32	31	30	30	33	32	31

The transformation MixColumns(Y) acts upon each column c_i in block Y, i.e. upon each machine word, $i = 0, 1, 2, 3$, by the rule

$$c_i(y) \leftarrow a(y) \cdot c_i(y) \bmod (y^4 + 1)$$

where $a(y) = 3y^3 + y^2 + y + 2$. This operation can be written in the matrix form

$$c_i = \begin{bmatrix} c_{0,i} \\ c_{1,i} \\ c_{2,i} \\ c_{3,i} \end{bmatrix} \leftarrow \begin{bmatrix} 2 & 3 & 1 & 1 \\ 1 & 2 & 3 & 1 \\ 1 & 1 & 2 & 3 \\ 3 & 1 & 1 & 2 \end{bmatrix} \cdot \begin{bmatrix} c_{0,i} \\ c_{1,i} \\ c_{2,i} \\ c_{3,i} \end{bmatrix}. \tag{8.8}$$

Here all "elementary" operations are performed on binary polynomials modulo $m(x)$.

It is obvious that the operation SubBytes can be swapped with ShiftRows without affecting the result since these transformations act upon individual bytes. Using the distributive property of polynomial multiplication we can write

$$\text{MixColumns}(Y \oplus W_i) = \text{MixColumns}(Y) \oplus \text{MixColumns}(W_i).$$

So, the MixColumns transformation and the key addition can also be swapped under the condition that the corresponding blocks of the round key (except the first and last) were subjected to the inverse transformation $\text{MixColumns}^{-1}(W_i)$. All this proves the identity of operation sequences (8.6) and (8.7) with the modified key. As a result, we obtain the following algorithm for the inverse cipher.

Algorithm 8.7 RIJNDAEL: DECRYPTION

INPUT: Block Y, round key W.
OUTPUT: Block X.
  1. $X \leftarrow Y \oplus W_r$;
  2.   FOR $i = r - 1, r - 2, \ldots, 1$ DO
  3. $X \leftarrow \text{SubBytes}^{-1}(X)$,
  4. $X \leftarrow \text{ShiftRows}^{-1}(X)$,
  5. $X \leftarrow \text{MixColumns}^{-1}(X)$,
  6. $X \leftarrow X \oplus W_i$;
  7. $X \leftarrow \text{SubBytes}^{-1}(X)$,
  8. $X \leftarrow \text{ShiftRows}^{-1}(X)$,
  9. $X \leftarrow X \oplus W_0$;
 10.   RETURN X.

The inverse transformations used in the algorithm are defined in the natural way.

The transformation $\text{SubBytes}^{-1}(X)$ is applied to each byte b in X:

$$b(x) \leftarrow (b(x) - (x^7 + x^6 + x^2 + x))(x^7 + x^5 + x^2) \bmod (x^8 + 1),$$

$$b(x) \leftarrow b^{-1}(x) \bmod m(x) \quad (0 \leftarrow 0),$$

where $x^7 + x^5 + x^2 = (x^7 + x^6 + x^5 + x^4 + 1)^{-1} \bmod (x^8 + 1)$. The results are stored in the table S^{-1}. The contents of the table S^{-1} are explicitly given in [Daemen and Rijmen (2003)].

The transformation $\text{ShiftRows}^{-1}(X)$ acts upon each row r_i in block X according to the rule

$$r_i \leftarrow (r_i \hookrightarrow i)$$

(here $\hookrightarrow$ denotes the cyclic shift right by i bytes).

The transformation $\text{MixColumns}^{-1}(X)$ acts upon each column c_i in block X by the rule

$$c_i(y) \leftarrow a^{-1}(y) \cdot c_i(y) \bmod (y^4 + 1)$$

where $a^{-1}(y) = 11y^3 + 13y^2 + 9y + 14$. In the matrix form,

$$c_i = \begin{bmatrix} c_{0,i} \\ c_{1,i} \\ c_{2,i} \\ c_{3,i} \end{bmatrix} \leftarrow \begin{bmatrix} 14 & 11 & 13 & 09 \\ 09 & 14 & 11 & 13 \\ 13 & 09 & 14 & 11 \\ 11 & 13 & 09 & 14 \end{bmatrix} \cdot \begin{bmatrix} c_{0,i} \\ c_{1,i} \\ c_{2,i} \\ c_{3,i} \end{bmatrix}. \tag{8.9}$$

Now proceed to the efficient tabular implementation which we consider only for the case of a 32-bit computer. Denote the state of the block by U. The sequence of steps 3–6 of the encryption algorithm converts the data block from the state U to a new state Y. Taking into account the transformations performed at steps 3–6, we can write the computation of each jth word (i.e. each column) in Y:

$$\begin{bmatrix} Y_{0,j} \\ Y_{1,j} \\ Y_{2,j} \\ Y_{3,j} \end{bmatrix} = \begin{bmatrix} 2 & 3 & 1 & 1 \\ 1 & 2 & 3 & 1 \\ 1 & 1 & 2 & 3 \\ 3 & 1 & 1 & 2 \end{bmatrix} \cdot \begin{bmatrix} S[U_{0,j}] \\ S[U_{1,j-1}] \\ S[U_{2,j-2}] \\ S[U_{3,j-3}] \end{bmatrix} \oplus \begin{bmatrix} W_{i,0,j} \\ W_{i,1,j} \\ W_{i,2,j} \\ W_{i,3,j} \end{bmatrix}$$

(the rightmost column in the expression is the jth word of W_i). Uncovering the matrix multiplication we obtain

$$Y_j = S[U_{0,j}] \cdot \begin{bmatrix} 2 \\ 1 \\ 1 \\ 3 \end{bmatrix} \oplus S[U_{1,j-1}] \cdot \begin{bmatrix} 3 \\ 2 \\ 1 \\ 1 \end{bmatrix}$$

$$\oplus S[U_{2,j-2}] \cdot \begin{bmatrix} 1 \\ 3 \\ 2 \\ 1 \end{bmatrix} \oplus S[U_{0,j-3}] \cdot \begin{bmatrix} 1 \\ 1 \\ 3 \\ 2 \end{bmatrix} \oplus W_{i,j}.$$

Define the four tables

$$
T_0[b] = \begin{bmatrix} S[b] \cdot 2 \\ S[b] \\ S[b] \\ S[b] \cdot 3 \end{bmatrix}, \quad
T_1[b] = \begin{bmatrix} S[b] \cdot 3 \\ S[b] \cdot 2 \\ S[b] \\ S[b] \end{bmatrix},
$$

$$
T_2[b] = \begin{bmatrix} S[b] \\ S[b] \cdot 3 \\ S[b] \cdot 2 \\ S[b] \end{bmatrix}, \quad
T_3[b] = \begin{bmatrix} S[b] \\ S[b] \\ S[b] \cdot 3 \\ S[b] \cdot 2 \end{bmatrix}.
$$

Each table is built for b running from 0 to 255 and consists of 256 4-byte words. The multiplication operation in the computations is a binary polynomial multiplication modulo $m(x)$. Tables T_i do not depend on either the key or the data and can be computed in advance. Using these tables we can build the jth word of the block as follows:

$$
Y_j = T_0[U_{0,j}] \oplus T_1[U_{1,j-1}] \oplus T_2[U_{2,j-2}] \oplus T_3[U_{3,j-3}] \oplus W_{i,j}.
$$

Now we are ready to write the algorithm in the tabular form (Algorithm 8.8).

Algorithm 8.8 RIJNDAEL: ENCRYPTION (FAST VERSION)

INPUT: Block X, round key W.
OUTPUT: Block Y.
1. $U \leftarrow X \oplus W_0$;
2.   FOR $i = 1, 2, \ldots, r - 1$ DO
3.   FOR $j = 0, 1, 2, 3$ DO
4. $Y_j \leftarrow T_0[U_{0,j}] \oplus T_1[U_{1,j-1}] \oplus T_2[U_{2,j-2}]$
                                  $\oplus \, T_3[U_{3,j-3}] \oplus W_{i,j}$;
5. $U \leftarrow Y$;
6.   FOR $i = 0, 1, 2, 3$ DO
7.   FOR $j = 0, 1, 2, 3$ DO
8. $Y_{i,j} \leftarrow S[U_{i,j-i}]$;
9. $Y \leftarrow Y \oplus W_r$;
10.   RETURN Y.

Note that many S-boxes are contained in the tables T_i. For instance, for the S-box at step 8, one can use the low-order bytes of table T_2.

To construct a tabular version for the inverse cipher we must review the observations given above with respect to the inverse transformations. As a result, we obtain the inverse tables T_i^{-1}:

$$T_0^{-1}[b] = \begin{bmatrix} S^{-1}[b] \cdot 14 \\ S^{-1}[b] \cdot 9 \\ S^{-1}[b] \cdot 13 \\ S^{-1}[b] \cdot 11 \end{bmatrix}, \quad T_1^{-1}[b] = \begin{bmatrix} S^{-1}[b] \cdot 11 \\ S^{-1}[b] \cdot 14 \\ S^{-1}[b] \cdot 9 \\ S^{-1}[b] \cdot 13 \end{bmatrix},$$

$$T_2^{-1}[b] = \begin{bmatrix} S^{-1}[b] \cdot 13 \\ S^{-1}[b] \cdot 11 \\ S^{-1}[b] \cdot 14 \\ S^{-1}[b] \cdot 9 \end{bmatrix}, \quad T_3^{-1}[b] = \begin{bmatrix} S^{-1}[b] \cdot 9 \\ S^{-1}[b] \cdot 13 \\ S^{-1}[b] \cdot 11 \\ S^{-1}[b] \cdot 14 \end{bmatrix}.$$

Given these inverse tables we can write down the decrypting algorithm (Algorithm 8.9). Note once again that all the tables may be found in [Daemen and Rijmen (2003)] in a ready-to-use form.

Algorithm 8.9 RIJNDAEL: DECRYPTION (FAST VERSION)

INPUT: Block Y, round key W.
OUTPUT: Decrypted block X.

1. $U \leftarrow Y \oplus W_0$;
2.   FOR $i = r - 1, r - 2, \ldots, 1$ DO
3.   FOR $j = 0, 1, 2, 3$ DO
4. $X_j \leftarrow T_0^{-1}[U_{0,j}] \oplus T_1^{-1}[U_{1,j+1}] \oplus T_2^{-1}[U_{2,j+2}]$
                                    $\oplus T_3^{-1}[U_{3,j+3}] \oplus W_{i,j}$;

5. $U \leftarrow X$;
6.   FOR $i = 0, 1, 2, 3$ DO
7.   FOR $j = 0, 1, 2, 3$ DO
8. $X_{i,j} \leftarrow S^{-1}[U_{i,j+i}]$;
9. $X \leftarrow X \oplus W_r$;
10.   RETURN X.

The last thing to consider is the formation of the round key. In the direct and inverse ciphers, it is convenient to divide the round key W into 4-word blocks. However, the formation of the key must be done in the word mode, so let's denote by the letter w with a subscript a distinct word in W, with numbering that starts from zero. As follows from the encryption and decryption algorithms, the round key W must consist of $r + 1$ blocks where

r is the number of rounds. So the number of words in W equals $4(r+1)$. In its turn, the number of words in the secret key K, which we shall denote by c, may be 4, 6, or 8.

In the round key schedule algorithm, SubWord(t) is a function applying the S-box of the cipher to each byte of the word t

$$[t_0, t_1, t_2, t_3] \longrightarrow [S[t_1], S[t_2], S[t_3], S[t_0]].$$

The transformation RotWord(t) is performed by the cyclic shift of the word t left by one byte

$$[t_0, t_1, t_2, t_3] \longrightarrow [t_1, t_2, t_3, t_0].$$

The array of round constants Rcon contains the words

$$\text{Rcon}[i] = [y_i, 0, 0, 0]$$

where

$$y_i = x^{i-1} \bmod m(x).$$

Algorithm 8.10 RIJNDAEL: ROUND KEY SCHEDULE

INPUT: Secret key K of c words.
OUTPUT: Round key W of $4(r+1)$ words.
1. $W \leftarrow K$ (c words);
2.   FOR $i = c, c+1, \ldots, 4(r+1) - 1$ DO
3. $t \leftarrow W_{i-1}$;
4.   IF $i \bmod c = 0$ THEN
5. $t \leftarrow \text{SubWord}(\text{RotWord}(t)) \oplus \text{Rcon}[i \text{ div } c]$;
6.   ELSE IF $c = 8$ AND $i \bmod c = 4$ THEN
7. $t \leftarrow \text{SubWord}(t)$;
8. $w_i \leftarrow W_{i-c} \oplus t$;
9.   RETURN $W_0 \cdots W_{4(r+1)-1}$.

The chosen method for the round key schedule must facilitate the solving of the following problems:

(1) to impede the attack to the cipher if the secret key is partially known or related keys (connected by the common rules of construction) are used;
(2) to eliminate any symmetries within the cipher round and between the rounds (the array of round constants Rcon is used for that purpose).

As we have noted when considering the inverse cipher, to produce the round key for decryption one has to apply the transformation MixColumns^{-1} to the blocks of W from the first to the next-to-last.

8.2.4 *The Kuznyechik (Grasshopper) Cipher*

The Kuznyechik (Grasshopper) cipher is a new algorithm that is part of the GOST R 34.12-2015 [RFC 7801 (2016)]. The cipher was developed by the Russian Federal Security Service with the company Infotecs (infotecs.ru) and first presented in [Shishkin *et al.* (2014)]. The main parameters of Kuznyechik are the following: a key length of 256 bits, a block size of 128 bits, and 9 rounds. The block consists of 16 bytes which we number 0 to 15, $Y = (y_0, y_1, \ldots, y_{15})$.

The structure of Kuznyechik is the same that of Rijndael. In each round, as in Rijndael, three layers may be distinguished (though the cipher designers do not use this terminology):

(1) the linear mixing layer based on a linear byte transformation;
(2) the non-linear layer implemented with byte-wise S-boxes;
(3) the key addition layer.

Consider first these basic transformations. Begin with non-linear substitution. We have a byte array S with elements S[0], S[1], ..., S[255]:

$$S = (252, 238, 221, 017, 207, 110, 049, 022, 251, 196, 250, 218, 035, 197, 004, 077,$$

$$233, 119, 240, 219, 147, 046, 153, 186, 023, 054, 241, 187, 020, 205, 095, 193,$$

$$249, 024, 101, 090, 226, 092, 239, 033, 129, 028, 060, 066, 139, 001, 142, 079,$$

$$005, 132, 002, 174, 227, 106, 143, 160, 006, 011, 237, 152, 127, 212, 211, 031,$$

$$235, 052, 044, 081, 234, 200, 072, 171, 242, 042, 104, 162, 253, 058, 206, 204,$$

$$181, 112, 014, 086, 008, 012, 118, 018, 191, 114, 019, 071, 156, 183, 093, 135,$$

$$021, 161, 150, 041, 016, 123, 154, 199, 243, 145, 120, 111, 157, 158, 178, 177,$$

$$050, 117, 025, 061, 255, 053, 138, 126, 109, 084, 198, 128, 195, 189, 013, 087,$$

$$223, 245, 036, 169, 062, 168, 067, 201, 215, 121, 214, 246, 124, 034, 185, 003,$$

$$224, 015, 236, 222, 122, 148, 176, 188, 220, 232, 040, 080, 078, 051, 010, 074,$$

$$167, 151, 096, 115, 030, 000, 098, 068, 026, 184, 056, 130, 100, 159, 038, 065,$$

$$173, 069, 070, 146, 039, 094, 085, 047, 140, 163, 165, 125, 105, 213, 149, 059,$$

$$007, 088, 179, 064, 134, 172, 029, 247, 048, 055, 107, 228, 136, 217, 231, 137,$$

225, 027, 131, 073, 076, 063, 248, 254, 141, 083, 170, 144, 202, 216, 133, 097,

032, 113, 103, 164, 045, 043, 009, 091, 203, 155, 037, 208, 190, 229, 108, 082,

089, 166, 116, 210, 230, 244, 180, 192, 209, 102, 175, 194, 057, 075, 099, 182).

The content of array S may be treated as some "random" permutation of all possible bytes (however, in [Biryukov *et al.* (2016)] an algorithm generating this permutation was found). Denote the non-linear transformation of block Y by $S(Y)$. It is done by substituting each separate byte in the block according to the scheme

$$b \leftarrow S[b].$$

To describe the linear transformation, introduce a function lm. This function computes a linear combination of the bytes of the block Y with the following formula:

$$\text{lm}(Y) = 148 \cdot y_0 \oplus 32 \cdot y_1 \oplus 133 \cdot y_2 \oplus 16 \cdot y_3 \oplus 194 \cdot y_4 \oplus 192 \cdot y_5$$

$$\oplus y_6 \oplus 251 \cdot y_7 \oplus y_8 \oplus 192 \cdot y_9 \oplus 194 \cdot y_{10} \oplus 16 \cdot y_{11}$$

$$\oplus 133 \cdot y_{12} \oplus 32 \cdot y_{13} \oplus 148 \cdot y_{14} \oplus y_{15}, \tag{8.10}$$

where the operator $\cdot$ denotes byte-polynomial multiplication modulo $m(x) = x^8 + x^7 + x^6 + x + 1$ (here Algorithm 8.6 may be used). Now the linear transformation of the block, denoted $L(Y)$, is written down as the following algorithm (operation $\hookrightarrow$ is a cyclic right shift of the block per 1 byte).

INPUT: Block $Y = (y_0, y_1, \ldots, y_{15})$.
OUTPUT: $L(Y)$.
        DO 16 times
            $b \leftarrow \text{lm}(Y); \; Y \leftarrow Y \hookrightarrow 1; \; y_0 \leftarrow b.$
        RETURN Y.

The round key $W = W_0, W_1, \ldots, W_9$ consists of 10 blocks of 128 bits each and is derived from the secret key K by the algorithm described later.

The S-box for inverse transformation $S^{-1}(X)$ is a byte permutation inverse with respect to S:

$$S^{-1}[S[b]] = b, \quad b = 0, 1, \ldots, 255.$$

The inverse linear transformation $L^{-1}(X)$ is done using the following algorithm (operation $\hookleftarrow$ is a cyclic left shift of the block by 1 byte).

INPUT: Block $X = (x_0, x_1, \ldots, x_{15})$.
OUTPUT: $L^{-1}(X)$.
          DO 16 times
              $X \leftarrow X \hookleftarrow 1;\ b \leftarrow \text{lm}(X);\ x_{15} \leftarrow b.$
          RETURN X.

Now we are ready to write down the encryption and decryption algorithms.

Algorithm 8.11 KUZNYECHIK: ENCRYPTION

INPUT: Block X, round key W.
OUTPUT: Block Y.
1. $Y \leftarrow X \oplus W_0;$
2.   FOR $i = 1, 2, \ldots, 9$ DO
3. $Y \leftarrow S(Y),$
4. $Y \leftarrow L(Y),$
5. $Y \leftarrow Y \oplus W_i.$
6.   RETURN Y.

Algorithm 8.12 KUZNYECHIK: DECRYPTION

INPUT: Block Y, round key W.
OUTPUT: Block X.
1. $X \leftarrow Y \oplus W_9;$
2.   FOR $i = 8, 7, \ldots, 0$ DO
3. $X \leftarrow L^{-1}(X),$
4. $X \leftarrow S^{-1}(X),$
5. $X \leftarrow X \oplus W_i.$
6.   RETURN X.

(For decryption, it is necessary to perform all the operations in reverse order using inverse transformations.)

The round key is formed using the same transformations as in encryption. Every single element of the secret and round keys is a word of 128 bits (the block size).

Algorithm 8.13 KUZNYECHIK: ROUND KEY SCHEDULE

INPUT: Secret key $K = K_0, K_1$.
OUTPUT: Round key $W = W_0, W_1, \ldots, W_9$.

1. FOR $i = 0, 2, 4, 6$ DO
2. $W_i \leftarrow K_0, W_{i+1} \leftarrow K_1$;
3.   FOR $j = 1, 2, \ldots, 8$ DO
4. $X \leftarrow K_0 \oplus L(4i + j)$,
5. $X \leftarrow S(X)$,
6. $X \leftarrow L(X)$,
7. $X \leftarrow X \oplus K_1$,
8. $K_1 \leftarrow K_0, K_0 \leftarrow X$;
9. $W_8 \leftarrow K_0, W_9 \leftarrow K_1$.
10. RETURN W.

We can see that most operations in Kuznyechik involve the processing of single bytes. This is quite inefficient in modern computers and even microcontrollers whose machine word size is 32 or 64 bits. Fortunately, the Kuznyechik cipher, similarly to Rijndael, allows for fast implementation on 32- and 64-bit platforms using look-up tables computed beforehand and stored in memory. A method of tabular speed-up was suggested in [Borodin *et al.* (2014)]. Let us describe the method.

Since the $L(Y)$ transformation is linear, the matrix A exists such that

$$
L(Y) = YA = (y_0, y_1, \ldots, y_{15}) \cdot
\begin{pmatrix}
a_{0,0} & a_{0,1} & \cdots & a_{0,15} \\
a_{1,0} & a_{1,1} & \cdots & a_{1,15} \\
& & \cdots & \\
a_{15,0} & a_{15,1} & \cdots & a_{15,15}
\end{pmatrix}. \tag{8.11}
$$

In accordance with the L transformation algorithm, multiplication of the vector by the matrix is performed using polynomial arithmetic rules where individual byte-polynomials are added and multiplied modulo $m(x) = x^8 + x^7 + x^6 + x + 1$. The matrix A can be easily obtained by applying the L transformation to blocks that contain a single unit byte. Indeed,

$$
\begin{aligned}
L(1, 0, 0, \ldots, 0) &= (a_{0,0}, a_{0,1}, \ldots, a_{0,15}), \\
L(0, 1, 0, \ldots, 0) &= (a_{1,0}, a_{1,1}, \ldots, a_{1,15}),
\end{aligned}
$$

$$
\cdots
$$

$$
L(0, 0, \ldots, 0, 1) = (a_{15,0}, a_{15,1}, \ldots, a_{15,15}).
$$

By rearranging the terms in the vector by matrix product (8.11) we can write

$$L(Y) = L_0(y_0) \oplus L_1(y_1) \oplus \cdots \oplus L_{15}(y_{15}),$$

where

$$L_i(b) = (a_{i,0} \cdot b, a_{i,1} \cdot b, \ldots, a_{i,15} \cdot b).$$

We can compute in advance the values of vectors L_i for all possible bytes b from 0 to 255.

Observe now that in block encryption, the L transformation goes after the S one which substitutes every byte in the block with the corresponding byte from table S. We can combine successive transformations S and L and compute in advance 16 tables $T_0, \ldots, T_{15}$ following the rule

$$T_i[b] = L_i(S(b)),$$

i.e.

$$T_i[0] = (a_{i,0} \cdot S[0], a_{i,1} \cdot S[0], \ldots, a_{i,15} \cdot S[0]),$$

$$\cdots$$

$$T_i[255] = (a_{i,0} \cdot S[255], a_{i,1} \cdot S[255], \ldots, a_{i,15} \cdot S[255]).$$

The tabular version of the encryption algorithm is given below.

Note that every element in the tables T has a length equal to the block size (128 bits). So the tabular implementation of the cipher can fully use the ability of modern processors to fetch from memory and operate under words of 32, 64 or even 128 bits.

The sequence of transformations S and L can be similarly optimized in the algorithm of the round key schedule. The constants $L(1)$, $L(2), \ldots, L(32)$ needed in the 4th line of the algorithm can also be computed in advance and stored in memory.

Algorithm 8.14 Kuznyechik: encryption (fast version)

INPUT: Block X, round key W.
OUTPUT: Block Y.
1. $Y \leftarrow X \oplus W_0$;
2.   FOR $i = 1, 2, \ldots, 9$ DO
3. $Y \leftarrow T_0[y_0] \oplus T_1[y_1] \oplus \cdots \oplus T_{15}[y_{15}]$,
4. $Y \leftarrow Y \oplus W_i$.
6.   RETURN Y.

Consider now the ways we can approach the tabular implementation of decryption. Here the same observations apply but the problem is that the S^{-1} transformation takes place *after* the L^{-1} transformation and we cannot combine them in the same way as we do in encryption. To combine these inverse transformations, we need to slightly change the structure of the inverse cipher.

Write down in a chain the operations performed in decryption by unfolding the loop in Algorithm 8.12:

$$W_9 \quad L^{-1}S^{-1}W_8 \quad L^{-1}S^{-1}W_7 \quad \ldots L^{-1}S^{-1}W_0.$$

Operations are performed from left to right, W_i denotes addition with the corresponding word of the round key, and spaces are inserted to show the grouping of operations. Now prepend the chain with two mutually compensating transformations S and S^{-1} and group the operations differently:

$$S \quad S^{-1}W_9L^{-1} \quad S^{-1}W_8L^{-1} \quad S^{-1}W_7\ldots L^{-1} \quad S^{-1}W_0.$$

Consider the triple $S^{-1}W_iL^{-1}$. This chain of operations computes for the current state of block X $L^{-1}(S^{-1}(X) \oplus W_i)$. Due to the linearity of L^{-1} the following equality is valid [Borodin *et al.* (2014)]:

$$L^{-1}(S^{-1}(X) \oplus W_i) = L^{-1}(S^{-1}(X)) \oplus L^{-1}(W_i).$$

As a result, we obtain a bunch in which S^{-1} precedes L^{-1}. Now by analogy with how it was done in encryption, we can compute 16 look-up tables for fast implementation of the sequence of transformations $S^{-1}L^{-1}$ in decryption. Denote these tables by $T_0^{-1}, \ldots, T_{15}^{-1}$. We are ready to write down the decryption algorithm in tabular version.

Algorithm 8.15 KUZNYECHIK: DECRYPTION (FAST VERSION)

INPUT: Block Y, round key W.
OUTPUT: Block X.
1. $X \leftarrow S(Y)$;
2.   FOR $i = 9, 8, \ldots, 1$ DO
3. $X \leftarrow T_0^{-1}[x_0] \oplus T_1^{-1}[x_1] \oplus \cdots \oplus T_{15}^{-1}[x_{15}]$,
4. $X \leftarrow X \oplus L^{-1}(W_i)$;
5. $X \leftarrow S^{-1}(X)$;
6. $X \leftarrow X \oplus W_0$.
7.   RETURN X.

We can see that, compared to the tabular encryption algorithm, two extra non-linear transformations are added here. The transformed round key words $L^{-1}(W_1), \ldots, L^{-1}(W_9)$ can be computed in advance (at the round key formation). The word W_0 remains intact.

8.3   Main Modes of Operation of Block Ciphers

The block ciphers are used for solving many problems in cryptography. In this section, we shall consider the main modes of their usage.

In the previous section, examples of real block ciphers were given. Now we can think of an (idealized) block cipher as a transformation of input block X into output block Y depending on secret key K,

$$Y = E_K(X),$$

the following requirements being fulfilled:

(1) given a known Y, but unknown K, it is practically impossible to recover X;
(2) given arbitrary known X and Y, but unknown K, it is practically impossible to learn K.

First we consider the classical problem of encrypting messages with the use of block ciphers.

8.3.1   *ECB Mode*

The acronym ECB comes from Electronic Code Book. In this mode, the message X is split into the blocks $X = X_1, X_2, \ldots, X_t$. Each block is encrypted by the block cipher

$$Y_i = E_K(X_i), \quad 1 \leq i \leq t.$$

We obtain the ciphertext $Y = Y_1, Y_2, \ldots, Y_t$. Decryption is carried out by the scheme

$$X_i = E_K^{-1}(Y_i), \quad 1 \leq i \leq t.$$

It is easy to see that one can perform decryption by selecting the ciphertext blocks in arbitrary order. This mode is convenient in many cases because it is easy to change or delete some fragments of data independently of the others and to decrypt starting at any point. This is particularly important for database applications.

However, there may be problems in some situations because the similar records will have similar ciphertexts. We can say that the ECB mode preserves the data pattern. It may provide some information to the adversary. For instance, if the number of *different* records in a database is small then the adversary can make a dictionary of ciphertexts and break the database using the frequency analysis. Note that she will not need to break the cipher.

8.3.2   *CBC Mode*

The acronym CBC comes from Cipher-Block Chaining. In this mode, the ciphertext is produced by the following rule:

$$Y_i = E_K(X_i \oplus Y_{i-1}), \quad 1 \leq i \leq t,$$

i.e. each successive plaintext block is covered by the previous ciphertext block prior to encryption. The word Y_0 (often called the *initialization vector*) must be specified in advance and known to both encrypter and decrypter. The resulting ciphertext can be decrypted in the following way:

$$X_i = Y_{i-1} \oplus E_K^{-1}(Y_i), \quad 1 \leq i \leq t.$$

With the CBC mode, we obtain the ciphertext in which each successive block depends on all of the previous ones. This mode destroys any data patterns. Even if all the plaintext blocks are identical, the ciphertext will consist of different blocks. The CBC mode is preferable when encrypting the messages whose length exceeds the block size. The drawback, however, is the absence of direct access capability: the message can be decrypted only sequentially, starting at the first block.

Two other block cipher modes will be considered in the context of the stream ciphers.

8.4 Stream Ciphers

In Sec. 7.3, we have considered the one-time pad cipher and established its perfect secrecy, i.e. the property that ensures that the adversary intercepting the ciphertext obtains no information about the message. In the one-time pad, the ciphertext $y_1, y_2, \ldots, y_k$ is produced from the message $x_1, x_2, \ldots, x_k$ under the key $z_1, z_2, \ldots, z_k$ by the following encrypting operation:

$$y_i = x_i \oplus z_i, \quad i = 1, 2, \ldots, k. \tag{8.12}$$

This cipher is perfect only if the key $z_1, z_2, \ldots, z_k$ consists of equiprobable and independent bits and is used only once. This leads to the necessity of generating random sequences of very large size and transmitting them over secure channels, which is highly difficult. Therefore, the idea arose to use sequences generated by the so-called *pseudo-random number generators* instead of truly random sequences. In this case, one may use the initial state of the generator as the secret key. Of course, the resulting cryptosystem will not be perfect anymore. The maximum of what we may expect is that breaking such a cryptosystem will require an enormous amount of time (e.g. it will require an exhaustive search through all possible initial states of the generator). As compensation for the loss of perfection we obtain the possibility of using short secret keys (say, of several hundred bits) which are significantly easier to maintain and distribute (e.g. they may be created by means of public-key techniques).

The cipher based upon (8.12) where the key sequence $z_1, z_2, \ldots, z_k$ is generated by some deterministic algorithm (e.g. a pseudo-random number generator) is called the *stream cipher*.

As a rule, the source message and the key sequence are independent streams of bits. Since the encrypting and decrypting transformations are the same for all stream ciphers, the latter differ only in the way of the construction of pseudo-random number generators. Indeed, to recover the message $x_1, x_2, \ldots, x_k$ from the ciphertext $y_1, y_2, \ldots, y_k$ produced by (8.12) one needs to generate the same sequence $z_1, z_2, \ldots, z_k$ as in encryption, and use the formula

$$x_i = y_i \oplus z_i, \quad i = 1, 2, \ldots, k. \tag{8.13}$$

Consider an example. One of the simplest pseudo-random number generators, called the *linear congruential generator*, operates according to the recurrence

$$u_{i+1} = (au_i + b) \bmod c, \qquad (8.14)$$

where a, b, c are some constants and u_i, u_{i+1} the elements of the produced pseudo-random sequence. The initial state is u_0. Take, for instance, $a = 5$, $b = 12$, $c = 23$, and let $u_0 = 4$. Compute several elements of the sequence:

$$u_1 = (4 \cdot 5 + 12) \bmod 23 = 9,$$

$$u_2 = (9 \cdot 5 + 12) \bmod 23 = 11,$$

$$u_3 = (11 \cdot 5 + 12) \bmod 23 = 21,$$

$$u_4 = (21 \cdot 5 + 12) \bmod 23 = 2,$$

$$u_5 = (2 \cdot 5 + 12) \bmod 23 = 22,$$

$$u_6 = (22 \cdot 5 + 12) \bmod 23 = 7,$$

$$u_7 = (7 \cdot 5 + 12) \bmod 23 = 1.$$

The produced sequence looks much like it is random (it can be converted to a bit stream by using binary representations of numbers, or by extracting particular bits, etc.).

For its use in cryptographic applications, the generator must meet the following main requirements:

(1) the period of the generated sequence must be large;
(2) the determination of z_{i+1} given the preceding elements of the sequence must be a hard, infeasible problem;
(3) the sequence generated must be indistinguishable from a truly random sequence by statistical tests.

The linear congruential generator considered above is completely unsuitable for cryptographic purposes since the algorithms that allow us to recover all the generator's parameters by examining only a few elements of the sequence generated are known [Plumstead (1982)].

As examples of cryptographically secure pseudo-random number generators, we shall consider the OFB and CTR block cipher modes and the algorithms RC4 and HC-128.

But first, let's pay attention to one peculiarity which is important for all stream ciphers. For encrypting any other message, one must use a different key K and/or initialization vector Y_0. Otherwise, several messages will be encrypted using the same sequence z and such a cipher can be disclosed. Let's explain the essence of the problem. Let two messages $u_1, u_2, \ldots, u_k$ and $v_1, v_2, \ldots, v_k$ be encrypted using the same sequence z. Then the ciphertexts will be of the form:

$$u_1 \oplus z_1, u_2 \oplus z_2, \ldots, u_k \oplus z_k \quad \text{and}$$

$$v_1 \oplus z_1, v_2 \oplus z_2, \ldots, v_k \oplus z_k.$$

Add one ciphertext to the other and, taking into account the equalities $z_i \oplus z_i = 0$, obtain the sequence

$$u_1 \oplus v_1, u_2 \oplus v_2, \ldots, u_k \oplus v_k.$$

We have obtained the analogue of the so-called *running-key cipher* in which one text is encrypted using another text taken from a certain place in a certain book. It is known that this cipher is insecure although it was used in the past [Menezes *et al.* (1996)]. The statistical analysis based on the redundancy of the texts allows us to recover both messages in most cases (we have considered this problem in detail in Sec. 7.6).

8.4.1   *The OFB Block Cipher Mode*

The acronym OFB comes from Output FeedBack. In this mode, the block cipher, parametrized by the secret key K and initialization vector Y_0, produces a pseudo-random sequence of r-bit numbers $z_1, z_2, \ldots, z_k$ which can be used in (8.12) and (8.13) for encryption and decryption, respectively. We shall assume, as before, that the block size of the cipher is n bits.

The pseudo-random sequence is produced by the scheme

$$Y_i = E_K(Y_{i-1}),$$

$$z_i = r \text{ high-order bits of } Y_i, \quad 1 \le i \le k$$

(here r, $1 \le r \le n$, is a parameter of the method).

If a secure block cipher is used, we obtain a secure generator that meets all the requirements given above. More exactly, the average value of the sequence's period (under randomly chosen K and Y_0) is about $r2^{n-1}$ bits (see [Menezes *et al.* (1996)]). Besides, the pseudo-random sequence is unpredictable in the sense that the adversary cannot predict (or compute) z_{i+1} if she has $z_1, \ldots, z_i$. The possibility of such a prediction would mean that the block cipher is insecure with respect to the known-plaintext attack. The prediction of z_{i+1} is an even more difficult problem than breaking the block cipher if $r < n$ [Menezes *et al.* (1996)].

In the OFB mode, the decryption can be carried out only from the beginning since it is not possible to obtain an arbitrary element of the sequence z without having computed the preceding elements. In this sense, the mode is similar to CBC. The advantage of the OFB mode is that the sequence z can be formed in advance in order to encrypt or decrypt data maximally fast when the elements arrive. It is of importance for the systems processing data in real time.

8.4.2 *The CTR Block Cipher Mode*

The name of this mode comes from the word CounTeR. This mode resembles the OFB. The difference is that a counter is enciphered rather than the previous output of the cipher. More exactly, the scheme is

$$z_i = r \text{ high-order bits of } E_K(Y_0 + i), \quad i = 1, 2, 3, \ldots$$

where r and Y_0 are parameters.

If the "ideal" block cipher is used, this mode ensures the same security level as the OFB mode. The advantage of the CTR mode is the possibility of the direct computation of any element of the sequence z. It allows us to encrypt and decrypt any fragments of the message independently of each other.

8.4.3 *The RC4 Algorithm*

The algorithm RC4 suggested by Rivest in 1994 (see [Schneier (1996)]) is a representative of a class of customized methods designed specially for stream ciphers. The pseudo-random generators constructed using such algorithms are usually much faster than the generators based on block ciphers.

The RC4 algorithm operates with n-bit words (usually, $n = 8$). All computations are performed modulo 2^n (the remainder $x \bmod 2^n$ is computed extremely fast by masking all but n low-order bits in x using the logical "and" operation). RC4 uses the L-word key $K = K_0 K_1 \ldots K_{L-1}$ and generates the sequence of words $\bar{u} = u_1 u_2 u_3 \ldots$ determined by that K.

The state of the generator is defined by the table S, which contains 2^n words, and by the two variables i and j. At each time instance table S contains all the n-bit numbers (from 0 to $2^n - 1$) but they are somehow mixed. Since every element of the table may take on values in the interval $[0,\ 2^n - 1]$, it may be treated in two ways, either as a number or as an index to another element in the table. The secret key determines only the initial permutation of numbers in the table. This initial permutation is formed using the following algorithm:

$$j \leftarrow 0, \quad S \leftarrow (0, 1, \ldots, 2^n - 1);$$
$$\text{FOR } i = 0, 1, \ldots, 2^n - 1 \text{ DO}$$
$$\qquad j \leftarrow (j + S_i + K_{i \bmod L}) \bmod 2^n,$$
$$\qquad S_j \leftrightarrow S_i;$$
$$i \leftarrow 0, \quad j \leftarrow 0.$$

After this is done, the generator is ready to work. The generation of a pseudo-random word u_i, $i = 1, 2, 3, \ldots$ is performed by using the following algorithm:

$$i \leftarrow (i + 1) \bmod 2^n;$$
$$j \leftarrow (j + S_i) \bmod 2^n;$$
$$S_j \leftrightarrow S_i;$$
$$t \leftarrow (S_i + S_j) \bmod 2^n;$$
$$u_i \leftarrow S_t.$$

Consider an example. Let $n = 3$, $K = (25)_8$ ($L = 2$). Form the initial permutation of numbers in table S (perform all computations modulo 8):

$$
\begin{aligned}
&& j = 0, && S = (0, 1, 2, 3, 4, 5, 6, 7), \\
i = 0, && j = 0 + 0 + 2 = 2, && S = (2, 1, 0, 3, 4, 5, 6, 7), \\
i = 1, && j = 2 + 1 + 5 = 0, && S = (1, 2, 0, 3, 4, 5, 6, 7), \\
i = 2, && j = 0 + 0 + 2 = 2, && S = (1, 2, 0, 3, 4, 5, 6, 7), \\
i = 3, && j = 2 + 3 + 5 = 2, && S = (1, 2, 3, 0, 4, 5, 6, 7), \\
i = 4, && j = 2 + 4 + 2 = 0, && S = (4, 2, 3, 0, 1, 5, 6, 7), \\
i = 5, && j = 0 + 5 + 5 = 2, && S = (4, 2, 5, 0, 1, 3, 6, 7), \\
i = 6, && j = 2 + 6 + 2 = 2, && S = (4, 2, 6, 0, 1, 3, 5, 7), \\
i = 7, && j = 2 + 7 + 5 = 6, && S = (4, 2, 6, 0, 1, 3, 7, 5).
\end{aligned}
$$

Now compute several elements of the pseudo-random sequence $\bar{u}$:

$$i = 1, \quad j = 0 + 2 = 2, \quad S = (4, 6, 2, 0, 1, 3, 7, 5), \quad t = 2 + 6 = 0, \quad u_1 = 4,$$

$$i = 2, \quad j = 2 + 2 = 4, \quad S = (4, 6, 1, 0, 2, 3, 7, 5), \quad t = 1 + 2 = 3, \quad u_2 = 0,$$

$$i = 3, \quad j = 4 + 0 = 4, \quad S = (4, 6, 1, 2, 0, 3, 7, 5), \quad t = 2 + 0 = 2, \quad u_3 = 1,$$

$$i = 4, \quad j = 4 + 0 = 4, \quad S = (4, 6, 1, 2, 0, 3, 7, 5), \quad t = 0 + 0 = 0, \quad u_4 = 4,$$

$$i = 5, \quad j = 4 + 3 = 7, \quad S = (4, 6, 1, 2, 0, 5, 7, 3), \quad t = 5 + 3 = 0, \quad u_5 = 4,$$

$$i = 6, \quad j = 7 + 7 = 6, \quad S = (4, 6, 1, 2, 0, 5, 7, 3), \quad t = 7 + 7 = 6, \quad u_6 = 7.$$

To apply Eq. (8.12) for encrypting write the numbers u_i in binary system. In our example, each number u_i is represented by 3 bits, so we obtain

$$\bar{z} = 1\,0\,0\,0\,0\,0\,0\,0\,1\,1\,0\,0\,1\,0\,0\,1\,1\,1 \ldots$$

8.4.4 *The HC-128 Algorithm*

There is no standardization of methods in the field of stream ciphers as strong as the ones we can see in other branches of cryptography. However, we must mention an attempt to issue an European standard that occurred as the result of an open project competition called eSTREAM [eSTREAM] organized in 2006. The competition ended in 2008 and 7 stream ciphers have become its winners (4 ciphers for software implementation and 3 for hardware). All the winners are recommended for wide practical use. One of the winners is the HC-128 stream cipher which is described in detail in this subsection. The author of HC-128 [Wu (2004)] is Hongjun Wu who was then working in the Catholic University of Leuven, Belgium.

The HC-128 cipher operates under a 128-bit secret key K and a 128-bit initialization vector IV. The cipher construction resembles that of RC4. There are two tables of 512 32-bit words that play the role of S-boxes, denoted by P and Q. The table elements are indexed from 0 to 511. One word in the tables is updated on each step due to a non-linear function, all words being updated every 1024 steps. On each step, 32 bits of pseudorandom sequence z_i are generated, where i is the step number. The following operations are used in HC-128:

+ addition of words modulo 2^{32} (i.e. 32-bit addition with loss of carry);
− subtraction modulo 512 (for the calculation of table indices, subtract and leave the 9 least significant bits with logical AND);
⊕ bitwise "exclusive or" of two words (the sum modulo 2);
≫ right shift of a word by a specified number of bits;

$\ll$ left shift of a word by a specified number of bits;
$\hookrightarrow$ cyclic right shift by a specified number of bits;
$\hookleftarrow$ cyclic left shift by a specified number of bits.

The word x consists of 4 bytes: $x = (x_3, x_2, x_1, x_0)$, where x_0 is the least significant byte. There are 6 functions defined over the words:

$$f_1(x) = (x \hookrightarrow 7) \oplus (x \hookrightarrow 18) \oplus (x \gg 3),$$

$$f_2(x) = (x \hookrightarrow 17) \oplus (x \hookrightarrow 19) \oplus (x \gg 10),$$

$$g_1(x, y, z) = ((x \hookrightarrow 10) \oplus (z \hookrightarrow 23)) + (y \hookrightarrow 8),$$

$$g_2(x, y, z) = ((x \hookleftarrow 10) \oplus (z \hookleftarrow 23)) + (y \hookleftarrow 8),$$

$$h_1(x) = Q[x_0] + Q[256 + x_2],$$

$$h_2(x) = P[x_0] + P[256 + x_2].$$

The f functions are borrowed from the SHA-256 hashing algorithm. The functions' non-linearity is determined by combining operations from different algebraic groups ($+$ and $\oplus$, arithmetic and cycle shifts).

As in RC4, HC-128 has an initialization phase in which the initial content of tables P and Q is created using the secret key and initialization vector. An auxiliary array W of 1280 words is needed for the phase.

Algorithm 8.16   HC-128: INITIALIZATION

INPUT: Secret key $K = K_0, K_1, K_2, K_3$,
           initialization vector $IV = IV_0, IV_1, IV_2, IV_3$.
OUTPUT: Initialized tables P, Q.
1. $W_0, \ldots, W_7 \leftarrow K_0, \ldots, K_3, K_0, \ldots, K_3$;
2. $W_8, \ldots, W_{15} \leftarrow IV_0, \ldots, IV_3, IV_0, \ldots, IV_3$;
3.   FOR $i = 16, 17, \ldots, 1279$ DO
4. $W_i \leftarrow f_2(W_{i-2}) + W_{i-7} + f_1(W_{i-15}) + W_{i-16} + i$;
5.   FOR $i = 0, 1, \ldots, 511$ DO
6. $P[i] \leftarrow W_{256+i}, \; Q[i] \leftarrow W_{768+i}$;
7.   FOR $i = 0, 1, \ldots, 511$ DO
8. $P[i] \leftarrow (P[i] + g_1(P[i - 3], P[i - 10], P[i - 511]))$
            $\oplus h_1(P[i - 12])$;
9.   FOR $i = 0, 1, \ldots, 511$ DO
10. $Q[i] \leftarrow (Q[i] + g_2(Q[i - 3], Q[i - 10], Q[i - 511]))$
            $\oplus h_2(Q[i - 12])$;
11.   RETURN P, Q.

Now a pseudorandom sequence z_0, z_1, z_2, ... may be generated word-by-word via the following simple algorithm:

Algorithm 8.17 HC-128: KEY-STREAM WORD GENERATION

INPUT: Word number i ($i = 0, 1, 2, \ldots$).

OUTPUT: Word z_i.

1. $j \leftarrow i \bmod 512$;
2.   IF ($i \bmod 1024$) < 512 THEN
3. $P[j] \leftarrow P[j] + g_1(P[j-3], P[j-10], P[j-511])$,
4. $z_i \leftarrow h_1(P[i-12]) \oplus P[j]$;
5.   ELSE
6. $Q[j] \leftarrow Q[j] + g_2(Q[j-3], Q[j-10], Q[j-511])$,
7. $z_i \leftarrow h_2(Q[j-12]) \oplus Q[j]$;
8.   RETURN z_i.

So 32 bits of pseudorandom sequence are generated and one table element is updated on each step. More precisely, table P is updated during the first 512 steps while Q is used as an S-box (via h_1 function). During the next 512 steps, the tables change roles: Q is updated and P is used as an S-box (via h_2 function).

According to the HC-128 author's investigation, 2^{64} bits can be generated for each pair of K and IV before deviation from randomness is detected by statistical tests; there are no weak keys, the key may be found only by exhaustive search. Under the proper program realization, the speed of key-stream generation is 3.05 cycles per byte on a Pentium M processor. This is about 5–6 times faster than when using AES on the same processor.

8.5 Cryptographic Hash Functions

We have already met the notion of the hash function in Chap. 4 where hash functions were parts of digital signature schemes. In those schemes, hash functions were used as the "digests" or "representatives" of the messages to be signed. The signature was actually produced on the hash function value and it was assumed that this value essentially depends on all symbols of the message and one cannot alter the message without affecting the hash function value.

As a matter of fact, hash functions have a wider use in cryptography. For example, the problem of secure password storage and the "friend or foe" protocol considered in Sec. 2.1 can be efficiently solved with the aid of hash functions. In Chap. 9, the application of hash functions to ensuring unique data identification and integrity, as well as to solving the problem of "proof of work" will be studied. Hash functions can be used to construct cryptographically secure pseudorandom number generators and many other things.

In this section, we shall formulate the requirements more strictly and consider the basic methods of the construction of cryptographic hash functions.

Definition 8.1. Any function $y = h(x_1 x_2 \ldots x_n)$ which maps the string (message) $x_1 x_2 \ldots x_n$ of *arbitrary* length n into the word (or number) y of a *fixed* length is called the *hash function*.

The example of the hash function is the checksum for the message. In this case

$$h(x_1 x_2 \ldots x_n) = (x_1 + x_2 + \cdots + x_n) \bmod 2^w,$$

where w is the size of machine word. The length of the number that contains the value of this function is w bits regardless of the length of the message. The checksums are often used for detecting unintentional (random) errors in the message (it is assumed that, if an error occurs, there is a high probability that the checksum will change). Nevertheless it is very easy to make an intentional error preserving the checksum value. If such a hash function had been used in a digital signature scheme, it would have been possible to alter the signed document. Therefore, the presented checksum hash function is unsuitable for cryptographic use.

Let's formulate the main requirements that any cryptographically secure hash function must meet. Let x be some string (message). Then

(1) for any given x, the computation $h(x)$ must be relatively fast;
(2) given y, it must be computationally infeasible to find a message x such that $y = h(x)$;
(3) given x, it must be computationally infeasible to find any other $x' \neq x$ such that $h(x') = h(x)$;
(4) it must be computationally infeasible to find any pair of distinct messages x and x' for which $h(x') = h(x)$.

Notice that the first requirement must always be fulfilled since, otherwise, the hash function loses any practical meaning. The other requirements are important for various applications. For instance, if the passwords are stored in the form of hash function values then the hash function must meet the second requirement. For the digital signature schemes, the third requirement is important. The fourth requirement is needed in some cryptographic protocols. Notice that the fourth requirement is stronger than the third (i.e. the fulfillment of the fourth implies the fulfillment of the third).

The value of the hash function is often referred to as the *hash value* or *message digest*. For cryptographic applications, the length of the hash value is important. We shall measure this length in bits and denote it by t. When a hash function satisfies the 2nd and 3rd properties, the best algorithm that can find the argument x requires $O(2^t)$ operations. When a hash function satisfies the 4th property, the best algorithm that can find an arbitrary pair of arguments that lead to the same hash value requires $O(2^{t/2})$ operations (due to the birthday paradox, see, e.g., [Menezes *et al.* (1996)]). It is generally accepted that for the state of computing equipment, a computationally infeasible number of operations is about 2^{80}. Therefore, to satisfy the 4th requirement, the length of the hash value must be not less than 160 bits.

Designing hash functions that would meet all four requirements is not a simple task. Nowadays, numerous hash functions are built upon several basic constructions that are suggested and used in practice.

The first, the oldest and the most studied construction is named after Mercle and Damgård (Mercle and Damgård (1979), see, e.g., [Menezes *et al.* (1996)]). It is based on a so-called "compression function" which can be realized via a block cipher or similar algorithm (it is desired that the compression function be irreversible). Consider two variants of the approach using a block cipher. Let there be given a block cipher E which maps the input block X onto the output block Y under the key K,

$$Y = E_K(X).$$

We present two algorithms for which the length of the hash function value equals the block size of the cipher but note that constructions are known which allow for the length of the hash value to be of several block sizes.

In the first algorithm, the message is represented as a sequence of blocks $X_1, X_2, \ldots, X_n$. The last block is padded with some bit string. The standard padding is formed of zeros followed by 1 and the message length is represented in binary with a fixed bit depth (say, 64 bits). The number of zeros is chosen so that the total length of the padded message is a multiple of the block size. The value of the hash function h results from the following iterative process:

$$h \leftarrow 0;$$
$$\text{FOR } i = 1, 2, \ldots, n \text{ DO}$$
$$h \leftarrow E_h(X_i) \oplus X_i.$$

The initial value of h may be some "magic" number rather than zero, but it is not important. In this algorithm, the value of h obtained in the previous iteration is used as the key to the cipher in the next iteration. Therefore, it is assumed implicitly that the length of the key is equal to the block size. Adding the source block to the enciphered one makes the compression function irreversible.

As we have seen in case of RC6, the length of the key can be significantly greater than the block size (in RC6 the length of the key can be as large as 255 bytes). In such cases the second algorithm is more appropriate.

In the second algorithm, the message is represented as a sequence $X_1, X_2, \ldots, X_m$ in which the length of each element equals the length of the cipher key. The last element is padded in the same way as in the first algorithm. The value of the hash function h is computed as follows:

$$h \leftarrow 0;$$
$$\text{FOR } i = 1, 2, \ldots, m \text{ DO}$$
$$h \leftarrow E_{X_i}(h) \oplus h.$$

Here the message elements play the role of keys for the cipher.

The presented algorithms satisfy all the requirements of cryptographic hash functions provided the underlying block ciphers are secure (see [Goldwasser and Bellare (2008); Menezes *et al.* (1996)]). However, one obstacle arises: block ciphers are usually explored under the assumption that the key is unknown. But everything is known in the presented constructions: the plaintext, the ciphertext and the key. Therefore additional requirements are applied to the block cipher, e.g., the absence of weak or related keys (i.e. the keys that result in almost identical ciphertexts). We have to date several broken hash functions based upon the Mercle–Damgård construction that have been actively used in the past. The search for alternative constructions continues.

One of these alternatives is a sponge construction. It was first presented in 2007 [Bertoni *et al.* (2007)]. The sponge construction is built upon the bit array (state) S, which is divided into two parts such that $S = (S^r, S^c)$ of

r and c bits, respectively (r and c are the method parameters), and a permutation (or transformation) f which acts upon the whole state: $S \leftarrow f(S)$. The message is represented as a sequence of r-bit blocks $X_1, X_2, \ldots, X_k$, the last block padded in the ordinal way. The hash value is formed in two phases: the phase of absorption where the message blocks are absorbed by the sponge, and the phase of squeezing where the sponge is squeezed to extract a needed number of bits as the result. The phase of absorption works with the following algorithm:

$$S \leftarrow 0;$$
$$\text{FOR } i = 1, 2, \ldots, k \text{ DO}$$
$$S^r \leftarrow S^r \oplus X_i,$$
$$S \leftarrow f(S).$$

The sponge squeezing is done as follows:

$$\text{FOR } i = 1, 2, \ldots, t/r \text{ DO}$$
$$h_i \leftarrow S^r,$$
$$S \leftarrow f(S).$$

The result is the t-bit hash value $h = h_1, h_2, \ldots, h_{t/r}$, made of distinct r-bit blocks. Here we implicitly assumed that t is a multiple of r, which is usually the case. If it is not so, the last block of the result may be cut to obtain the desired hash length.

Notice that the part of the sponge S^c never directly interacts with either input or output. It participates only in permuting transformation f. This part of the state constitutes the internal capacity of the sponge. The construction authors show that to achieve the t-bit security of the hash function, the equality $c = 2t$ must hold. Of course, the security substantially depends on the choice of transformation f, as well. The theoretical properties of the sponge construction were justified under the assumption that f is a completely random permutation. But in practice this permutation must surely be deterministic, determined by a certain algorithm.

Let us present a brief survey of the most popular hash functions, embracing, for the sake of completeness, those that have gone out of use but, which have greatly impacted the development in the field.

The first series of hash functions is presented by the algorithms MD2, MD4, MD5 and MD6. Here MD has a twofold meaning: on the one hand, it means Message Digest, on the other hand, it refers to the Mercle–Damgård construction which is the basis of these algorithms. The series was developed under R. Rivest. The hash function MD2 came to life in 1989 and since that time has been actively employed in various Internet protocols. A number of theoretical attacks against the algorithm that had been found led gradually to its rejection. The MD4 algorithm has not found wide application both because some vulnerabilities were promptly discovered and because a more advanced variant, MD5, was developed.

The MD5 hash function with a 128-bit hash value was suggested in 1991 and became a de facto standard for many information security systems [Rivest (1992)]. It is still in use as a cryptographic checksum to control data integrity and as a method of storing passwords in computers. But this hash function is associated with one of the most dramatic stories of breaking cryptographic algorithms. In [Wang *et al.* (2004)], a practically feasible method of finding collisions in MD5 was suggested. In a number of subsequent works, even faster algorithms were developed which in the end led to the ability to find collisions in just one minute on a personal computer. This situation has stimulated a transition to longer hash values (of about 256 bits and higher) and a search for alternative constructions.

The last in the series, the MD6 hash function [Rivest *et al.* (2008)] was developed in 2008. It obviates the flaws of MD5, has a hash value of up to 512 bits and allows for parallel computation due to a tree structure of intermediate hash values (which is its most distinctive feature). But MD6 did not pass the first round of the NIST hash function competition (see below) and is not widely used today.

The next important hash function series is the series of US standards developed under the National Institute of Standards and Technology of the USA (NIST). The series comprises four generations of algorithms: SHA-0, SHA-1, SHA-2 and SHA-3. Here SHA stands for Secure Hash Algorithm. The first two algorithms (SHA-0 and SHA-1) have left the scene due to the same reasons as MD5. The third generation (SHA-2) [FIPS 180-4 (2015)] consists of four hash functions named SHA-224, SHA-256, SHA-384 and SHA-512. These hash functions were developed in response to the failure of MD5 and the supposed failure of SHA-1 [FIPS 180-1 (1995)], for which collisions were indeed found later, though with a more time-consuming algorithm. The SHA-2 family, as well as its predecessors, is built upon the Mercle–Damgård construction and has an increased length of hash values denoted by the extension to the word SHA (in bits). Currently, the SHA-2 hash functions are considered as secure, as only attacks on their weakened versions (with reduced numbers of rounds) are described in the literature. But the history of predecessors, which are based on similar constructions, has raised the question of whether we should create new algorithms which are able to ensure forward security for centuries.

In 2007 NIST launched an open competition for a new generation of hash functions known as SHA-3 — the NIST Hash Function Competition. Several dozens of development teams all over the world took part in the competition. After several rounds of selection, in 2012, a family of algorithms Keccak developed with a Belgian team was announced the winner. The family is based on the sponge construction. There are 6 variants of hash function in the SHA-3 standard: SHA3-224, SHA3-256, SHA3-284, SHA3-512, SHAKE128 and SHAKE256. In all the variants, the length of the sponge state is 1600 bits (in previous notation, $r + c = 1600$). The first four variants have the hash value length indicated by an extension to the word SHA3. The sponge capacity, as we have said above, must be twice the length of the hash value. From this condition, the values of r and c for all variants are easily obtained. For instance, for SHA3-224 we have $c = 2 \times 224 = 448$, $r = 1600 - 448 = 1152$. Note that r is always greater than the length of the hash value. This means that there are no iterations on the squeezing phase: the value of the hash function is taken from S^r with the truncation of excess bits. The last two algorithms allow for the generation of hash values of arbitrary length which is achieved by multiple sponge squeezing (several iterations in the squeezing phase). However the cryptographic security is determined not by the hash value length but by the capacity $c = 256$ in the case of SHAKE128 and $c = 512$ in the case of SHAKE256.

The next series of hash functions – RIPEMD, RIPEMD-160, RIPEMD-256 and RIPEMD-320 [Preneel *et al.* (1991); Dobbertin *et al.* (1996)] was developed by a team from the Catholic University of Leuven, Belgium, and is often regarded as an unofficial European standard as its development started in the framework of the RACE (Research in Advanced Communications in Europe) program. All the hash functions in this series are built upon the Mercle–Damgård construction. The first hash function of the series (RIPEMD) was successfully attacked together with MD5 [Wang *et al.* (2004)] and has gone out of use. The rest of the hash functions in the series are based on modified algorithms with increased lengths of hash values (that are indicated by the number in the name). These algorithms are considered secure, as only attacks on their weakened versions have been suggested.

The series is less popular than SHA but finds applications in some modern systems. For instance, RIPEMD-160 is used in Bitcoin (Chap. 9) for hashing public keys.

We should say some words about Russian hash function standards GOST R 34.11-94 [RFC 4491 (2006)] and GOST R 43.11.2012 (Streebog) [RFC 6986 (2013)]. These standards are obligatory for use in Russia. Both hash functions are built upon the Mercle–Damgård construction. The hash function GOST R 34.11-94 was developed by the Federal Agency of Government Communications and Information, Russia. As a compression function, the Magma cipher is used with the unspecified and freely chosen content of S-boxes. This hash function has been officially removed from use since 2013, when a new standard, GOST R 43.11.2012, was enacted. The new hash function, named Streebog after the Slavic god, was developed by the Federal Security Service of the Russian Federation, and involved the Infotecs company (recall that the same team are the developers of the new Russian cipher Kuznyechik). Streebog can produce hashes of two lengths, 256 and 512 bits, using the same algorithm. The compression function is ideologically close to the Kuznyechik cipher, in particular, it uses the same S-box to make a non-linear layer. As opposed to many of the hash functions described above, the Streebog algorithm was not created in response to open programs or competitions. Just after the announcement of its creation, the papers began to report about attacks on the algorithm. In response to these publications, Infotecs launched an open competition for the best attack against Streebog. The winner was proclaimed in 2015 to be the paper [Guo *et al.* (2014)] in which a second preimage attack (i.e. the attack breaking the third property of cryptographic hash functions, see the beginning of this section) was carried out that required 2^{266} invocations of the compression function for messages of more than 2^{259} blocks. It is clear that such a complexity makes the attack infeasible in practice, but, it is much less than an initially supposed complexity of about 2^{512} operations.

Similar to Streebog in construction, the Whirlpool hash function [Barreto and Rijmen (2008)] uses a modified version of the AES block cipher as the compression function. This hash function was developed by one of the authors of AES (Rijndael), V. Rijmen, and P. Barreto during the course of the research project NESSIE (New European Schemes for Signatures, Integrity and Encryption), which was carried out in 2000–2003 as a European alternative to AES. The Whirlpool hash function was recommended by NESSIE and entered the standard ISO/IEC 10118-3 mutually adopted by the International Organization for Standardization and the International

Electrotechnical Commission. The Whirlpool hash value length is 512 bits. No attacks against Whirlpool have been known to date.

Finally, we mention one more interesting hash function series – BLAKE and BLAKE2. These hash functions were developed by an international team of cryptographers. The BLAKE hash function [Aumasson *et al.* (2010)] took part in the SHA-3 competition and passed to the finals where it conceded to Keccak. Then a version that was optimized for speed was designed, called BLAKE2, [Aumasson *et al.* (2019)] which is employed nowadays. Hash functions of the BLAKE series are built upon another alternative construction HAIFA [Biham and Dunkelman (2007)] that involves a stream rather than a block cipher, namely, the ChaCha stream cipher [Bernstein (2008)]. The BLAKE2 family of hash functions, like SHA-3, provides different, sometimes arbitrary, hash lengths as well as implementation variants for processors with a word size from 8 to 64 bits, and affords parallel computation on multi-core processors. The authors position these hash functions as faster than MD5, SHA-1, SHA-2 and SHA-3 — for more information, visit the official site https://blake2.net. To this date no successful attacks have been published against the BLAKE hash function series. These hash functions are employed in numerous software solutions including the GNU projects, OpenSSL, WhatsApp and WinRAR.

We remark in the end that all cryptographic hash functions considered in our survey, except MD6, are not patented and are available for free use.

Chapter 9

Cryptocurrencies and the Blockchain

9.1 Introduction

In recent years, some cryptographic methods and the systems based thereon have found application in economics and financial markets, as well as society. We mark among them the blockchain technology and cryptocurrencies, as Bitcoin is truly famous all over the world.

The Bitcoin cryptocurrency uses some cryptographic techniques that are interesting as such. So, in this chapter, we first describe these techniques on their own and, in the last sections, show how they are employed in the construction of the Bitcoin cryptocurrency.

9.2 Proof-of-work and the Hashcash

Apparently, the first "proof of work" scheme was suggested in [Dwork and Naor (1993)] as a means for combating spam. Recall that spammers send out the same advertisement text to thousands or even millions of addresses, littering the post boxes of e-mail users.

Consider the interaction between a mail server and its clients who wish to send electronic letters. In [Dwork and Naor (1993)], a scheme was suggested in which every client who requests that the server send a letter has first to solve some computational problem (in other words, to do some work) which requires a certain amount of time (say, several seconds). The problem is chosen so as to make it easy for the server to check the results.

It is assumed that spending several seconds on solving a problem in order to send a letter will not complicate the life of an "honest" client, while it will be a severe barrier for the spammer who sends thousands of copies, as she has to solve a proof-of-work problem for every copy of a letter which she sends, and consequently the total time expended would be enormous.

Although this method of combating spam does not find any practical application, it has proven to be useful for constructing cryptocurrencies and solving some other problems, so there are various implementations nowadays. In this section, we consider in detail one such algorithm suggested in 2002 by A. Back [Back (2002)] and called "the Hashcash".

There are two participants in the Hashcash protocol, the server and the client. The client wishes to get some service from the server but the server, before providing the service, requires the client to solve a complex problem. (Example of such a service include sending an electronic letter, providing access to a database and so on). We assume that the client and server are connected by a computer network and are able to use a specific cryptographic hash function h. Proceed to the step-by-step description.

Step 1. The client tells the server that it wishes to get some service.

Step 2. The server generates a random word s and sends it to the client together with an integer number k. (In real working protocols, the length of s is several hundred bits and the length of k is several dozen bits).

Step 3 (client's "work"). The client finds a word x such that

$$h(s\|x)|_1^k = 00\ldots0, \tag{9.1}$$

where $w|_1^k$ denotes the first k bits of w, $a\|b$ being a concatenation of the words a and b, and $00\ldots0$ is a word of k zeros.

Step 4. The client sends the word x to the server. The server computes the value of $h(s\|x)$ and if the first k bits are zeros, provides the service to the client, otherwise finishes without the service.

Examine the properties of this protocol starting from the third step, which is the principal. The main question is how to find a word x satisfying (9.1). It turns out that for the "ideal" hash function there is no better approach than the sequential computation of values $h(s\|x_1)$, $h(s\|x_2)$, $h(s\|x_3), \ldots$, where $x_1, x_2, x_3, \ldots$ are randomly generated words (in practice, these could just be the sequential numbers $1, 2, 3, \ldots$).

In order to estimate the working time of the described protocol, we need the following proposition.

Proposition 9.1. *Let the probability of the occurrence of event A in a single experiment be p. Let the experiments be independent and repeat until* *the first occurrence of A, ν being a random variable equal to the number of such experiments. Then*

$$E(\nu) = 1/p, \tag{9.2}$$

$$P\{\nu \geq n\} = q^{n-1}, \tag{9.3}$$

where $E(\nu)$ is the expected value of ν, $q = 1 - p$, and n is an integer.

Proof. It is plain that $P\{\nu = n\} = pq^{n-1}$. (Indeed, $\nu = n$ if A does not occur $n - 1$ times, the probability of this being q^{n-1}, and then does occur, the probability of this being p). These probabilities set a so-called geometric distribution for which the expected value equals (9.2), see [Feller (1968)]. Equation (9.3) is derived from the chain of equalities

$$P\{\nu \geq n\} = p \sum_{i=n-1}^{\infty} q^i = pq^{n-1} \sum_{i=0}^{\infty} q^i = pq^{n-1}(1/(1-q)) = q^{n-1}.$$

(Here we used the formula for the sum of geometric series and the fact that $p + q = 1$.) □

Taking into account that $\lim_{p \to 0}(1 - p)^{1/p} = e^{-1}$, we may rewrite the result of Proposition 9.1 for small p in the form

$$P\{\nu \geq n\} \approx e^{-np}, \tag{9.4}$$

where $e = 2.71828\ldots$ is the Euler number.

Let us now return to the protocol under consideration and obtain a useful corollary.

Corollary 9.1. *Suppose that the search for x in Step 3 until the condition 9.1 is satisfied is carried out so that the condition is true with probability 2^{-k}. Then the average number of attempts to find the required x is equal to $1/2^{-k} = 2^k$ and the probability that more than $\lambda 2^k$ hash function evaluations will be needed equals approximately $e^{-\lambda}$.*

The proof follows from 9.2 and 9.4 when $p = 2^{-k}$.

The protocol described has many quite useful properties. First, the required amount of computations for solving the problem can be easily varied by changing the value of k since the average number of operations is proportional to 2^k, see Corollary 9.1.

Second, though we described the protocol in interactive form when the client and server exchange several messages, it can be easily made non-interactive. To do this, the server may require the client to execute Step 2 by itself, i.e. the client must generate both s and x (in this case the pair $s\|x$ can be generated as a single word u). The client, having found a value u such that $h(u)|_1^k = 00\ldots0$, can send it to the server to get the service. There is no need for a preliminary exchange.

There are, however, two easily surpassed obstacles. The client may try to use the word u several times once it is found. To avoid this, the server may store the list of words received earlier and check whether a newly received word is in the list. The service is granted only if u is distinct from all the words received earlier. Otherwise the service is denied.

Another similar obstacle is the attempt of the client to use the word u found for one server to get service from other servers. To rule this out the server may require that the client prepend the server name to the word u and ensure k initial bits in $h(\text{servername}\|u)$ be zeros. It is assumed that the server name is widely known, e.g. it is posted on its website. In this case the client will not be able to use the word servername$\|u$ for other servers.

At the end of this section, we consider one more scheme of proof-of-work that is widely used in practice. In the previous scheme, the complexity of the problem was determined by the number of initial bits in the hash value, and it was concluded that 2^k hash function evaluations should be made on average. As we mentioned above, sometimes the necessity of increasing the complexity arises, e.g. if more powerful computers come to the scene. The increase can be provided by the transition from k to $k+1$ which ensures the doubling of the average number of hash function evaluations up to 2^{k+1}. In some situations such an increase in complexity may appear too big and smoother growth may be desired. The method to do this is known and is also based on hash functions.

Consider a hash function h whose values are words of α bits. Notice that the values can be treated as integer numbers within the interval from 0 to $2^\alpha - 1$ (in contemporary hash function standards $\alpha = 256$ or 512 bits). Replace Step 3 in the protocol described above in the following way:

Step 3* (client's "work"). The client finds a word x such that

$$h(s\|x) \leq \Omega, \tag{9.5}$$

where the integer number Ω is a method parameter satisfying the inequalities $0 \leq \Omega \leq 2^\alpha - 1$. It is clear that under the random selection of the word $s\|x$ the probability of 9.5 being true is $\Omega/2^\alpha$ and, consequently, that this probability decreases per $1/2^\alpha$ as Ω is decremented by 1. If $\alpha = 256$ or 512 this value is small enough to provide very smooth changes of probability and hence the average number of hash function evaluations (i.e. the amount of work). Note that the first described system (with k zeros at the beginning of the hash value) is in fact a special case of the second one if we set $\Omega = 2^k$.

9.3 Time-Stamping of Documents

Various companies, organizations, banks, and even particular persons keep records that register their income and expenses. Before "paper-free" technologies appeared, such records were collected in so-called ledgers which were kept in such a way as to eliminate the possibility of replacement or substitution of already filed papers (e.g., the pages were flashed and sealed, stored in safes and so on). Note that the necessity to reliably store the records of some events arises not only in financial spheres but also for many other organizations, such as organizations registering marriages and divorces, organizations providing notarial services, hospitals that keep trace of medical history, patent offices, and others.

With the advent of the information era, records of successions of events have begun to be stored in computer databases. Organizing these databases in such a way that it became impossible to replace particular records became a task for specialists in information security.

One of the first solutions was suggested in the 1990s in the works of D. Bayer, S. Haber and W. S. Stornetta [Haber and Stornetta (1991); Bayer *et al.* (1993)] who considered the problem of time-stamping digital documents, i.e., marking the documents with the date of their creation. Time-stamping resembles the application of a stamp on an envelope at the post office to indicate the date it has been sent. We start this section by considering the problem of digital document time-stamping since it is of independent practical interest and has led to the discovery of new methods that are now used in many cryptographic systems.

Consider a community whose members are producing, from time to time, some documents $x_1, x_2, \ldots$, which are represented as digital files. For example, this could be a stock exchange with brokers and traders concluding sale contracts, or a counting house producing financial documents and so on. Our task is to construct a system in which every document is dated, i.e., marked with information about its time of creation, so that nobody can create a document "from the past", i.e., with the date marking that document corresponding to a time in the past.

First consider a solution involving a trusted third party (TTP) which is called a time-stamping authority (TSA) in this case. We assume that all the participants and the TSA can communicate over a computer network, they agree to use a hash function h, and the TSA has its own digital signature verifiable by any of the participants. (We studied digital signatures in detail in Chap. 4. Recall that to use digital signature, the TSA must have a pair of private and public keys. For signing messages, the private key is used. The public key must be known to all the participants so that any participant can verify the signature of the TSA applying this key.) Denote the TSA signature for document u by $\Sigma_{\text{TSA}}(u)$, then a signed document will be $u \| \Sigma_{\text{TSA}}(u)$.

Describe a time-stamping protocol. Let one of the participants, Alice, create a document x. Now she must time-stamp it. There are four steps:

Step 1. Alice computes the hash $h(x)$ and sends it to the TSA.

Step 2. The TSA, having received the hash $h(x)$, forms the word $h(x) \| t_x$, where t_x is the time (and date) of receiving x (say, formatted as YEAR: MONTH: DAY: HOUR: MINUTE: SECOND).

Step 3. The TSA signs the word $h(x) \| t_x$, i.e., computes a signature $\Sigma_{\text{TSA}}(h(x) \| t_x)$, and sends it to Alice together with t_x.

Step 4. Alice, having received the TSA signature and time (and date), forms a document with the time stamp $w(x) = x \| t_x \| y$ with $y = \Sigma_{\text{TSA}}(h(x) \| t_x)$.

Any participant, say, Bob, can verify the authenticity of the date in some document $w^\star = x^\star \| t_x^\star \| y^\star$. To do that Bob computes $h(x^\star)$ and verifies the signature by taking into account that $y^\star = \Sigma_{\text{TSA}}(h(x^\star) \| t_x^\star)$.

If the document passes the verification, Bob concludes that the document $x^\star$ was actually created at $t_x^\star$ time. Otherwise Bob concludes that the document was forged and (or) created after $t_x^\star$. This is justified by the following proposition.

Proposition 9.2. *In the system described, none of the participants can form a document at time T_1 with the date T_2 preceding T_1.*

Proof. Dates for each document are assigned by the TSA only, and the TSA does it honestly by definition. So the only way to attach a wrong date to a document is to do that without the TSA. But this is impossible because one needs to forge the TSA's signature.   □

So we have solved the problem of reliable time-stamping. The system constructed is quite simple and it finds application in practice. However the reliability of the system depends not only on the security of the cryptographic methods used (hash function, digital signature) but also on the honesty of the TSA. Therefore the natural question that arises is whether it is possible to construct a reliable time-stamping system which does not depend on the honesty of the TSA. A positive answer was given in the first works on time-stamping [Haber and Stornetta (1991); Bayer *et al.* (1993)], with two different methods being suggested. One of them relies on the ability to detect a dishonest TSA, thus ensuring that the TSA is honest. The other totally excludes the TSA.

In the following section, we consider a time-stamping system, suggested in [Haber and Stornetta (1991); Bayer *et al.* (1993)], in which the TSA cannot stamp a false time, i.e., it must be honest. It is worth noting that the idea of a chain of linked data (the blockchain) first appeared in that system and is now widely used in cryptocurrencies and many other applications.

9.4 The Blockchain

The technology described in this section has wide practical use. Consequently, major IT companies have developed specific applications which have been deployed by large banks and even the governments of some countries. We describe the construction of a blockchain as a result of the evolution of the time-stamping system. The resulting system will possess a unique property — nobody, including the TSA, will be able to alter any document. More precisely, such an attempt will be immediately discovered by all participants. Such a system would without a doubt be useful for ledgers maintained by banks or companies to register financial transactions, medical organizations which store the documents of patient treatment, and many other organizations.

So let Alice create a document x, which she wants to mark with a certified date. In the system considered, the time-stamping of the document will be done by the TSA who sends Alice a corresponding certificate. For example, the TSA is a bank, Alice is its client, who has a bank account, and the document is an order of payment for something. The bank stamps the document with the date of its execution.

The TSA assigns each document a serial number n so that it will be convenient to denote the nth client by ID_n (client's identifier) and the document by x_n. The sequence of actions is the following:

Step 1. Alice computes the hash $h(x)$ and tells the TSA about her wish to time-stamp the document.

Step 2. The TSA, upon the receipt of $h(x)$, assigns a serial number to the request (let it be n) and forms a certificate

$$C_n = (n, t_n, ID_n, y_n, L_n), s_n = \Sigma_{\text{TSA}}(C_n), \qquad (9.6)$$

where, as earlier, s_n is the TSA signature to C_n, t_n is the time (the date) of receipt of $h(x)$, $ID_n = $ Alice, $y_n = h(x)$, and L_n is a piece of linking information (a "link" for brevity):

$$L_n = (t_{n-1}, ID_{n-1}, y_{n-1}, h(L_{n-1})). \qquad (9.7)$$

After that the TSA waits for the next request, which is assigned the serial number $n + 1$, and sends Alice C_n, s_n and the name of the next client ID_{n+1}.

Step 3. Alice having received C_n, s_n, ID_{n+1}, can check the correctness of the time-stamping by verifying that the time (and date) t_n is correct, that y_n equals the $h(x)$ that she has sent, and that the TSA signature s_n is valid.

We remark that in this scheme all documents are linked in one chain in the order of their formation by the TSA via L_n: the nth document is tied to the $(n-1)$th.

Suppose now that Bob needs to verify the validity of the date on Alice's document x. He asks Alice for the certificate C_n, s_n and ID_{n+1}. First, he checks the signature of the TSA s_n. If the signature is not valid, he decides that the time stamp must have been forged. The validity of the signature would have been enough if Bob had trusted the TSA. But Bob assumes that both Alice and the TSA may be dishonest. For that reason Bob continues the examination. He computes $h(L_n) = h^*$ and asks for the certificate of the user ID_{n+1} who sends him C_{n+1}, s_{n+1} and ID_{n+2}. From C_{n+1} Bob finds L_{n+1} and hence $h(L_n)$, see (9.7). Now he can compare this value with the h^* computed earlier. If they are not equal then Alice and the TSA must have forged the date. Even if these values are equal Bob can carry out an additional check: by analogy with the previous check he can compute $h^*(L_{n+1})$, and ask for the certificate from ID_{n+2} who will send C_{n+2}, s_{n+2}, and ID_{n+3}. From these data Bob will find $h(L_{n+1})$ and compare it to $h^*(L_{n+1})$. If they match but Bob still has doubts he may similarly obtain and compare $h(L_{n+2})$ with $h^*(L_{n+2})$. If desired, he may proceed further along the chain of informationally-linked documents up to the last time-stamped document. This is important to note that by examining the chain of certificates Bob does not obtain information about the content of the time-stamped documents since the certificates contain only hashes (but not the documents).

So the described method of chaining documents via links (L_n) has the following property: if the ith certificate C_i is altered (corrupted, forged) then all subsequent certificates C_{i+1}, C_{i+2},... become invalid. This is because the link L_{i+1} is tied to the preceding link L_i, see (9.7).

Consider now two generalizations of the described scheme. First, we can create a certificate not only for one document, x_n, but for a group of documents combining in one block those received in some time interval (say, 10 minutes). In this case the certificate (9.6) shall contain several ID and their corresponding y supplied by a single L. It is natural to speak of these linked blocks as a "blockchain".

Another generalization comes from the replacement of the chain with a tree. Assume that the sequence of blocks (and corresponding certificates) grows as a binary tree so that some nodes have two children. Every block that corresponds to the child node is tied via the link (9.7) with the parent's node L but is not linked with the sibling. The trees with nodes linked via hash functions are called Merkle trees. In contrast to the system where all blocks are linked in a linear chain, the tree structure allows us not to have to examine all the data subsequent to the block under verification but to check only a piece of the tree descended from that block. There are situations when this contraction provides some computational gain, perhaps at the expense of reducing security — a short chain is easier to forge.

In the construction presented, altering one element implies that the certificates of all the subsequent blocks become invalid, which allows us to detect a corrupted block. If one wishes to conceal changes in a block, she must re-compute the certificates in all subsequent blocks. In order to make this task computationally hard, a Hashcash-like approach was suggested in [Nakamoto (2008)]. The idea is to change the linking information in (9.7) in the following way:

$$L_n = (t_{n-1}, ID_{n-1}, y_{n-1}, h(L_{n-1}), \text{nonce}_n), \qquad (9.8)$$

where nonce_n is a binary word that is chosen so as to make the first k bits of $h(L_n)$ equal to zero. In other words, we have used the Hashcash method to ensure that the average number of words to be tried until nonce_n is found equals 2^k. Now, after having altered the nth block in the chain, the adversary has to find nonce_{n+1}, nonce_{n+2}, nonce_{n+3} and so on till the end of the chain which requires a large amount of computation when k is big enough. This increases the reliability of the blockchain.

Presently, a number of blockchain implementations are known that differ in the rules of block formation and some other details. In the next section, we shall describe a variant of blockchain used in the cryptocurrency called Bitcoin. It is worth noting that its security has been proven both theoretically and practically, the Bitcoin system having successfully functioned since 2009.

9.5   Bitcoin and Cryptocurrencies

The Bitcoin cryptocurrency suggested in the seminal work of Satoshi Nakamoto [Nakamoto (2008)] in 2008 has quite interesting origins and has turned into a powerful payment system. In [Narayanan et al. (2016)] one can find a description of the history of the emerging ideas and constructions connected with cryptocurrencies.

In this book, we have already considered the problem of organizing anonymous payments over computer networks and presented a solution where even the bank itself has no knowledge of the destination of its client's payments. However, in that system, the client interests are not protected against any "incorrect" behavior of the bank. For example, the bank may go bankrupt and the client's assets will be lost. The central bank may mint money "out of thin air" thus devaluing the money, which decreases the client's real savings. (There are cases in the history of many countries when such minting took place and savings got lost due to inflation.) So the problem arises of constructing a payment system in which no participant can damage the interests of another (we speak, of course, about cash payments over computer networks and not about using gold coins or so). Such a system, called Bitcoin, was suggested in [Nakamoto (2008)] and realized in practice and the current section is devoted to its description.

Briefly, the Bitcoin system is a blockchain maintained by numerous participants. Physically, the participants are represented by the nodes of so-called peer-to-peer computer networks where each participant (peer) grants the others access to the stored data. All nodes have equal rights and there is no center of control. The blockchain can be seen as a ledger which stores information about the assets of participants and allows them to conduct mutual payments. Every participant stores a copy of the blockchain.

The currency that is used for payments has a unit called bitcoin with a minimal fraction of 10^{-8} bitcoin called Satoshi. Since the name of the whole system coincides with the name of a currency unit, to avoid ambiguity, we shall use the denomination BTC for bitcoin as a currency unit. The question of creating new coins (minting, or mining) will be discussed later on. Now we proceed to the system description mostly following [Nakamoto (2008)].

9.5.1 Transactions and Bitcoins

Every participant has a private and public key which we denote by skey_{name} and okey_{name}, respectively. All participants use the same digital signature method ECDSA and the same hash function SHA-256 (to be more exact, a so-called SHA-256d is computed by applying SHA-256 twice: first to the initial message and then to the hash value, i.e., given a message x we compute $h(h(x))$).

Payments are executed per transactions. Transactions, in the main part, are the records on transferring bitcoins from one participant to another (for buying some goods, services and so on). The recipient of the payment is identified by his public key. We show below that a bitcoin is determined as a sequence of digital signatures as it passes from one owner to another.

Some words about the anonymity of participants should be said. In fact, any one participant is only represented by his public key. Moreover, one physical person can be represented by several different public keys. But for the sake of convenience we shall use two names, Alice and Bob.

We now describe a transaction involving transferring money in the form of a protocol. Let Alice (the customer) wish to transfer 1 BTC to Bob (the vendor). Assume that Alice has obtained this bitcoin via transaction t_{n-1} where $n - 1$ is a serial number.

Step 1. Alice forms the following message:

$$u_n = (t_{n-1}, 1\text{BTC}, \text{okey}_{\text{Bob}}). \tag{9.9}$$

This message virtually means "take one bitcoin that I've received in transaction t_{n-1} and transfer it to Bob".

Step 2. Alice signs u_n using her private key $\text{skey}_{\text{Alice}}$ and forms a transaction

$$t_n = (u_n, s_n), \tag{9.10}$$

where s_n is Alice's signature to u_n.

Step 3. Alice sends t_n to Bob and the other participants of the network. (Further, after verification, t_n will be put in the ledger, see the next subsection).

Let us show how Bob (and any other participant) can verify the validity of t_n. He starts with a search of t_{n-1} (referenced by t_n, see (9.9)) in the common ledger and sees that 1 BTC was indeed transferred to Alice in t_{n-1}. After that he checks the signature in t_n using Alice's public key $okey_{Alice}$.

It is important that Alice alone can use the bitcoin transferred to her in transaction t_{n-1} since nobody else knows the secret key $skey_{Alice}$ required to generate a valid signature in t_n. Note also that Bob only uses public information (public keys and the common ledger) so any other participant can similarly verify the correctness of transaction t_n.

We can see that a coin in the system is in fact a chain of transactions t_1, $t_2, \ldots, t_n$ (the creation of the initial coin in t_1 will be explained below). We number only the transactions in which a particular coin is involved. Thus in between, e.g., t_2 and t_3, thousands of transactions with other coins may have been executed.

It is necessary to say that transactions with several senders (inputs) and/or receivers (outputs) are also possible. These transactions are used to exchange and consolidate coins. For example, 10 BTC gained in one transaction may be transferred to different addresses as 5 BTC, 3 BTC and 2 BTC in another transaction (in this case the latter transaction has 1 input and 3 outputs). Several payments gained in multiple transactions may be transferred to several addresses. For example, 3 BTC and 5 BTC may be transferred as 4 BTC, 2 BTC and 2 BTC (the transaction has 2 inputs and 3 outputs). For the transaction to be correct it is necessary that the sum of the input be not less than the sum of the output (i.e., money must not be created out of thin air).

Unfortunately, the verification considered is not sufficient to eliminate the possibility of fraud. Alice may attempt to deceive Bob in the following way: she may try to pay the same coin several times. We have seen how this problem is solved if there is a bank that keeps the serial numbers of all the used coins and checks if a coin has already been used. But there is no bank in Bitcoin. The problem of double spending is solved because the list of all transactions (i.e., a copy of the ledger) is stored by every participant. So any attempts at fraud will be seen by all and stopped.

Finally, note that the Bitcoin system is developing and changing. Its software is being updated and new proposals of improvement discussed (there is a series of design documents known as Bitcoin Improvement Proposals). There appear new types of transactions delivering new possibilities, in particular, increasing the level of anonymity. However all these transaction types have methods of validation close to the considered one.

We proceed now to a more detailed description of the ledger.

9.5.2 *Ledger Maintenance and Mining Bitcoins*

In the process of Bitcoin system functioning, new transactions are collected in blocks supplied with the time-stamping and proof-of-work facilities described in the previous sections, from which the blockchain is formed.

Let us look at the formation of new blocks in the blockchain in more detail. Every participant keeps a copy of the whole ledger (blockchain) and is able to form a new block on his own. To do this, he has to find such a nonce that the hash value does not exceed a certain threshold Ω, see (9.5), which, of course, requires computing power and takes some time.

A participant occupied with block formation is called a miner, and the process itself is mining. In order to make mining profitable, this work is paid for, first, by deductions from transactions collected in a block, and, second, by direct reward with an appropriate amount of bitcoins. The first transaction in a block generates bitcoins to reward the miner who creates that block.

So, in order to mint new coins, it is necessary to perform many computations which consumes technical resources and electricity. Here we can make an analogy to mining gold or silver for minting (physical) coins. The work of prospectors turns into money. Then it is natural to call miners those who create bitcoins and who receive bitcoins in return as payment for maintaining the blockchain. However, in Bitcoin, the process of minting new coins is limited: after the formation of every 210000 blocks the miner reward is halved. As the initial miner reward was 50 BTC per block, it became 25 BTC in 2012, 12.5 BTC in 2016, and 6.25 BTC nowadays. As the reward is being reduced in geometric series, the moment will occur when it becomes less than 1 Satoshi (10^{-8} BTC). At that moment, the creation of new coins will have stopped and the overall number of bitcoins will not exceed 21 million. Then the work of miners will be paid for by transaction fees only. A transaction fee is the difference between the amount of inputs and outputs. For example, if Alice wishes to pay 1 BTC to Bob, she may specify 1.001 BTC as the input and 1 BTC as the output. The difference of 0.001 BTC is a transaction fee and it will be earned by the miner who succeeds in creating the block that contains this transaction. (Notice that transaction fees are usual in ordinary banks.)

Having formed a new block, the miner sends it to all the Bitcoin network participants. Upon the receipt of the block every participants checks the condition

$$h(h(\text{block}\|\text{nonce})) \leq \Omega, \qquad (9.11)$$

where Ω is the variable that determines the amount of computations in the proof-of-work, see definition in (9.5) (here, as usually, the hash value is considered as a number). If the condition is not satisfied, the block is discarded. Otherwise, every participant verifies the validity of all the transactions contained in the block (as it is described in the previous subsection), as well as any attempts to double spend. If all is correct, the block is added to the blockchain. Every added block is linked with the previous block in the blockchain.

The blockchain in Bitcoin cannot have branches, i.e., it must be a chain, not a tree. But a situation in which the blockchain has branches is possible when different miners end up with creating blocks almost simultaneously. So there are two valid blocks but only one of them should be added to the blockchain. To resolve a collision, a so-called block complexity is used. Recall that for each block condition (9.11) is satisfied. A value

$$\alpha = 1/h(h(\text{block}\|\text{nonce}))$$

is said to be the block complexity (sometimes complexity is an increasing function of this value). The block complexity is closely related to the average number of nonces to be tried until one is found that satisfies (9.11).

So, let the miner receive two blocks B^1 and B^2 almost simultaneously. In this case he adds to the blockchain the block whose complexity is higher. Let it be B^1. However, if he later receives blocks that are linked to B^2 and the branch based on B^2 grows faster than that based on B^1, he discards the branch based on B^1 and continues with that based on B^2. The transactions contained in B^1 are not lost, they are included by miners in other blocks. But the payment to the miner for the creation of B^1 disappears and no extra coins emerge in the system.

Generally, the rule for branches may be the following. If we have two or more alternative branches, we may decide to continue the blockchain with the branch that has a maximal sum of block complexities.

9.5.3   *Stability of the Bitcoin System*

It is known that computing devices are developing quite rapidly. If some problem can be solved, say, in 10 minutes today, it is very likely that, in a year, a computer of the same class will solve this problem faster, say, in 7 minutes. In order to have the time taken to find a nonce (and hence the creation of a block) roughly constant independently of the progress in computers and the number of miners (who may join or leave deliberately), the Bitcoin system provides a mechanism for changing the complexity of block formation. This is done in the following way: after adding every 2016 blocks the average time of block creation is assessed. If the average time is less than 10 minutes, the value of Ω decreases and hence the complexity of block creation increases (i.e., the number of trials for finding an appropriate nonce increases since the average number of trials equals $1/\Omega$, see (9.5)). Due to this procedure the average time taken to create a block remains constant (10 minutes) despite more and more powerful computing facilities being involved in mining. A similar correction of Ω is performed if the average time of block creation becomes greater than 10 minutes (e.g., because the miners leave). Of course, in this case Ω is increased.

Another threat to the system is an adversary (Eve) who generates false blocks faster than honest miners do. If Eve succeeds in her attempts then the blockchain will grow with her blocks only and the blocks created by honest miners will not be added to the blockchain. It is only possible if the overall computing power of honest miners is less than Eve's computing power. In general, we may consider a case when Eve is not a single person but a large group of dishonest miners. In this case, the system will be resistant to the attack if the overall computing power of honest miners is greater than that of dishonest miners. Sometimes this condition is shortened: the system is secure if honest miners are more numerous than dishonest miners.

Chapter 10

Random Numbers in Cryptography

10.1 Introduction

We have seen in the previous chapters that random and pseudo-random numbers play an important role in cryptography. Actually, all cryptosystems that we have described rely on the random choice of the keys and various parameters. Recall also that the perfect secrecy of the one-time pad is based on the claim that the key sequence consists of equiprobable and independent bits. Finally, we have shown how pseudo-random sequences are used in stream ciphers to encrypt messages. It is natural then that the problem of generating random and pseudo-random numbers is of great interest to the designers of cryptosystems. Moreover, it occurs that many fundamental problems of cryptography are closely connected with generating and testing random numbers. For instance, the theoretical possibility to construct secure pseudo-random generators depends on the existence of one-way functions, and one of the attacks on block ciphers is based on statistical tests designed to detect deviations from randomness.

In this chapter, we shall consider some problems, ideas, and methods in cryptography connected with the generation and testing of random numbers. We begin with the main question: what is the random number or, more generally, the sequence of random numbers? One of the possible definitions is the following. This is a (binary) sequence obtained by fair coin tossing if the sides of the coin are marked by 0 and 1. More formally the random sequence may be defined as a sequence consisting of independent zeros and ones whose probabilities are equal. Sometimes such sequences are called *completely* random but we shall usually omit the adverb for brevity. Other random numbers, say, random integers from some interval, can easily be produced from binary random sequences and we shall not discuss this issue.

The next question is how to generate random numbers in a computing environment? It is clear that such "manual" methods as coin tossing and drawing cards can hardly be applied. What is really useful is digitizing the physical processes that are known to contain randomness. These may be noises in electrical circuits or electronic components (such as diodes), physical particle counters, or computer mouse motions. One of the main problems here is the conversion of physical measurements into completely random sequences of bits. This problem will be addressed in the next section.

Very often, we use pseudo-random numbers instead of random. We have already considered the problem of generating cryptographically secure pseudo-random sequences in Sec. 8.4. We shall return to this problem in Sec. 10.3 to discuss some extra issues.

The demands regarding the quality of random and pseudo-random numbers in cryptography are extremely high. First of all, any statistical deviations from the standard must be left out, i.e. zeros and ones must be equiprobable and independent. To detect the deviations, special statistical tests are used. The US National Institute of Standards and Technology (NIST) recommends 16 tests for use in cryptography [Rukhin *et al.* (2010)]. In Sec. 10.4 we shall consider some methods that outperform the NIST tests.

As we have noted in the beginning of the chapter, various branches of cryptography are usually connected but this is not always obvious. An example of such a connection will be given in the last section where we describe an attack on block ciphers that is closely connected with random numbers and statistical tests.

10.2   Refining Physical Random Number Generators

Assume that we have a physical generator that produces a sequence of random zeros and ones but the bits of the sequence are not equiprobable and/or exhibit some correlations. Our task is to convert this sequence into a completely random one. This conversion is often referred to as the *refinement* of the generator. There are two classes of refinement algorithms. The algorithms of the first class are built on the assumption that the source bits are independent but, perhaps, not equiprobable. The second class algorithms assume that bits may also be correlated (more exactly, that they may obey some correlation model). We shall consider only the first class algorithms.

The methods of the second class go beyond the scope of the book for two reasons: first, for many physical generators (e.g. based on noise diodes), the measurements made at distant time instances may be considered as independent; second, the methods eliminating dependences, as a rule, can do that only approximately (i.e. the resulting bits are only "almost" independent), their description is complicated and today they are rarely used in practice. But it is worth noting that there exist interesting and elegant methods in this field described in the literature on cryptography and computational complexity (see, e.g. [Nisan and Zuckerman (1996)] and the survey [Nisan and Ta-Shma (1999)]).

So, in the rest of the section, we consider the methods which refine the sequences of independent but not equiprobable zeros and ones.

The first algorithm for solving this problem was discovered by John von Neumann (see [Elias (1987)]). For a description of the algorithm, we introduce the necessary notation. Let a memoryless source be given generating letters over the alphabet $\{0, 1\}$ with probabilities $1 - p$ and p, respectively. The probability p may be unknown. It is necessary to convert the sequence generated by the source into a completely random sequence.

Von Neumann suggested the following method. The source sequence is split into 2-bit blocks that are encoded by the rule

$$00 \to \Lambda, \quad 01 \to 0, \quad 10 \to 1, \quad 11 \to \Lambda, \qquad (10.1)$$

where Λ denotes an empty word.

Consider an example. Let the source sequence be $\bar{m} = 1101110110$. We split it into 2-bit blocks (delimited by commas): $\bar{m} = 11, 01, 11, 01, 10$. Now we apply the mapping (10.1) and obtain a completely random sequence $\bar{z} = \Lambda, 0, \Lambda, 0, 1 = 001$. So, we have "extracted" 3 completely random bits from a 10-bit source sequence.

For justification of the method, notice that the probabilities of the blocks 01 and 10 are equal since they are $p(1 - p)$ and $(1 - p)p$, respectively. Therefore, the resulting sequence consists of equiprobable zeros and ones, as required.

The given example demonstrates the disadvantage of the method defined in (10.1): the resulting sequence is much shorter than the source one. More exactly, it is easy to see that given t source symbols we obtain $tp(1 - p)$ output bits on average. For example, if p is close to $1/2$ then we obtain, on average, about $t/4$ output bits.

Peter Elias refinement method suggested a conversion method which spends less source bits [Elias (1987)]. This is achieved by encoding blocks of length n, where $n > 2$ (if $n = 2$, the methods of Elias and von Neumann coincide). To measure the effectiveness of the algorithm, Elias introduced the quantity η_n, defined as the ratio of the mean length of the resulting codeword to the block length n. He showed that the natural upper bound for η_n is the source entropy $h(p)$. Recall from Sec. 7.4, Eq. (7.7), that in binary case, $h(p) = -(p \log p + (1 - p) \log(1 - p))$. (It is easy to understand why $h(p)$ is the maximum possible value for the ratio between the lengths of the output and input sequences. Informally, on the one hand, the entropy is a measure of the uncertainty or randomness of the input sequence. On the other hand, the entropy of the output completely random sequence is equal to its length, since the entropy of one completely random bit is 1.)

In fact, the idea of Elias's approach can be illustrated by one algorithm we have already discussed. Revert to the description of the ideal cipher construction in Sec. 7.8. There a message generated by a binary memoryless source with unknown statistics (i.e. our input to a refinement algorithm, in terms of the present section) was transformed into the sequence

$$u(\bar{m}_1)v(\bar{m}_1)w(\bar{m}_1)u(\bar{m}_2)v(\bar{m}_2)w(\bar{m}_2)\ldots$$

where $\bar{m}_i$, $i = 1, 2, \ldots$, denote the input blocks of n bits and $u(\cdot)$, $v(\cdot)$, $w(\cdot)$ some transformations, $w(\bar{m}_i)$ being completely random. Now the output of Elias's algorithm can be obtained by simply discarding the words $u(\bar{m}_i)$ and $v(\bar{m}_i)$, i.e. it will consist of concatenated words $w(\bar{m}_i)$. We may summarize that using this approach we gain the following refinement conversion of the source sequence:

$$\bar{m}_1\bar{m}_2\bar{m}_3 \ldots \longrightarrow w(\bar{m}_1)w(\bar{m}_2)w(\bar{m}_3)\ldots.$$

For example, let the same message as above be generated, $\bar{m} = 1101110110$. Split it into 5-bit blocks: $\bar{m} = 11011, 10110$, where $\bar{m}_1 = 11011$, $\bar{m}_2 = 10110$. Apply to these blocks the coding method described in Sec. 7.8 (with the obvious substitution of a_1 for 0 and a_2 for 1). We obtain $w(\bar{m}_1) = (10)_2$ and $w(\bar{m}_2) = (110)_2$, see p. 138. Hence, the source message $\bar{m}$ converts to the completely random sequence $w(\bar{m}_1)w(\bar{m}_2)$:

$$1101110110 \longrightarrow 10110.$$

So, we have extracted 5 completely random bits.

By Proposition 7.5 the average length of each word $w(\bar{m}_i)$ is greater than $nh(p) - 2\log(n+1)$. Hence we obtain the lower bound for η_n,

$$\eta_n > \frac{nh(p) - 2\log(n+1)}{n} = h(p) - \frac{2\log(n+1)}{n}.$$

It is clearly seen that if n increases, η_n approaches $h(p)$.

So, the Elias algorithm allows for the effectiveness η_n to approach the upper bound (Shannon entropy) if the block size n increases. But, at the same time, it requires the memory size to grow to 2^n which makes the algorithm intractable for large n. In [Ryabko and Matchikina (2000)], a significantly more efficient method was suggested, with the memory size growing to $n\log^2 n$. We refer the interested reader to the cited paper for more details.

10.3 Pseudo-Random Number Generators

In Sec. 8.4, we have already considered pseudo-random number generators used for constructing stream ciphers and discussed the requirements of cryptographically secure generators. In this section, we shall briefly touch on some additional issues.

First, we comment on the last two requirements given on page 172. They claim that (a) the determination of the next element of the sequence given the preceding elements should be an infeasible problem and (b) the sequence produced by the generator should be indistinguishable from a completely random sequence by any statistical test. It is clear that computational complexity here is crucial. For example, if we are not computationally bounded, then any pseudo-random generator can be predicted. Suppose we have a generated sequence $z_1, z_2, \ldots, z_i$ and wish to predict (to guess) the z_{i+1}. We know that the whole sequence depends on some initial (secret) state of the generator which can be represented as an integer s. We can try one value of s after another until such s is found that makes the generator produce exactly $z_1, z_2, \ldots, z_i$. Now knowing s we can easily compute z_{i+1}. If the length of s is $|s|$ bits, this approach requires about $2^{|s|}$ computations and is infeasible if $|s|$ is about 100 bits or greater.

The problem with practical pseudo-random generators, such as RC4, is that computational bounds for their security are not strictly determined mathematically. In the case of the block-cipher-based generators the computational bounds for their security is proved to be exponential if the underlying block cipher is "ideal". But, in turn, for practical block ciphers, the

correspondence to the "ideality" conditions is not proved. So, many inves-
tigators are engaged in searching for new algorithms of statistical testing
and prediction in the hope that they will find some breaches in the generators' constructions. Some recent results in the field will be presented in the
following sections.

However, there exists an elegant theory that allows one to connect
the above problem with other branches of cryptography and with complexity theory. A detailed exposition of this theory can be found, e.g. in
[Goldwasser and Bellare (2008)] but we shall only point out some basic
results. First, it is shown that pseudo-random number generators exist
which produce sequences indistinguishable from completely random ones by
any polynomial-time test. This means, in particular, that such sequences
can securely substitute for completely random sequences in polynomial-
time algorithms. Second, it is shown that both the requirements of generated sequences, marked (a) and (b) above, are equivalent if we deal with
polynomial-time algorithms. Third, a connection is established between
pseudo-random number generators and one-way functions which, in particular, allows us to construct "provably secure" generators based on one-way
functions. The quoted phrase here means that the proofs are valid under
certain conditions typical for complexity theory, e.g. are based on unproved
assumptions about the one-wayness of certain functions. We shall describe
one of such provably secure generators based on RSA.

The parameters of the RSA-based generator are two large primes P
and Q ($P \neq Q$), their product $N = PQ$, and a number $e \geq 3$ coprime to
$(P-1)(Q-1)$. The initial state x_0 is a randomly chosen number from the
interval $(1, N-1)$. The generator produces a sequence of bits $z_1, z_2, \ldots, z_k$
according to the following scheme:

$$x_i \leftarrow x_{i-1}^e \bmod N,$$

$$z_i \leftarrow \text{least significant bit of } x_i, \quad i = 1, 2, \ldots, k.$$

Note that the number e can be 3 which simplifies exponentiation.

The described generator is proved to be cryptographically secure under
the assumption that RSA cannot be broken. This generator is significantly
slower than the generators described in Sec. 8.4 and is therefore unsuitable
for stream ciphers. However, it may be used successfully in other tasks
where high security is paramount. For example, it may be used to generate
parameters for cryptographic protocols based on a relatively small random
number x_0. Other generators that make use of one-way functions may be

found in the literature, see, e.g. [Goldwasser and Bellare (2008); Menezes *et al.* (1996)].

10.4 Statistical Tests for Random and Pseudo-Random Number Generators

Random and pseudo-random numbers are widely used not only in cryptography but also in other fields such as computational mathematics, modeling and simulation. This highlights the problem of constructing efficient statistical tests aimed at detecting possible deviations from randomness. Thus the US National Institute of Standards and Technology (NIST) has carried out an investigation of known statistical tests for random and pseudo-random numbers. The results and recommendations for practical usage were published in 2001, the last revision being made in [Rukhin *et al.* (2010)]. Particularly, 16 methods were recommended for use in cryptography. It is important to note that these tests were selected as a result of a comprehensive theoretical and experimental analysis and may be considered as the state-of-the-art in randomness testing. In a series of works [Ryabko and Pestunov (2004); Ryabko *et al.* (2004); Ryabko and Monarev (2004)] a number of new tests were suggested. The performance of these tests was significantly greater than that of the NIST tests. In this section, we describe one of these new methods.

In a statistical test for randomness, we consider the main hypothesis H_0 that a bit sequence is generated by a memoryless source with equal probabilities of zeros and ones. Associated with this null hypothesis is the alternative hypothesis H_1 that the sequence is generated by a stationary ergodic source which differs from the source under H_0, $H_1 = \neg H_0$.

Let's describe the test suggested in [Ryabko and Pestunov (2004)]. In this test, the input sequence $x_1, x_2, \ldots, x_n$ is divided into subwords $x_1, x_2, \ldots, x_s$, $x_{s+1}, x_{s+2}, \ldots, x_{2s}$, $\ldots$, $s \geq 1$, and the hypothesis H_0^* that the subwords obey the uniform distribution (i.e. that each subword is generated with the probability 2^{-s}) is tested against $H_1^* = \neg H_0^*$. It is clear that H_0^* is true if H_0 is true. The key idea of the test is as follows. All subwords from the set $\{0, 1\}^s$ are ordered and this order changes after processing each subword $x_{js+1}, x_{js+2}, \ldots, x_{js+s}$, $j = 0, 1, \ldots$, in such a way that, loosely speaking, the more frequent subwords have small ordinals. Then the frequencies of different ordinals are estimated (instead of the frequencies of the subwords as, say, for a chi-square test [Kendall and Stuart (1961);

Knuth (1981)]). The test is based on the construction of adaptive code suggested in [Ryabko (1980)] and called *book stack*.

We shall consider the input sequence as generated by a source over the alphabet $A = \{a_1, \ldots, a_S\}$ (in practice, $S = 2^s$ but it is not necessary). Suppose we are given a sample $u_1, u_2, \ldots, u_n$ generated by the source.

In the book stack test, all letters from A are ordered from 1 to S and this order is changed after observing each letter u_t according to the formula

$$\nu^{t+1}(a) = \begin{cases} 1, & \text{if } u_t = a, \\ \nu^t(a) + 1, & \text{if } \nu^t(a) < \nu^t(u_t), \\ \nu^t(a), & \text{if } \nu^t(a) > \nu^t(u_t) \end{cases} \quad (10.2)$$

where ν^t is the order after observing $u_1, u_2, \ldots, u_t$, $t = 1, \ldots, n$, ν^1 being defined arbitrarily. (For example, we can define $\nu^1 = (a_1, \ldots, a_S)$.)

Let us explain informally (10.2). Suppose that the letters from A are arranged in a stack, like a stack of books, and $\nu^1(a)$ is the position of a in the stack. Let the first letter u_1 of the word $u_1, u_2, \ldots, u_n$ be a. If it occupies the i_1-th position in the stack ($\nu^1(a) = i_1$), then extract a out of the stack and push it to the top. (It means that the order is changed according to (10.2).) Repeat the procedure with the second letter u_2 and the stack obtained, etc.

It can help us to understand the main idea of the suggested method if we take into account that, if H_1 is true, the frequent letters from A (as frequently used books) will have relatively small ordinals (will spend more time near the top of the stack). On the other hand, if H_0 is true, the probability of finding each letter u_i at each position j is equal to $1/S$.

Let's continue the description of the test. The set of all indexes $\{1, \ldots, S\}$ is divided into the subsets where $r \geq 2$, and where the subsets are $A_1 = \{1, 2, \ldots, k_1\}$, $A_2 = \{k_1 + 1, \ldots, k_2\}, \ldots, A_r = \{k_{r-1} + 1, \ldots, k_r\}$. Then, using $u_1, u_2, \ldots, u_n$, we calculate how many $\nu^t(x_t)$, $t = 1, \ldots, n$, belong to a subset A_k, $k = 1, \ldots, r$. We denote this number by n_k. More formally,

$$n_k = |\{t : \nu^t(x_t) \in A_k, t = 1, \ldots, n\}|, \quad k = 1, \ldots, r.$$

Obviously, if H_0^* is true, the probability of the event $\nu^t(x_t) \in A_k$ is equal to $|A_j|/S$. Then, using the usual chi-square test, we test the hypothesis

$$\hat{H}_0 = P\{\nu^t(x_t) \in A_k\} = |A_j|/S$$

which is based on the empirical frequencies $n_1, \ldots, n_r$, against $\hat{H}_1 = \neg \hat{H}_0$. Let us recall that the value

$$x^2 = \sum_{i=1}^{r} \frac{(n_i - n(|A_i|/S))^2}{n(|A_i|/S)} \tag{10.3}$$

is computed, when the chi-square test is applied, see, e.g. [Kendall and Stuart (1961); Knuth (1981)]. It is known that x^2 asymptotically follows the chi-square distribution with $(k-1)$ degrees of freedom (χ^2_{k-1}) if $\hat{H}_0$ is true. If the level of significance (or a Type I error) of the chi-square test is α, where $0 < \alpha < 1$, the hypothesis $\hat{H}_0$ is accepted when x^2 from (10.3) is less than the $(1 - \alpha)$-value of the χ^2_{k-1} distribution.

We do not describe any rule for constructing the subsets $A_1, \ldots, A_r$, but recommend the implementation of some experiments for finding the parameters which make the sample size minimal (or, at least, acceptable). The point is that there are many cryptographic applications where it is possible to implement some experiments for optimizing the parameter values and, then, to test the hypothesis based on independent data. For example, in the case in which a pseudo-random number generator is tested it is possible to seek suitable parameters using a part of a generated sequence and then to test the generator using a new part of the sequence.

Let us consider an example. Let

$$A = \{a_1, \ldots, a_6\}, \quad u_1 \ldots u_8 = a_3 a_6 a_3 a_3 a_6 a_1 a_6 a_1,$$

$$r = 2, \quad A_1 = \{1, 2, 3\}, \quad A_2 = \{4, 5, 6\},$$

$$\nu^1 = (a_1, a_2, a_3, a_4, a_5, a_6).$$

Then

$$\nu^1 = (a_1, a_2, a_3, a_4, a_5, a_6), \quad n_1 = 0, \quad n_2 = 0;$$

$$\nu^2 = (a_3, a_1, a_2, a_4, a_5, a_6), \quad n_1 = 1;$$

$$\nu^3 = (a_6, a_3, a_1, a_2, a_4, a_5), \quad n_2 = 1;$$

$$\nu^4 = (a_3, a_6, a_1, a_2, a_4, a_5), \quad n_1 = 2;$$

$$\nu^5 = (a_3, a_6, a_1, a_2, a_4, a_5), \quad n_1 = 3;$$

$$\nu^6 = (a_6, a_3, a_1, a_2, a_4, a_5), \quad n_1 = 4;$$

$$\nu^7 = (a_1, a_6, a_3, a_2, a_4, a_5), \quad n_1 = 5;$$

$$\nu^8 = (a_6, a_1, a_3, a_2, a_4, a_5), \quad n_1 = 6;$$

$$\nu^9 = (a_1, a_6, a_3, a_2, a_4, a_5), \quad n_1 = 7.$$

We can see that the letters a_3 and a_6 are quite frequent and the book stack test indicates this non-uniformity quite well. Indeed, the average values of n_1 and n_2 are equal to 4, whereas the real values are 7 and 1, respectively.

Let us make two notes here. First, we pay attention to the complexity of this algorithm. The "naive" method of transformation according to (10.2) would take a number of operations proportional to S, but there exist algorithms which can perform all operations in (10.2) in $O(\log S)$ time. Such algorithms can be based on AVL trees, see, e.g. [Aho *et al.* (1976)]. Also, even faster methods may be connected with ideas of hashing to speed up computations. An efficient program implementation of the book stack test with 2 subsets ($r = 2$) based on hashing is due to Alexey Lubkin and is available at https://github.com/book-stack-test/bs.

The second comment concerns with the name of the method. The book stack structure is quite popular in information theory and computer science. In information theory, this structure was first suggested as the basis of a universal code in [Ryabko (1980)] and then rediscovered in [Bently *et al.* (1986)]. In the literature this code is frequently called the "move-to-front" (MTF) scheme as was suggested in [Bently *et al.* (1986)].

As we have already noted, in [Ryabko and Pestunov (2004); Ryabko and Monarev (2004)], the book stack test was compared to the NIST tests. The power of the book stack test was shown to be significantly greater than that of all 16 tests recommended by NIST; see the cited papers for details.

10.5   Distinguishing Attack on Stream Ciphers

We have mentioned in the sections devoted to stream ciphers and pseudo-random number generators (Secs. 8.4 and 10.3, respectively) that pseudo-random sequences generated therein must be statistically indistinguishable from the sequences of equiprobable and independent zeros and ones which we agreed to call "completely random". The distinguishing attack aims to detect deviations from randomness for generated sequences. If the deviation can be detected in a reasonable time, the corresponding generator or stream cipher is considered weak, unsuitable for cryptographic applications. Therefore all known and newly developed stream ciphers (or more precisely, the pseudo-random number generators they are based upon) are analyzed for deviation from randomness by means of various statistical tests.

In this section, we present the results of distinguishing attacks [Doroshenko *et al.* (2007)] carried out with the aid of the book stack test described in Sec. 10.4 against RC4 and ZK-Crypt stream ciphers. The RC4 cipher was discussed in Sec. 8.4. As for another cipher, ZK-Crypt, it was suggested as a participant of the ECRYPT Stream Cipher Project (eSTREAM), an open contest held by the European Union from 2004 to 2008 with the goal of identifying new stream ciphers suitable for widespread adoption [eSTREAM].

The key stream of the RC4 cipher was tested for randomness in the most popular mode of the cipher where the length of word was 8 bits. A collection of 100 randomly selected keys was used to generate bit sequences. The book stack test was used with the following parameters: a word size of 16 bits, two index subsets with the size of the upper part being 16 elements (in this case, the rest of the $2^{16} - 16$ elements are not to be stored in memory). Key-stream sequences of different lengths were generated for every key. Each sequence was tested with the level of significance $\alpha = 0.05$. This means that if the null hypothesis H_0 is true then, on average, only 5 sequences out of 100 may be declared non-random. The results obtained are given in Table 10.1. We can see that starting from the sequence length 2^{31} bits H_0 should be rejected, i.e. that the generated sequences were not completely random.

The key-stream sequences generated by ZK-Crypt were tested in a similar way but with different parameters of the book stack test: a word size of 32 bits, two index subsets with the size of the upper part being 2^{16} elements, a level of significance of $\alpha = 0.001$ (H_0 being true, on average, only 1 sequence out of 1000 may be declared non-random). The results obtained are given in Table 10.2. We can see that starting from the sequence length 2^{24} bits H_0 should be rejected since the generated sequences were far from random.

The results of tests sent to the eSTREAM committee became an important factor in the rejection of ZK-Crypt. In fairness, we should note that

Table 10.1   Testing RC4.

Key-stream length, bits	2^{31}	2^{32}	2^{33}	2^{34}	2^{35}	2^{36}	2^{37}	2^{38}	2^{39}
The number rejected	6	12	17	23	37	74	95	99	100

Table 10.2   Testing ZK-Crypt.

Key-stream length, bits	2^{24}	2^{26}	2^{28}	2^{30}
The number rejected	25	51	97	100

the attempts of the participants of the contest to find deviations from randomness with the aid of the book stack test as well as other tests (such as adaptive chi-square [Ryabko *et al.* (2004)]) developed by the authors of this book, in other stream ciphers, were not successful. In particular, no deviations were found in the ciphers selected as the winners, see [eSTREAM]. As for the RC4 stream cipher, it was broken in a number of other works, see, e.g., [Crowley (2003)], but there were considerably longer key-stream lengths of about 2^{55} bits which required the power of a supercomputer to crack them.

10.6   Statistical Attack on Block Ciphers

The cryptanalysis of block ciphers attracts much research, and new results in the field are always beneficial for improving the construction of the ciphers. Sometimes the complexity of a new attack (measured in the number of memory units and operations required for mounting such an attack) might be quite large. Nevertheless, even if a relatively small decrease in attack complexity is achieved, in comparison with previously known methods, this can motivate further development of the cipher design. Thus linear cryptanalysis of DES (see [Menezes *et al.* (1996)]) requires 2^{43} known plaintext–ciphertext pairs and is generally considered infeasible in practice. But it has made an important impact on the design principles of modern block ciphers, that are now resistant to this kind of attack. In this section, we describe a new attack on block ciphers, referred to as a "gradient statistical attack". This attack connects such different problems as randomness testing and block cipher cryptanalysis.

Consider a block cipher with the block length n, key length s, and encryption function $E(x, K)$, where $x \in \{0, 1\}^n$ denotes a plaintext block, and $K \in \{0, 1\}^s$ a secret key (we need to change the notation slightly as compared to Sec. 8.2). The typical values of n and s for modern block ciphers are $n = 64$ or $n = 128$, $s = 128$ bits or $s = 256$ bits (see Sec. 8.2). The majority of block ciphers are iterated, i.e. they involve many rounds of transformations usually bracketed by some prologue and epilogue. Either of these, in turn, can sometimes be divided into a number of more simple steps. In respect of this iterated structure, the secret key K is expanded into a sequence of subkeys or round keys $k_1, k_2, \ldots, k_t$, where t is the number of "simple steps" in a block cipher. Denote by x_0 the initial state of block x, and by x_i the state after the i-th step. So the complete encryption is $x_t = E(x_0, K)$ and this can be written as

$$x_1 = E_1(x_0, k_1), \quad \ldots, \quad x_t = E_t(x_{t-1}, k_t), \tag{10.4}$$

where E_i denotes the encrypting transformation at the i-th step.

The described attack belongs to a class of chosen-plaintext attacks. Upon starting that kind of attack, a cryptanalyst is able to input any information into the cipher and observe the corresponding output. Her aim is to recover the secret key or the round keys, which is almost the same. Such attacks are of practical interest and it is assumed that the block ciphers must be secure against them. We consider a chosen-plaintext attack for the cipher which can be represented by (10.4) with relatively small subkeys. Denote the lengths of the secret key and each subkey by $|K|$ and $|k|$, respectively. The exhaustive key-search requires $O(2^{|K|})$ operations (decrypt with $K = 0, 1, \ldots$ until a known x is obtained). Meanwhile, the described attack requires $O(mt2^{|k|})$ operations, where m is the number of ciphertext blocks sufficient for statistical analysis. The attack succeeds in finding the correct subkeys (instead of K itself), provided the statistical test is able to detect deviations from randomness in a sequence of m blocks. It is essential to use new efficient statistical tests like those presented in Sec. 10.4.

As we consider the block ciphers that can be described by (10.4), notice that the sequence corresponding to (10.4) for decryption is

$$x_{t-1} = D_t(x_t, k_t), \quad \ldots, \quad x_0 = D_1(x_1, k_1), \tag{10.5}$$

where D_i denotes the decrypting transformation inverse to E_i.

One of the requirements of a block cipher is that, given a sequence of different blocks as input, the cipher must output a sequence of bits that looks completely random (see CTR block cipher mode on page 174). We shall loosely call bit sequences "more random" or "less random" depending on how much they differ from a completely random sequence. One way to measure randomness is to use some statistic on the sequence with the property that less random sequences have greater statistics (to within some probability of error in decision). This may be a well-known x^2 statistic subjected to χ^2 distribution. Denote such a statistic by $\gamma(x)$, where x is a bit sequence.

Denote by $\alpha_1, \alpha_2, \ldots, \alpha_m$ a sequence of input blocks. Let all the blocks be non-random and pairwise different. A possible example would be $\alpha_1 = 1$, $\alpha_2 = 2, \ldots, \alpha_m = m$, where the numbers are written as n-bit words. For a good block cipher, the encrypted sequence

$$E(\alpha_1, K), \quad E(\alpha_2, K), \quad \ldots, \quad E(\alpha_m, K)$$

must look random, for any K. Now recall (10.4). Apply only one step of encryption to the input sequence, denoting the result by $\beta_1, \beta_2, \ldots, \beta_m$:

$$\beta_1 = E_1(\alpha_1, k_1), \quad \ldots, \quad \beta_m = E_1(\alpha_m, k_1).$$

We claim that the sequence β is more random than the sequence α, i.e. $\gamma(\beta) < \gamma(\alpha)$. After the second step of encryption, the sequence

$$E_2(\beta_1, k_2), \quad E_2(\beta_2, k_2), \quad \ldots, \quad E_2(\beta_m, k_2)$$

is more random than β, and so on. Each step of encryption increases the degree of randomness.

Notice the obvious consequence: in decryption according to (10.5), the randomness of the data decreases from step to step. For example, the sequence

$$D_1(\beta_1, k_1), \quad D_1(\beta_2, k_1), \quad \ldots, \quad D_1(\beta_m, k_1),$$

which is α, is less random than β. But here is what is important: this is true only if the decryption is done with the valid key. If the key is not valid, denote it by k_1', then the sequence

$$\alpha_1' = D_1(\beta_1, k_1'), \quad \ldots, \quad \alpha_m' = D_1(\beta_m, k_1')$$

will be *more* random than β, $\gamma(\alpha') < \gamma(\beta)$. This is because decrypting with a different key corresponds to further encrypting with that key, which is the well-known multiple encryption principle [Menezes *et al.* (1996)]. So, generally, decryption with an invalid round key increases randomness, while decryption with the valid round key decreases randomness. This difference can be detected by a statistical test.

The suggested gradient statistical attack is mounted as follows. First encrypt the sequence $\alpha_1, \alpha_2, \ldots, \alpha_m$, defined above. Denote the output sequence by ω,

$$\omega_1 = E(\alpha_1, K), \quad \ldots, \quad \omega_m = E(\alpha_m, K).$$

(Recall that the cipher involves t rounds or steps, and the length of subkey at each step is $|k|$.)

Now begin the main procedure of key search. For all $u \in \{0,1\}^{|k|}$ compute a sequence

$$\Gamma_t(u) = D_t(\omega_1, u), \quad D_t(\omega_2, u), \quad \ldots, \quad D_t(\omega_m, u)$$

and estimate its randomness, i.e. compute $\gamma(\Gamma_t(u))$. Find such u^* for which $\gamma(\Gamma_t(u^*))$ is maximal. Assume that the unknown subkey $k_t = u^*$. Note that the number of operations at this stage is proportional to $m2^{|k|}$.

After that, based upon the sequence $\Gamma_t(k_t)$, repeat the similar computations to find subkey k_{t-1}. Use $\Gamma_{t-1}(k_{t-1})$ to find k_{t-2}, and so on down to k_1. The total number of operations to recover all subkeys is proportional to $mt2^{|k|}$.

We have described the idea of the attack in a pure form. Now let's discuss some implementation variants.

(1) The measure of randomness γ is a parameter. One may apply different measures not only for different ciphers, but also for different rounds of the same cipher. As stated above, any statistical test applicable to checking the main hypothesis H_0 that the binary sequence is truly random, versus the opposite hypothesis H_1 that the sequence is not, may be used for that purpose.

(2) The sequence length m was chosen to be constant for simplicity of description. In fact, this length may vary in each round. More lengthy sequences are needed when a cipher's output becomes more random, i.e. in the last rounds. The value of m depends on the power of the statistical test and the cipher and can usually be determined experimentally.

(3) Some division of the encryption process into simple steps may result in a situation where, at a particular step, only part of the block is affected. This may reduce the effective length of the sequence to be tested.

(4) When searching for a relevant subkey, it is reasonable to keep not a single but several candidate subkeys, say, c different values of $u \in \{0,1\}^{|k|}$ for which $\gamma(\Gamma_j(u))$ is maximal. Besides, when searching for simple sequences and subkeys, the sequential methods, analogous to sequential criteria in statistics, are appropriate.

(5) The initial non-random sequence $\alpha_1, \alpha_2, \ldots, \alpha_m$ may be constructed in different ways. For example, it seems to make sense to choose the sequence in which consecutive words (α_i, α_{i+1}) not only contain many equal bits but differ in at most one bit (so-called Gray code). Other choices may reflect the peculiarities of a particular cipher.

(6) The last modification may be connected with the fact that many modern ciphers with a great number of rounds convert even absolutely

non-random input sequences into something "quite random" (at least not distinguishable from a truly random sequence by known tests in an acceptable time frame). Let, for instance, the cipher have r rounds and for some simple initial sequence $\alpha_1^0, \alpha_2^0, \ldots, \alpha_m^0$ the sequences

$$\alpha^1 = E_1(\alpha_1^0, k_1), \quad E_1(\alpha_2^0, k_1), \quad \ldots, \quad E_1(\alpha_m^0, k_1),$$

$$\alpha^2 = E_2(\alpha_1^1, k_2), \quad E_2(\alpha_2^1, k_2), \quad \ldots, \quad E_2(\alpha_m^1, k_2),$$

$$\ldots$$

$$\alpha^d = E_d(\alpha_1^{d-1}, k_d), \quad \ldots, \quad E_d(\alpha_m^{d-1}, k_d)$$

are not random under all subkeys $k_1, \ldots, k_d$, where $d < r$. Then the suggested attack may be modified in the following manner. For each set of subkeys $k_{d+1}, \ldots, k_r$ of rounds $d+1, \ldots, r$ apply the main procedure described above and find unknown subkeys $k_1, \ldots, k_d$. In other words, find subkeys $k_{d+1}, \ldots, k_r$ by exhaustive search, and $k_1, \ldots, k_d$ by the gradient statistical test. To maintain this combined attack, $O(m2^{(r-d)|k|}d2^{|k|})$ operations are required, which, depending on certain parameters, can be smaller than $O(2^{|K|})$ for exhaustive key search.

Let us describe a concrete application of the attack to one of the modern ciphers that belongs to the family of so-called lightweight block ciphers. In recent years, a large number of lightweight cryptographic algorithms have been proposed. They have been widely adopted for devices with low computing power. Examples of these highly constrained devices are RFID tags, sensors in wireless sensor networks, small Internet-enabled appliances in the Internet of Things (IoT), etc. Due to serious limitations on the computational resources of these devices, it is often impossible to use conventional cryptographic algorithms, such as standard block ciphers, so there is a need for developing lightweight algorithms that would meet those limitations.

We consider the CHAM 64/128 cipher with 64-bit block and 128-bit secret key. The number of rounds for CHAM 64/128 is 80, internal words and round keys are 16-bit. For detailed description of CHAM refer to [Koo *et al.* (2017)]. The cipher designers carried out investigations in which they showed the maximum number of rounds that are defeated by the most prominent attacks. For CHAM 64/128, the most successful are related-key boomerang attacks (56 rounds), related-key differential attacks (51 rounds), linear attacks (49 rounds) and related-key differential-linear attacks (51 rounds).

CHAM 64/128 is an iterated block cipher which means that we can apply the gradient statistical attack to a reduced number of rounds. Since the round key size is 16 bits, in order to find the correct round key, we need to decrypt the ciphertext one round lower, and analyze its randomness when there are 2^{16} possible round keys.

The input to the cipher was made of Gray code sequences of different lengths. We note that these input sequences are completely non-random: any two adjacent blocks differ in only one bit. Therefore the probability of distinguishing encrypted data from a random sequence increases significantly. For decryption, we used round keys of the form $000X$, where $0 \leq X \leq 15$ is called the rank. Of course, the round keys of that form are wrong in most cases, and decrypting with those keys increases the randomness in comparison with decrypting with the right key. However, for CHAM 64/128, we show experimentally that the key with only 4 bits correct provides less randomness than other keys of that rank (the ranks of other sizes were less "distinguishing" in our experiments). We did 1000 independent tests for 1000 randomly selected 16-bit keys. Obviously the probability of finding the round key with correct rank X is $P_{000X} = Q_{000X}/1000$, where Q is the number of cases in which the randomness of a sequence decrypted using a round key with correct rank X is the smallest. A similar pattern was found for round keys of the form $00X0$, $0X00$ and $X000$, where $0 \leq X \leq 15$. Notice that all these patterns are independent.

As an example, Table 10.3 shows the probabilities of finding a round key with correct rank X for the 13th round, S being the length of the sequence (in bytes).

We note that the book stack parameters w, u are different. The set of optimal parameters for the test essentially depends on the sequence size, number of rounds and type of round key, and we have to select it experimentally for each case. Note also, that if we increase the length of the analyzed sample, the probability of finding the correct rank X also increases (compare the values of P for $S = 2^{20}$ and $S = 2^{26}$).

Denote by P_{000X}, P_{00X0}, P_{0X00}, P_{X000} the probabilities of finding a round key with correct rank X. In order to calculate the

Table 10.3 The probabilities of finding the correct rank X for 13th round.

	$000X$	$00X0$	$0X00$	$X000$	$000X$	$00X0$	$0X00$	$X000$
w	16	8	8	8	4	4	8	8
u	28672	17	153	89	13	14	169	57
$P = Q/N$	0.8	0.99	0.788	0.92	1	1	0.9	1
S	2^{20}	2^{20}	2^{20}	2^{20}	2^{26}	2^{26}	2^{26}	2^{26}

Table 10.4   The probabilities of finding a round key for 10 to 21 rounds, if the sample size is 2^{24} bytes.

Round	10	11	$\cdots$	15	16	17	18	19	20	21
Prob.	1	0.93		0.51	0.84	0.71	0.66	0.21	0.68	0.41

Table 10.5   The probabilities of finding a round key for 10 to 21 rounds, if the sample size is 2^{29} bytes.

Round	10	11	$\cdots$	15	16	17	18	19	20	21
Prob.	1	0.96		0.67	0.89	0.87	0.86	0.37	0.76	0.61

probability of finding the correct round key we multiply them: $P_i = P_{000X} P_{00X0} P_{0X00} P_{X000}$. As a result, we find the correct round key with probability P_i by searching not through 2^{16} candidate keys but only through $4 \times 2^4 = 2^6$.

Similar calculations were performed for other rounds.

Table 10.4 shows the probability of finding a correct round key for 10 to 21 rounds if the sample size is $S = 2^{24}$ bytes.

Table 10.5 shows the probability of finding a correct round key for 10 to 21 rounds if the sample size is $S = 2^{29}$ bytes.

It was experimentally verified that the probability of finding a round key does not depend on other rounds. Thus, the probability to find all the round keys is

$$P_{\mathrm{RK}} = \prod_{i=1}^{r} P_i,$$

where P_i is the probability of finding a correct round key on the ith round.

In Table 10.6 we present the number of rounds after which the probability of finding all the round keys was 0.01, 0.05 and 0.1, and the minimum length (in bytes) of input sequence required for the search.

From Table 10.6 we can see that the maximum number of rounds after which the probability of finding all the round keys is more than 0.01 is 23.

Let us estimate the complexity of the attack for 23 rounds. The length of the input sample is 2^{31}. The empirical estimation of the book stack test complexity is:

$$T_{\mathrm{bookstack}} = CS, \tag{10.6}$$

where S is the length of the input sample (in bytes) and C is a constant which depends on the hardware parameters and book stack parameters w, u.

Table 10.6 The number of rounds and sample lengths after which the probability of finding all the round keys is 0.01, 0.05 and 0.1.

Round	$P = 0.01$ Length	$P = 0.05$ Length	$P = 0.1$ Length
12	2^{17}	2^{19}	2^{20}
13	2^{18}	2^{20}	2^{22}
14	2^{18}	2^{20}	2^{22}
15	2^{20}	2^{23}	2^{24}
16	2^{21}	2^{23}	2^{25}
17	2^{22}	2^{24}	2^{27}
18	2^{23}	2^{26}	2^{27}
19	2^{25}	2^{28}	2^{30}
20	2^{26}	2^{29}	no data
21	2^{27}	2^{32}	no data
22	2^{28}	no data	no data
23	2^{31}	no data	no data

According to (10.6) the complexity of attack

$$T = CS_r \times 2^6,$$

where S_r is the length of the input sample on the last round, and 2^6 is the number of round key iterations. So, the complexity of the attack for 23 rounds is $T = 2^{31} \times 2^6 = 2^{37}$.

If we increase the computational power, the number of rounds will grow. In order to estimate it, we extrapolate the theoretical length of the ciphertext required for a successful gradient statistical attack on later rounds for CHAM 64/128, by prediction for the case where the probability of finding all the round keys is 0.01. Denote by $\hat{S}_r$ an estimate of the sample length required to attack the cipher on round r. According to the recommendations of classical textbooks [Kendall and Stuart (1961); Förster and Rönz (1979)], the prediction and confidence intervals are constructed as follows:

$$\log_2 \hat{S}_r = ar^2 + br + c. \tag{10.7}$$

The parameters of the Eq. (10.7) are found by the ordinary least squares method (OLS) based on the data provided in Table 10.6 for $P = 0.01$. The regression Eq. (10.7) looks like

$$\log_2 \hat{S}_r = 0.036r^2 - 0.035r + 12.169.$$

Next, we find the confidence intervals for the predicted values.

Table 10.7   CHAM 64/128: Estimated number of
rounds and the minimum sample length for which
the gradient statistical attack is possible.

Round	Length	Complexity
25	$2^{32.5} \ldots 2^{35.1}$	$2^{38.5} \ldots 2^{41.1}$
35	$2^{53.1} \ldots 2^{57.0}$	$2^{59.1} \ldots 2^{63.0}$
50	$2^{97.3} \ldots 2^{107.6}$	$2^{103.3} \ldots 2^{113.6}$
55	$2^{115.6} \ldots 2^{122.7}$	$2^{121.6} \ldots 2^{128.7}$
56	$2^{119.4} \ldots 2^{126.8}$	$2^{125.4} \ldots 2^{132.8}$
57	$2^{123.4} \ldots 2^{130.9}$	$2^{129.4} \ldots 2^{136.9}$
58	$2^{127.4} \ldots 2^{135.1}$	$2^{133.4} \ldots 2^{141.1}$

The computed predicted results for later rounds of the CHAM 64/128
are shown in Table 10.7. We present the dependences of the sample size
and attack complexity on the number of rounds for which the probability
of finding round keys is equal to 0.01. Note that if we find the secret key
faster than the direct exhaustive key search, the attack is of interest to
cryptologists. Thus we considered the gradient statistical attack complexity
to be less than 2^{128}.

Our extrapolation for CHAM 64/128 shows that the gradient statistical
attack is possible for 57 rounds (the total number of rounds is 80) with
complexity lying in the confidence interval $2^{129.4} \ldots 2^{136.9}$ with probability
0.95. The probability of finding all the round keys is 0.01.

Note that the complexity of the gradient statistical attack shown above
may be lower than or commensurate with that of exhaustive key search.
Indeed, when searching keys, we first need to expand each key into round
keys, which is equivalent to 8 round function evaluations for CHAM 64/128,
then apply 57 rounds to obtain the ciphertext. Taking into account that
the total number of keys is equal to 2^{128} and that the probability of success
is the same at 0.01, we have $2^{128} \times 8 \times 57 \times 0.01 \approx 2^{130.2}$ round function
evaluations needed for an exhaustive key search attack. That is why we
stop at 57 rounds.

The other remark is connected with the complexity of a so-called dictionary attack, in which we compute a full dictionary containing all possible
plaintext–ciphertext pairs. The total number of such pairs caused by the
block size is 2^{64}. It may seem that the dictionary attack has less complexity than the suggested gradient statistical attack. However, to maintain
the dictionary attack one needs all the memory at once, which is currently, and in the near future, intractable for 2^{64} plaintext–ciphertext pairs.

Meanwhile, the time complexity of about 2^{130} is more tractable since one may start the attack right now and go ahead year after year with more and more powerful computational facilities. The space complexity of the gradient statistical attack is determined by the necessity of storing the upper part of the stack in the book stack test (parameter u in Table 10.3), which is quite small compared to the sample size.

So we conclude that the gradient statistical attack is the most effective attack on the cipher CHAM 64/128 at the moment of its publication.

Chapter 11

Steganography

11.1 Purpose of Steganography

Steganography is a science studying the methods of transmitting messages in such a way that the very fact of transmission is concealed from any observer. The alternative term for steganography used widely in the literature is "data hiding". The demand for covert data transmission distinguishes steganography from cryptography where the fact of the transmission of a secret (encrypted) message is known and not concealed from Eve. Note that this distinction is quite essential: in some cases, the very fact of secret message exchange may be considered as a proof of illegal activity or, at least, it raises suspicions. It is generally assumed that cryptography has emerged together with writing and cannot exist without it. In its turn, steganography may have emerged long before writing and, judging by works of fiction, may have been used for centuries by people unaware of writing. An example of such a stegosystem is the presence or absence of flowers on Alice's window sill which tells Bob about the possibility or impossibility of their rendezvous (we shall still call the participants exchanging messages Alice and Bob and the observer Eve).

The interesting fact of a real application of steganography is described in [Kahn (1967)]. During World War II a German spy communicated the following message from New York: "Apparently neutral's protest is thoroughly discounted and ignored. Isman hard hit. Blockade issue affects pretext for embargo on by-products, ejecting suets and vegetable oils". It is proposed in [Kahn (1967)] that this message looks completely innocuous, however, if we take the second letter of each word, we obtain the "spy" text: "Pershing sails from NY June I".

In steganography, the first text is called a covertext (simply "cover", or, depending on its nature, coverimage, coveraudio etc). The second text is called an embedded message (or hidden message, hidden data, hidden information).

Another well-known example of steganography application is an acrostic. Thus in the poem "Georgiana Augusta Keats" by John Keats

> Kind sister! aye, this third name says you are;
> Enchanted has it been the Lord knows where;
> And may it taste to you like good old wine,
> Take you to real happiness and give
> Sons, daughters and a home like honied hive.

the sequence of the first letters of the lines is read as KEATS.

Acrostics and other similar methods of embedding hidden information have been quite popular for centuries. It is believed that Epicharmus, a Greek dramatist and philosopher who lived in Syracuse in the fifth century BC, was an inventor of acrostics. He used acrostics for copyright protection by hiding his name in the texts he had written. Though various steganographic methods were discovered and used before our era in China, Greece and Rome, a real flourishing of this art occurred in the Middle Ages in Europe. At that time methods were invented to embed hidden messages in musical compositions, paintings, miscellaneous forms of text, etc. Many technical facilities, such as invisible ink were suggested, and several books devoted to steganography were published. Great attention were also paid to an antipodal science — steganalysis — which aims to detect the presence of hidden information. A detailed and interesting survey of steganography achievements in the "pre-information" era is presented in the paper [Petitcolas *et al.* (1999)] whose authors think it valuable for modern stegosystem designers to be acquainted with the history of invention and the "crash" of information hiding methods.

Further on, we shall consider a traditional scheme of steganography application where it is assumed that Alice sends Bob an innocuous message containing a hidden secret text. But all the methods considered are also applicable in the situation when Alice does not send anything and just exhibits some files so that anyone, including Bob, can see and read them. For instance, Alice posts a comment on an article on an Internet site and Bob, as a user of this site, browses this comment and extracts hidden information. Of course, Alice and Bob must agree in advance which Internet site, embedding method and key to properly extract hidden messages are to be used (in particular, which features will allow Bob to discern Alice's comments). In this case not only is the secret message concealed from Eve, but Eve does not even know that Alice is communicating with Bob (recall the example with the flowers on the window sill). It has been mentioned in the mass media that some terrorist groups have used this scheme to coordinate their actions.

Nowadays the methods of embedding hidden information are in the center of attraction for many researchers and engineers. Numerous conferences on information security are held with many talks devoted to steganography and steganalysis, and international scientific journals are issued where papers on covert data transmission and its applications are published. Among various survey papers and monographs on steganography we mark the works [Petitcolas *et al.* (1999); Katzenbeisser and Petitcolas (eds.) (1999); Kipper (2003); Cox *et al.* (2007); Shih (2017); Yahya (2018)] that can supplement this chapter. In addition there are computer programs freely available via the Internet for embedding hidden information, as well as for its detection, targeted for various types of data (digital images, movies, audio, texts etc).

Consider now the main fields of application of data hiding methods. The most obvious usage of data embedding is the covert transmission of information from Alice to Bob (sometimes it is this field that is called "steganography" whereas the other fields are referred to as "data hiding" or "data embedding"). The Internet is the main media for the implementation of such kinds of covert transmission.

The other, perhaps most widespread application of data hiding, is copyright protection. Like Epicharmus Syracusanus, the authors and owners of digital images, films, musical compositions and even computer programs (which we will generally refer to as digital objects) embed hidden data in those objects in the form of digital watermarks or fingerprints. A digital watermark is one and the same for all copies (like the watermark on banknotes of the same denomination). A watermark must possess the following property: it cannot be deleted without severe damage of the digital object it is embedded in. The purpose of watermarks has not changed from Epicharmus's time — when necessary, one can prove his/her authorship or ownership, say, in the court. As for digital fingerprints, they are different in every copy: they serve as identifiers of particular copies of digital object. The main purpose of fingerprints is for protection against unauthorized copying. Let us explain it with an example. Let the owner of a digital film sell the copies to different movie theaters with the rights to show the film at these theaters only. The owner of the digital film embeds a unique fingerprint in each copy. Then if one of the theaters illegally resells the film to some other theater, the illegally-sold film can be traced from its copy and the sellers brought to trial. A specific demand usually imposed on the fingerprint is that it must withstand the so-called coalition attack. Several purchasers can compare the digital content of their copies and reveal the places where fingerprint embedding occurs. Then they will be able to change the fingerprint in hope of concealing their identities while illegally reselling the copyrighted object. To prevent this kind of action the fingerprint must be designed so that any coalition, up to a specified size, is able to get only partial information about the fingerprint, and the remaining partial fingerprint is sufficient to trace at least one of the coalition members.

The third field of application of hidden data embedding methods is checking the integrity of digital documents or, more generally, the integrity of various digital objects. As a simple example, we may consider a file, which is a digital medium for some document, that contains a hidden digital mark representing, say, the value of the hash function of the document text. Then if some intruder changes a fragment of the document, the new hash function value will differ from the previous one. But this previous value is hidden in the file and the intruder does not know how and where it is hidden and thus cannot replace it with the new value. So the document modification will be detected by its creator or any other entity who knows the key for the hidden mark extraction.

Some other fields of application of data embedding methods can be found in the literature, but they are in essence close to the three mentioned above. For instance, it is reasonable to covertly store the names of patients in a medical history database. This refers also to any databases containing personal information of any type. It is believed that storing sensible data not just in encrypted form but also in a hidden way ensures greater security in some cases.

Consider in more detail certain kinds of attack on a stegosystem. We assume that Alice and Bob possess a secret key and are able to exchange innocuous messages (digital images, audio, video, e-mails etc). Eve may be interested in solving a number of different tasks and thus may launch the corresponding attacks on the stegosystem of Alice and Bob.

First, Eve may be interested in whether the messages communicated between Alice and Bob contain embedded secret information. This is the objective of steganalysis. To answer this question Eve can use various methods, some of which may be based just on common sense, while the others may rely on more formal constructions requiring computer-aided processing such as statistical analysis, hypothesis checking, neural networks, spectral analysis and so on.

Second, Eve may attempt to change the communicated data in order to destroy any hidden information within. For instance, let Alice send Bob a JPEG image which, perhaps, contains some hidden information. Eve can squeeze the image, with a certain loss of quality, and then reestablish the initial size. Under such a transformation, some fine details may disappear or be distorted which will probably destroy the hidden information that could have been present. In other words, Eve transforms the communicated covertext so that, on the one hand, she does not damage it noticeably and, on the other hand, she seriously distorts the anticipated hidden information. Such attacks are often developed for destroying watermarks and fingerprints.

In the third type of attack, Eve just substitutes messages sent by Alice with some other similar messages. For example, if Alice sends images of buildings of the city she lives in, Eve substitutes them with images made on her own in the same place with a similar camera. In this case Bob may not be able to detect the substitution and will be misled.

Yet other types of attack can be devised by Eve, including a previously described coalition attack, and so on.

It is natural to assume that robustness with respect to various kinds of attack is the main feature of steganographic systems. Another important question is the speed of covert data transmission which can be measured in the number of bits per a time unit, or as a ratio between the lengths of a hidden message and the covertext it is contained in (this characteristic is usually called the embedding rate). In this chapter, we consider basic methods of data embedding paying attention mainly to robustness with respect to an attack aimed at detecting the fact of hidden data presence.

It occurs that if the covertext is a sequence of independent symbols, a simply realizable perfect stegosystem can be constructed, i.e. a system which ensures that the presence of hidden data cannot be detected in principle. Such systems and their generalizations in cases when covertexts are generated by more complex sources, sources with finite memory, will be considered in Sec. 11.4.

But such covertexts as digital images, voice messages and many other "natural" digital objects have quite complex statistical structures. It can be said that, in a sense, the symbols that form such objects are generated by a source with very large or even infinite memory. Here even small distortions introduced to embed hidden data change the statistical structure of the covertext which is the leverage for steganalysis methods. So the problem of how to embed maximum possible information under a specified level of distortion arises. The methods of solving this problem will be considered in Sec. 11.3.

11.2   Basic Methods of Data Embedding

We begin with one of the oldest and most widespread steganographic methods called "LSB replacement". According to its name embedding is performed by replacing the least significant bits of covertext with the bits of data that are meant to be hidden. This method is used now to hide information in digital images, audio and video, but, as many other algorithms in steganography, it emerged in the Middle Ages. Before the advent of computers, tables of logarithms and other mathematical functions had been used for computations. These tables contained thousands of values of, say, decimal logarithms and were printed as booklets. The computation of tabular values was highly labor- and time-consuming which determined the high price of the booklets and the great importance of their copyright protection. It is because an adversary could easily copy the tables and sell them at reduced prices thus making the author bear a loss. To protect their rights, the authors of tables introduced small distortions (errors) by replacing the last digit in a logarithm value with an incorrect one (e.g. the value 0.2284938 could be replaced with 0.2284939). The changes were made to different values in different copies of the tables, so if a purchaser of a copy started reprinting and reselling it, the legal owner of the tables could trace the adversary from any "pirated" copy and bring him to court. To prove the authorship in court, it was sufficient for the legal owner to show the true values and introduced errors.

In the graphic format BMP, the audio format WAW, and many other formats, data samples are represented as binary numbers recorded by words of a certain length, usually a multiple of a byte. If secret data are embedded through LSB replacement, the quality of the content, say, the picture, does not change in a way that is perceptible to the human eye. However, if all of sufficiently many samples are touched, contemporary methods of staganalysis may detect the presence of hidden data. Therefore, usually only a small fraction of samples are used for embedding, selected by means of a pseudorandom number generator controlled by a key known to Alice and Bob.

Another widely used LSB method called "LSB matching" was described in [Ker and Lubenko (2009)]. The distinctive features of this method are, first, random selection in encoding and, second, the usage of the ordinary operation of adding numbers with carry propagation. To describe the method, we assume for certainty that each value is represented by a byte (a string of 8 bits) and denote the ith byte by x_i, its least significant bit by $\mathrm{LSB}(x_i)$, the bit to be embedded by m_i (its value is either 0 or 1) and a random number taking on values -1 and $+1$ with equal probabilities by r_i. Then the LSB matching is defined by the following equation:

$$\bar{x}_i = \begin{cases} x_i, & \text{if } \mathrm{LSB}(x_i) = m_i \\ x_i + r_i, & \text{if } \mathrm{LSB}(x_i) \neq m_i, \quad x_i \neq 0, \quad x_i \neq 255 \\ x_i + 1, & \text{if } \mathrm{LSB}(x_i) \neq m_i, \quad x_i = 0 \\ x_i - 1, & \text{if } \mathrm{LSB}(x_i) \neq m_i, \quad x_i = 255 \end{cases}$$

Here $\bar{x}_i$ is the byte value after embedding, and the last two lines are devoted to the rare cases where x_i takes the minimum or maximum value. Notice that the least significant bit of $\bar{x}_i$ is equal to the embedded bit m_i.

The LSB methods can also be used to embed hidden data in the covertexts where information is presented as arrays of coefficients obtained from the decomposition of signals over the set of orthogonal functions. These formats include JPEG images and MP3 audio. There are many program implementations available, their description may be found, e.g. in [Cox *et al.* (2007); Yahya (2018)]. The idea is quite simple: embedded data are stored in the least significant bits of decomposition coefficients because changes in these bits make only minor distortions and therefore they are difficult to detect. Some properties of cover data representations are taken into account. For example, for images, it is known that decomposition via discrete Fourier transform ensures that distortions in high-frequency harmonics are less perceptible, so low-frequency coefficients are not used for data embedding.

Quite different types of covertext are represented by texts in natural languages. Here LSB embedding does not work but many specific methods are described in the literature. We just present a couple of ideas which may be used. The first method is based on the selection of synonyms or, more generally, interchangeable words that do not considerably distort the purport of the text. For example, let Alice and Bob agree on the following pairs of interchangeable words: "green–red", "pen–pencil", "lay–lies" and "desk–table", where the choice of the first word in a pair encodes 0 and the choice of the second encodes 1. Then the binary message 0000 can be hidden in a sentence like "A green pen lay on the desk", while 1111 can be hidden in "A red pencil lies on the table". The reader can easily verify that all other 4-bit messages can be embedded in this way producing correct sentences.

The second approach utilizes algorithms for the automatic generation of texts in natural languages. The input to the generator is a sequence of zeros and ones (the secret message) and the output appears as a generated text. When Bob receives such a text, he performs the inverse transform and extracts the hidden message. It is important to note that such texts are grammatically correct sets of words, but man immediately understands their unnatural, artificial style (this refers to contemporary methods; it is possible that over time, algorithms will appear that generate meaningful texts). The point of using these methods is that their automatic (i.e., without human intervention) analysis to reveal the presence of hidden data can be a difficult task.

It is interesting that even computer programs may be used as covertexts for data embedding. At first glance it seems to be impossible because one may expect that any change in a computer program will inevitably spoil it. However it does not always occur so: there are some instruction sequences in computer programs that allow us to change the order of instructions without altering the computation result. For example, the following fragments written in programming language are equivalent:

$$c1 := 3;\ ff := 17 \text{ and } ff := 17;\ c1 := 3$$

Alice and Bob may use such sequences for covert data transmission. Say, they may agree that if the operations in a pair go in alphabetic order, they encode 0, otherwise they encode 1. Then in the above example the first pair encodes 0, the second 1. More detail on such kinds of methods can be found in [Anckaert *et al.* (2005); Nechta *et al.* (2009)].

11.3 Optimal Embedding under Given Level of Distortion

11.3.1 *Problem Setting*

As we have seen in the previous section, embedding hidden data is based on introducing some errors (distortion) in digital images, audio and similar "natural" objects. This distortion makes digital objects "less natural" which is the main hook for steganalysis that permits us to detect the presence of hidden data. So the question arises for stegosystem developers, how should they construct the methods that would allow them to embed the maximal amount of information under a given (admissible) level of distortion. Note that this problem cannot be solved "once and for all" since the level of undetected distortion becomes smaller and smaller with the progress in steganalysis.

To explain the essence of the problem, let us consider an example. Let Alice be able to transmit innocuous N-bit messages in which she can change no more than n bits. (It is supposed that Eve can detect the introduction of distortion if $n+1$ bits or more have been changed). One of the possible strategies for Alice is to select n positions (agreed with Bob) and replace them with the bits of a secret message (in real systems Alice and Bob often select those positions using identical pseudorandom number generators). In this case, Alice can transmit n-bit secret messages and the size of the set of all potentially possible secret messages is 2^n. As we know, the progress in steganalysis restricts the number of distorted bits n to be much less than the covertext size N. The ratio $\alpha = n/N$ is called the *embedding rate* and, for some covertexts, may be equal to few percent.

On the other hand, if Alice has freedom to select any n positions in the covertext, she has a set of possible messages of a size that is not 2^n but of a rather greater value $\binom{N}{n}$ (more precisely, $\sum_{i=0}^{n} \binom{N}{i}$ as she may not change n bits exactly but any of their number up to n bits). Consequently, Alice can potentially transmit secret messages of $\log \sum_{i=0}^{n} \binom{N}{i}$ bits which asymptotically, as N gets large, equals $Nh(\alpha)(1 + o(1))$, where $h(\alpha) = -(\alpha \log \alpha + (1-\alpha) \log(1-\alpha))$ is the binary Shannon entropy, see [Cover and Thomas (2006)]. We can see that even for small embedding rates $\alpha = n/N$, the length of the embedded message, asymptotically, can be much greater than n.

The idea of introducing distortion not in the fixed n positions of covertext but in "variable" positions determined by the embedded message, was in one form or another realized in stegosystems utilizing error-correcting codes. Such systems were first suggested in [Crandall (1998)] and then developed and generalized in [Westfeld (2001); Galand and Kabatiansky (2003); Bierbrauer and Fridrich (2008)] and many other works. We shall not describe these stegosystems but shall consider a more general class of stegosystems that incorporates, as special cases, methods essentially equivalent to those based on error-correcting codes [Ryabko and Fionov (2019)]. Running a few forward, we note that the stegosystems suggested in this paper allow us to transmit secret information of an amount asymptotically close to the maximum possible, i.e. $\log \sum_{i=0}^{n} \binom{N}{i}$.

We proceed to a formal description of the problem considered. Let there be a stegosystem with the set of covertexts $\hat{C}$ and the set of admissible distortions $\hat{D}$. Denote by $c * d$ a covertext c with the introduced distortion d. For instance, $\hat{C}$ may be a set of digital photos in full-color BMP format with a resolution of 1280×800 pixels (each pixel is encoded by three bytes, representing the intensities of red, green and blue color components (RGB)). Various admissible distortions may be accepted for various stegosystems. For example, in one stegosystem distortions of not more than 1% of the least significant bits (LSB) in any of the RGB components may be admitted. In this case the set of admissible distortions $\hat{D}$ may be composed of elements represented as three matrices (maps) of zeros and ones, each of size 1280×800, where ones indicate the positions which must be altered by LSB replacement or LSB matching, the share of ones being not greater than 1% in each matrix. An alternative demand may admit distortions of not more than 1% of LSB, as previously, but distortions in adjacent pixels are prohibited. In the third case, the distortions are admitted if in any 10×10 square (or a circle with a diameter of 10 pixels) there is not more than 1 bit changed. And so on. If the images are in JPEG format, different rules establishing the admissible distortions may be applied.

A natural question is related to the estimation of the amount of information which can be covertly transmitted in the system $\hat{C}, \hat{D}$. Let us call this value the capacity of the system and denote by γ. Then, evidently,

$$\gamma \leq \log |\hat{D}|, \tag{11.1}$$

where, as usually, $|\hat{D}|$ is the number of elements in $\hat{D}$. (Indeed, each distortion corresponds to one hidden message, so the number of words of length γ (which is 2^γ) cannot be greater than the number of admissible distortions $|\hat{D}|$, hence $2^\gamma \leq |\hat{D}|$).

11.3.2   *Stegosystem Based on Linear Hash Functions*

We can see in the examples considered that, in many cases, both covertexts and distortions may be represented as binary words of equal length and the process of applying the distortion d to the covertext c is reduced to bitwise addition modulo 2, i.e. the covertext with introduced distortion may be represented as $w = c \oplus d$. In this section, we describe a stegosystem Λ whose capacity is close to the upper bound (11.1). For this we need a so-called linear hash function λ defined over the set of words w with values in the set of binary words of a certain length γ_λ. We assume that the function λ, as any ordinary hash function, makes good mixing, and for any covertext $c \in \hat{C}$ and distortion $d \in \hat{D}$ the identity is valid

$$\lambda(c \oplus d) = \lambda(c) \oplus \lambda(d). \tag{11.2}$$

It is worth noting that the required hash function does not need to be cryptographically secure.

Describe now the sequence of the actions of Alice and Bob (or the protocol) defining the system Λ.

Let Alice have a covertext $c \in \hat{C}$, and let her wish to send it to Bob with embedded secret message $s \in \{0,1\}^{\gamma_\lambda}$. To do that Alice computes $u = \lambda(c)$, $v = u \oplus s$, and finds the distortion $d \in \hat{D}$ satisfying the identity $\lambda(d) = v$. Then Alice forms the stegotext $w = c \oplus d$ and sends it to Bob.

Bob, having received the stegotext w, computes $\lambda(w)$.

It occurs that $\lambda(w) = s$. That is, Bob can extract the secret message. More precisely, the following simple yet important theorem is valid:

Theorem 11.1. *Let the stegosystem Λ be used. If for every word $v \in \{0,1\}^{\gamma_\lambda}$ there exists $d \in \hat{D}$ for which $\lambda(d) = v$, then $\lambda(w) = s$ and the system capacity equals γ_λ.*

Proof. Indeed, from the linearity of λ it follows that $\lambda(w) = \lambda(c \oplus d) = \lambda(c) \oplus \lambda(d)$. Due to the system construction $\lambda(d) = v = u \oplus s$ and $\lambda(c) = u$ hence $\lambda(c \oplus d) = u \oplus (u \oplus s) = s$. The theorem is proved. $\qquad\square$

Remark 11.1. In order to fulfill the condition that $d \in \hat{D}$ for which $\lambda(d) = v$ exists, it is sufficient to require that the values of hash function λ cover entirely the set of γ_λ-bit words, i.e. the identity must hold $\{\lambda(d) : d \in D\} = \{0,1\}^{\gamma_\lambda}$. Then, evidently, for any $v \in \{0,1\}^{\gamma_\lambda}$ such $d \in \hat{D}$ can be found that $\lambda(d) = v$. Notice also that the system capacity equals γ_λ in this case.

11.3.3 *Linear Hash Functions over Binary Fields*

Complexity, performance, as well as the very existence of the described above stegosystem Λ depends primarily on linear hash function λ which we shall now consider. We consider only one class of such functions based on the abstract mathematical theory of Galois fields which finds wide practical application in the systems of information transmission and storage where it is used to construct cyclic redundancy check (CRC) codes. To describe the considered class of linear hash functions we assume that empty and filled covertext objects as well as distortions are represented by binary words of length N, $N > 0$. Every word $w = w_{N-1}w_{N-2} \ldots w_1 w_0 \in \{0,1\}^N$ may be seen as the polynomial

$$w(x) = w_{N-1}x^{N-1} + w_{N-2}x^{N-2} + \cdots + w_1 x + w_0. \qquad (11.3)$$

Let m be an integer and

$$g(x) = x^m + g_{m-1}x^{m-1} + g_{m-2}x^{m-2} + \cdots + g_1 x + g_0$$

be a degree m polynomial. We define the hash function $\lambda_G(w)$ as the remainder from the division of $w(x)$ by $g(x)$:

$$\lambda_G(w) = w(x) \bmod g(x), \qquad (11.4)$$

using this notation both for the polynomial and the word formed by its coefficients. Note immediately that from the elementary properties of polynomials it follows that $\lambda_G(w_1 \oplus w_2) = \lambda_G(w_1) \oplus \lambda_G(w_2)$, i.e. λ_G is a linear hash function.

Denote by Λ_G the described above stegosystem Λ in the case when the hash function λ_G is employed.

It is known that if $g(x)$ is an irreducible polynomial (i.e. the one that cannot be factored), then the set of all possible polynomials $\lambda_G(w)$ constitutes a binary field $\mathbb{F}_{2^m}$ (or a Galois field $GF(2^m)$ in alternative notation) whose definition and main properties can be found in many textbooks, see e.g. [Menezes *et al.* (1996)].

Consider an example. Let the covertexts be binary words of length $N = 2^m - 1$, $m \geq 1$, and the admissible distortion be 1 bit (in other words, Alice gets an N-bit word w in which she may change not more than 1 bit for hidden data transmission). Formally, the set of admissible distortions $\hat{D}$ may be represented as $\hat{D} = \{s_0, s_1, \ldots, s_N\}$, where s_i is a word having single 1 at the i-th position and zeros at the remaining positions (s_0 consisting of zeros only).

To construct the stegosystem Λ_G choose a primitive polynomial $g(x)$ of degree m that constitutes a binary field $\mathbb{F}_{2^m}$ and let hash function $\lambda_G(w)$ for a word $w \in \{0,1\}^N$ be defined by identities (11.3) and (11.4). (Note that the length of hash values is m bits.)

Proposition 11.1. *The capacity of the stegosystem Λ_G equals m bits which is the maximum possible value.*

Proof. Recall that $\hat{D} = \{s_0, s_1, \ldots, s_N\}$, hence the capacity of this stegosystem cannot exceed $\log|\hat{D}| = \log(N+1) = m$. Let us show now that the capacity equals m. Indeed, the capacity of stegosystem Λ_G is determined in the remark to Theorem 11.1. As it follows from the remark, it suffices to show that the values of hash function λ_G are different at all possible distortions $d \in \hat{D}$. We defined the set $\hat{D}$ so that any element s_i contains a single 1 bit in the i-th position (s_0 is all zeros). Consequently, $\lambda_G(s_i) = x^{i-1} \bmod g(x)$ for all $i = 1, 2, \ldots, N$, see (11.4). By definition, the polynomial $g(x)$ is primitive and the property of the binary field dictates that $x^{i-1} \bmod g(x)$ are non-zero and different for all $i = 1, 2, \ldots, N = 2^m - 1$, (they generate $2^m - 1$ different non-zero elements of the field). Hence all $\lambda_G(s_i)$ are different for $i = 1, 2, \ldots, N$ and also differ from $\lambda_G(s_0) = 0$. $\qquad\square$

Consider a more specific example. Let $m = 2$ and thus $N = 3$. In this case, the set of admissible distortions $\hat{D} = \{000, 001, 010, 100\}$ (we write the words in big-endian format, i.e. the least significant bit is the rightmost, for ease of association with polynomials). Assume that Alice and Bob choose the primitive polynomial $g(x) = x^2 + x + 1$. Then the hash function values for the elements of $\hat{D}$ are:

$$\lambda_G(000) = 00,$$

$$\lambda_G(001) = 1 \bmod g(x) = 01,$$

$$\lambda_G(010) = x \bmod g(x) = x = 10,$$

$$\lambda_G(100) = x^2 \bmod g(x) = x + 1 = 11.$$

Suppose Alice has the covertext $c = 101$ and wishes to transmit the secret message $s = 11$. By the protocol defining stegosystem Λ, Alice computes $u = \lambda_G(c) = \lambda_G(101) = (x^2 + 1) \bmod (x^2 + x + 1) = x = 10$. Then Alice finds $v = u \oplus s = 10 \oplus 11 = 01$ and determines $d \in \hat{D}$ for which $\lambda_G(d) = 01$: $d = 001$. Alice introduces distortion d in covertext c: $w = 101 \oplus 001 = 100$, and sends it to Bob. Bob, having received the distorted covertext w, computes $\lambda_G(100) = 11$ and gets the secret message $s = 11$.

We remark that with the admissible distortion of 1 bit, the considered stegosystem Λ_G has the same capacity as a stegosystem based on Hamming codes, see [Bierbrauer and Fridrich (2008)].

11.3.4 *Potential Capacity of Stegosystems Based on Linear Hash Functions*

In this subsection, we show that "almost any" stegosystem based on a linear hash function, generally speaking, has the capacity to be asymptotically close to the maximum possible value. To do this, we go back to considering the general system Λ. In this system, Alice transmits in one covertext object γ_λ bits of secret information which means, by definition, that the capacity equals γ_λ so the question of its evaluation plays an important role. Let us proceed to answer this question.

We start with clarifying the concept of hash function mixing property. Let λ be a function defined over the binary words of length N, and taking values in the set of binary words of length m, moreover, $N \geq m \geq 1$. We refer to this function as *mixing* if for any $v \in \{0,1\}^m$

$$P\{\lambda(w) = v\} = 2^{-m}, \tag{11.5}$$

if different w are picked from the set of words $\{0,1\}^N$ uniformly at random (with equal probabilities).

Assume now that the sets of covertexts $\hat{C}$ and admissible distortions $\hat{D}$ are given, their elements are represented by binary words of length N, and there is a hash function λ, of which is only known that it possesses the mixing property (11.5). Let us estimate the capacity γ_λ of this system. First, note that with any (non-zero) value of m and any hash function λ the situation is possible when the values of hash function $\lambda(d)$, $d \in \hat{D}$, do not completely cover the set $\{0,1\}^m$, i.e.

$$\{v : \lambda(d) = v, \ d \in \hat{D}\} \neq \{0,1\}^m.$$

Therefore the described system may have some (non-zero) capacity only with certain probability. Obviously, only those systems which have this probability close to 1, say, $1 - 10^{-8}$, are practically interesting.

It occurs that asymptotically under any arbitrarily small $\delta > 0$ the capacity γ_λ is close to the maximum possible capacity. More formally, the following holds:

Theorem 11.2. *Let the stegosystem Λ be defined on the set of covertexts $\hat{C}$ and the set of randomly selected admissible distortions $\hat{D}$, and let it use a hash function λ which possesses the mixing property (11.5). Then for large $|\hat{D}|$ and any $\delta > 0$ the inequality*

$$\gamma_\lambda \geq \log |\hat{D}| - \log \ln(|\hat{D}|/\delta) \tag{11.6}$$

holds with probability $1 - \delta$ (here $\log$ denotes binary and $\ln$ natural logarithms).

Proof. The proof is based on known solutions of the problem of distributing balls into boxes. The problem is formulated as follows. There are M

boxes into which K balls are to be distributed uniformly at random, besides, each box can stow an arbitrary number of balls. A random variable μ_0 is defined to be the number of boxes that remain empty after finishing the distribution of balls. It is shown in [Kolchin *et al.* (1978)] that

$$E(\mu_0) \leq M e^{-K/M}. \tag{11.7}$$

With respect to the stegosystem Λ, we may consider every word from the set $\{0,1\}^m$ as a box, and the elements of $\hat{D}$ as the balls. Besides, assume that the ball d is placed in the box $v \in \{0,1\}^m$, if $\lambda(d) = v$. Note that the mixing property (11.5) ensures the uniformity of distribution of balls into boxes. So

$$M = 2^m, \quad K = |\hat{D}|. \tag{11.8}$$

As the random variable μ_0 is not equal to zero, this means that the values of hash function $\lambda(d)$ do not cover entirely the set $\{0,1\}^m$ under the given $\hat{D}$. By the condition of the theorem, it is required that the probability of this event be equal to $1 - \delta$, i.e.

$$P\{\mu_0 = 0\} = 1 - \delta. \tag{11.9}$$

Notice now that, by definition,

$$E(\mu_0) = \sum_{j=1}^{\infty} j \times P\{\mu_0 = j\}.$$

It is plain that

$$E(\mu_0) \geq \sum_{j=1}^{\infty} 1 \times P\{\mu_0 = j\} = 1 - P\{\mu_0 = 0\}.$$

From this inequality and (11.7) we obtain

$$M e^{-K/M} \geq 1 - P\{\mu_0 = 0\},$$

consequently,

$$P\{\mu_0 = 0\} \geq 1 - M e^{-K/M}.$$

By substitution of (11.9) in the last inequality we obtain

$$1 - \delta \geq 1 - M e^{-K/M}.$$

Hence

$$K/M - \ln M \leq \ln(1/\delta).$$

Taking into account that the number of boxes M is less than the number of balls K (since, according to the theorem condition, we consider large $K = |\hat{D}|$), from the last inequality we obtain

$$K/M - \ln K \leq \ln(1/\delta).$$

By rearranging the last inequality we can see that

$$M \geq K/\ln(K/\delta).$$

Considering that this inequality holds with probability $1 - \delta$ and Eq. (11.8) is valid, taking logarithms we obtain

$$\gamma_\lambda \geq \log |\hat{D}| - \log \ln(|\hat{D}/\delta)|.$$

This completes the proof. □

11.3.5 *Methods of Constructing Stegosystems Based on Linear Hash Functions*

The problem of constructing the system with capacity r close to the maximum γ_λ given by (11.1) essentially depends on the size of the set $\hat{D}$. If this quantity is small and all elements of $\hat{D}$ may be counted in relatively short time, we can define a hash function λ' whose values may be recorded for all admissible distortions $d \in \hat{D}$. Then the maximal value of r can be found such that certain (e.g. initial) r bits of values of $\lambda'(d)$, $d \in \hat{D}$, cover entirely the set $\{0, 1\}^r$. In this case, we can slightly modify the hash function by making its value consist of those r bits. (It is easy to see that in the modified hash function the property of linearity is preserved.) The capacity of this stegosystem is obviously r bits. If Alice and Bob have enough time, they can exhaustively search through several hash functions to select one with maximal capacity and then use the selected hash function for stegosystem construction.

However, in many situations in practice the set of admissible distortions $\hat{D}$ is of very large size so the exhaustive search through all $d \in \hat{D}$ to find experimentally a hash function of maximal capacity is infeasible. Let, for instance, the placeholders for embedding be the least significant bits of relatively small images, represented as matrices of zeros and ones of dimensions 100×100 and let the admissible distortions amount to 2% of symbols. Then the number of admissible distortions equals $\sum_{i=0}^{200} \binom{10000}{i} \gg 2^{100}$ which precludes the exhaustive search.

We consider a well-known approach to solving this problem: divide the covertext in small pieces and use each piece as a separate covertext. Then the total amount of admissible distortions is distributed among the pieces. Thus for the example above the initial covertext of dimensions 100×100 can be divided into 200 equal-size pieces with an admissible distortion of 1 bit per piece. In this case the stegosystem is greatly simplified and we can use the method based on binary fields. Unfortunately, the capacity of the system with split covertexts may be essentially lower than that of the initial system. For the example considered, the potential capacity of the initial system is $\log \sum_{i=0}^{200} \binom{10000}{i} \sim 1400$ (see (11.1)), while the capacity of the system with split covertexts is only $200 \times \lfloor \log 51 \rfloor = 1000$.

Let us derive asymptotic estimates for both stegosystems that allow us to judge their capacities in the general case. Let the covertexts and admissible distortions be the sets of N-bit words and let each word of the admissible distortion set contains not more than n ones (in other words, distortions in not more than n symbols of covertext are admitted). So the rate of embedding $\alpha = n/N$. Then from (11.1) we can see that for any stegosystem Λ its capacity γ_λ does not exceed $\log \sum_{i=0}^{n} \binom{N}{i}$. Using known asymptotic estimates for large N and fixed α, see [Cover and Thomas (2006)], we may write

$$\gamma_\lambda \leq Nh(\alpha)(1 + o(1)), \tag{11.10}$$

where $h(\alpha) = -(\alpha \log \alpha + (1 - \alpha) \log(1 - \alpha))$.

Consider now a simple stegosystem λ^1 where each covertext is divided into n subwords of equal length N/n with admissible distortion 1 bit. We have seen that such a system can be built using binary fields and its capacity $\gamma_\lambda^1 = n \log(N/n)$, see Proposition 11.1. (We do not account for the necessity of rounding N/n since we are interested in asymptotic estimates.) The last equation can be presented as

$$\gamma_\lambda^1 = N(-\alpha \log \alpha)(1 + o(1)).$$

Comparing it with (11.10) we can see that, asymptotically, when implementing the stegosystem λ^1, the loss in capacity is

$$N(-(1 - \alpha) \log(1 - \alpha))(1 + o(1)).$$

Upon small α, this value tends to zero, hence the loss in implementing the simple stegosystem becomes negligible.

Some Properties of Binary Fields

We need the following properties of binary fields:

(1) The number of elements in $\mathbb{F}_{2^m}$ equals 2^m and the fields produced by different irreducible polynomials of degree m are isomorphic (a formal definition of isomorphism can be found in the literature, but informally, it means that all the fields are essentially identical). So one denomination $\mathbb{F}_{2^m}$ is used for any irreducible polynomial $g(x)$ of degree m.

(2) A so called generator x_g exists whose powers generate all non-zero elements of $\mathbb{F}_{2^m}$, i.e. the set

$$x_g^1 \bmod g(x), \quad x_g^2 \bmod g(x), \ldots, x_g^{2^m-1} \bmod g(x)$$

contains all non-zero elements of $\mathbb{F}_{2^m}$. For any field $\mathbb{F}_{2^m}$ there exists a so-called primitive generating polynomial for which $x_g = x$.

11.4 Asymptotically Optimal Perfect Stegosystems

In this section, we consider the construction of a perfect steganographic system, i.e. the system where messages carrying and not carrying hidden information (empty and filled covertexts) obey the same probability distribution and hence are statistically indistinguishable. This means that Eve will not be able in principle to distinguish between empty and filled covertexts. This system was suggested by B. Ryabko and D. Ryabko in [Ryabko and Ryabko (2007); Ryabko and Ryabko (2009)]. The system is also universal, i.e. it accepts covertexts with unknown statistics (yet it guarantees that after data embedding the initial probability distribution is preserved). The notions of perfect and universal stegosystems were introduced in [Cachin (1998)].

Let us introduce some notation to be used hereinafter. Consider a source of covertexts μ generating independent and identically distributed letters over an alphabet A which may be finite or infinite. There are two participants of information exchange, Alice and Bob, and Alice is going to use the source μ for the covert transmission of messages composed of symbols over the alphabet $B = \{0,1\}$ generated independently with equal probabilities. This second source we denote by ω and call it further the source of secret messages. Such a model of a source of secret messages is generally accepted since it is assumed that the secret messages have already been encrypted by Alice with a key known only to her and Bob. If Alice uses the one-time pad then the secret messages consist of equiprobable and independent bits; if a block or stream cipher is used, then, as we have seen in the previous sections, the messages must look like a sequences of equiprobable and independent bits (this may mean indistinguishability from randomness in polynomial time or confirmed by the statistical testing data available for all modern ciphers). As usually, we assume that Eve reads all data communicated between Alice and Bob and tries to detect the presence of hidden information. Remark once more that if the messages containing and not containing hidden information obey the same probability distribution, Eve (and anybody else) will not be able to distinguish such messages. Due to this property such stegosystems are said to be perfect.

We present a universal stegosystem construction which is perfect and, besides, the rate of hidden data transmission approaches the upper bound, i.e. the maximal possible value, the Shannon entropy of the source μ. It is important to note that the algorithms of embedding and extracting hidden data are quite simple, their complexity grows polynomially as the rate of hidden data transmission tends to the limit — the Shannon entropy.

In order to better explain the idea, we begin the description with the simplest case when the source of covertexts μ generates independent symbols with unknown probabilities over the alphabet $A = \{a, b\}$ (so the alphabet sizes of the covertext source μ and the source of secret messages ω are the same). Denote a secret message by $y^* = y_1 y_2 y_3 \ldots$ and a covertext by $x^* = x_1 x_2 x_3 \ldots$. For instance,

$$y^* = 0110\ldots, \quad x^* = aababaaaabbaaaaabb\ldots. \tag{11.11}$$

To embed y^*, the covertext x^* is transformed into a new sequence X such that (1) y^* can be correctly recovered from X and (2) the probability distribution of symbols in X is the same as in x^* (in other words, X and x^* are statistically indistinguishable). The process of producing X from x^* and y^* may be split into steps. First, partition all the symbols of x^* into pairs and, for convenience, denote all possible pairs in the following way:

$$aa = u, \quad bb = u, \quad ab = v_0, \quad ba = v_1.$$

For example, the sequence from (11.11) can be represented as

$$x^* = aa\,ba\,ba\,aa\,ab\,ba\,aa\,aa\,bb\ldots = uv_1v_1uv_0v_1uuu\ldots$$

(spaces are only inserted for ease of reading). The the sequence X is formed as follows: all pairs that correspond to u remain intact and the pairs that correspond to v_k are replaced sequentially by $v_{y_1} v_{y_2} v_{y_3} \ldots$. For the considered example (11.11) we obtain

$$X = aa\,ab\,ba\,aa\,ba\,ab\,aa\,aa\,bb\ldots.$$

The method of extracting is obvious: Bob partitions the received sequence X into pairs and extracts 0 from ab and 1 from ba while other pairs are ignored.

Denote the method described by St$_2$. An almost apparent property is given by the following

Proposition 11.2. *Let there be given a source μ generating independent identically distributed letters over the alphabet $A = \{a, b\}$ and let this source be used to covertly transmit messages consisting of equiprobable and independent bits by the method St$_2$. Then the probability distribution of output messages is the same as that of the input source μ.*

We do not give an evident proof of this proposition as it is a special case of the theorem provided below.

In Sec. 10.2, we have seen that a similar method was used by von Neuman for constructing a sequence of equiprobable bits. His method, as well as the described stegosystem, is based on the fact that the probabilities of symbol pairs ab and ba are equal.

The construction described above can be easily extended to an arbitrary alphabet A. Indeed, define some order on the set of all letters of A. (It is worth noting here that A may consist of graphic files or images but, in any case, these and all similar objects are represented in computer or communications systems as binary words and hence can be ordered, e.g. lexicographically). As earlier, to transmit a secret message $y^* = y_1 y_2 y_3 \ldots$, generated by the source of equiprobable and independent bits ω, a covertext sequence $x^* = x_1 x_2 x_3 \ldots$, generated by the source of independent symbols μ, $x_i \in A$, is partitioned in blocks of length 2. If a block $x_{2i-1} x_{2i}$ consists of the same letters, it is not used for the embedding and is transmitted without change. Otherwise, if a block $x_{2i-1} x_{2i}$ consists of different letters, say, α and β, then it is used for the embedding of y_k. Without loss of generality, assume that $\alpha < \beta$ under the given ordering. Then the transmitted block is $\alpha\beta$ if $y_k = 0$ and $\beta\alpha$ if $y_k = 1$. The rule of extraction is plain: if in a stegotext block $X_{2i-1} = X_{2i}$ the block is discarded; else if $X_{2i-1} < X_{2i}$ extract $y_k = 0$, else extract $y_k = 1$. Denote this stegosystem by St$_2(A)$.

Theorem 11.3. *Let a source μ be given generating independent identically distributed letters over some alphabet A and let the source be used for covert data transmission in the stegosystem St$_2(A)$. Then the probability distribution of messages on the stegosystem output is the same as that of μ and the average number of letters per one covert bit equals $2/(1 - \sum_{a \in A} \mu(a)^2)$.*

Proof. Take arbitrary $\alpha, \beta \in A$ and i and show that

$$P(X_{2i-1}X_{2i} = \alpha\beta) = \mu(\alpha\beta).$$

If $\alpha = \beta$ then $P(X_{2i-1}X_{2i}) = P(x_{2i-1}x_{2i})$, i.e. the probabilities in the source block and in the block containing hidden data are the same. Let then $\alpha < \beta$. In this case

$$P(X_{2i-1}X_{2i} = \alpha\beta) = P(y_k = 0)P(x_{2i}x_{2i+1} = \alpha\beta)$$

$$+P(y_k = 1)P(x_{2i}x_{2i+1} = \beta\alpha)$$

$$= (1/2)\,\mu(\alpha)\mu(\beta) + (1/2)\,\mu(\beta)\mu(\alpha) = \mu(\alpha)\mu(\beta).$$

The case $\beta > \alpha$ can be analyzed similarly. The second statement is obtained by the direct calculation of the probability that two letters in the block are the same. □

We remark that in practice, when the letters of A may be, say, image files, the size of A is quite large, so the average number of transmitted letters (images) per one hidden bit is close to 2.

Now we are ready to describe a general method. Let, as earlier, a secret message $y^* = y_1y_2y_3\ldots$ generated by the source of equiprobable independent bits ω be covertly transmitted and let there be a sequence $x^* = x_1x_2x_3\ldots$ generated by a source of independent identically distributed letters over an alphabet A denoted by μ. In this stegosystem, the sequence x^* is split into blocks of length n, where $n > 1$ is a method parameter. Each block is used to encode a certain number of symbols from y^* (for instance, in the above described stegosystem $St_2(A)$ each block of two symbols encodes either one letter from y^* or nothing). However, in the general case, one peculiarity is essential that does not arise in two-letter blocks: while the probabilities of words generated by the source of secret messages are negative powers of 2, the number of equiprobable blocks may not be a power of 2 and we need to agree somehow on the probabilities of blocks in x^* and y^*.

Denote by u the first n letters of x^*: $u = x_1\ldots x_n$ and let $\nu_u(a)$ be the number of occurrences of the letter a in the word u. By definition, the set S_u consists of all words of length n over the alphabet A having the same number of occurrences of letters as the word u, i.e. S_u consists of the words of the frequency class of u. Notice that the probabilities of all words of S_u are equal since μ is a source of independent and identically distributed letters. Let some order, known to Alice and Bob, be set on S_u

(say, a lexicographic order) and let $S_u = \{s_0, s_1, \ldots, s_{|S_u|-1}\}$ under this ordering.

Let $m = \lfloor \log_2 |S_u| \rfloor$. Then the binary expansion of the number $|S_u|$ is

$$|S_u| = (\alpha_m, \alpha_{m-1}, \ldots, \alpha_0),$$

where $\alpha_m = 1$, $\alpha_j \in \{0, 1\}$, $m > j \geq 0$. In other words,

$$|S_u| = 2^m + \alpha_{m-1} 2^{m-1} + \cdots + \alpha_0.$$

Denote by $\delta(u)$ the ordinal number of word u (under the ordering set on S_u) and let $(\lambda_m, \lambda_{m-1}, \ldots, \lambda_0)$ be the binary expansion of $\delta(u)$. Let $j(u)$ be the greatest number such that $\alpha_j \neq \lambda_j$. Alice having determined $j(u)$, reads $j(u)$ letters from the secret message y^* and let these letters form a binary number τ. Alice finds in the set S_u a word v whose ordinal in S_u equals $\sum_{j(u)<s\leq m} \alpha_s 2^s + \tau$ and sends the word v to Bob.

Bob, under the receipt of v, determines the set S_v (which coincides with S_u) and, in the same way as Alice, finds $j(v) = j(u)$ and τ and reads $j(v)$ bits from τ as a covertly transmitted secret message.

All subsequent n-letter words are encoded by Alice and decoded by Bob similarly. Denote this system by $\mathrm{St}_n(A)$.

Consider an example to illustrate the details of the method. Let $A = \{a, b, c\}$, $n = 3$, $u = bac$. Then $S_u = \{abc, acb, bac, bca, cab, cba\}$, $|S_u| = 6$, $m = 2$, $\alpha_2 = 1$, $\alpha_1 = 1$, $\alpha_0 = 0$, $\delta(u) = 2$, $\lambda_2 \lambda_1 \lambda_0 = 010$, $j(u) = 2$. Having computed these values, Alice reads $j(u) = 2$ bits from y^* which will then be covertly communicated. For certainty, let these bits be 11, so $\tau = 3$. Alice finds the ordinal number $\sum_{2<s\leq 2} \alpha_s 2^s + \tau = 0 + 3 = 3$ and let the correspondent word $v = bca$. Alice sends the word bca to Bob. Having received the word bca, Bob determines $S_v(=S_u)$, $j(v) = 2$, $\tau = 3$, and reads from τ the secret message 11.

Theorem 11.4. *Let a source μ be given generating independent identically distributed letters over some alphabet A and let the source be used for the covert transmission of messages consisting of independent and equiprobable binary digits according to the method $\mathrm{St}_n(A)$ with block size n, $n \geq 2$. Then the following statements are satisfied:*

(1) *The stegosystem output messages obey the distribution μ (i.e. the distributions of input and output sequences are the same and hence the stegosystem is perfect).*

(2) *The average number of covert bits per source letter* (L_n) *satisfies the inequality*

$$L_n \geq \frac{1}{n} \left(\sum_{u \in A^n} \mu(u) \log \frac{n!}{\prod_{a \in A} \nu_u(a)!} - 2 \right),$$

where $\mu(u)$ *is the probability of generating the word* u *by the source* μ *and* $\nu_u(a)$ *is the number of occurrences of letter* a *in the word* u.

(3) *If the alphabet* A *is finite and the block length* n *infinitely grows then the average number of covert bits per source letter* L_n *tends to the Shannon entropy of the source* μ

$$\lim_{n \to \infty} L_n = h(\mu) = - \sum_{a \in A} \mu(a) \log \mu(a).$$

Proof. To prove the first statement of the theorem, it suffices to show that for each n-letter word u from the input sequence the probability of any output word $v \in S_u$ equals $1/|S_u|$. The proof, as earlier, is based on the formula of total probability. As can be seen from the method description, upon $\alpha_j = 1$ the probability that j bits are read from the secret message, $j = 0, \ldots, m$, equals $2^j/|S_u|$, since the ordinal number of word u in S_u must satisfy the inequality

$$\sum_{j(u) < s \leq m} \alpha_s 2^s \leq \delta(u) < \sum_{j(u) \leq s \leq m} \alpha_s 2^s.$$

For certainty, let u and v be the first words of the input and output sequences, respectively. Then

$$P(X_1 \ldots X_n = v) = P(u \in S_v \quad \text{and} \quad j(v) = j(u)) 2^{-j(v)}.$$

Here the last term is the probability of reading from y^* the binary word of length $j(v)$ that determines v. From the last identity we obtain

$$P(X_1 \ldots X_n = v) = P(u \in S_v) P(j(v) = j(u) | u \in S_v) 2^{-j(v)}$$
$$= |S_v| \mu(u) (2^{j(v)}/|S_v|) 2^{-j(v)} = \mu(u).$$

Since both u and v belong to the same frequency class, from the last identity we can see that $P(X_1 \ldots X_n = v) = \mu(v)$.

To prove the second statement, define the quantity $\phi = 2^m/|S_u|$ and denote by $L(S_u)$ the average number of covertly transmitted bits per one word from S_u:

$$L(S_u) = \frac{1}{|S_u|} \sum_{i=0}^{m} \alpha_i i 2^i.$$

The following relations are true:

$$L(S_u) = \frac{1}{|S_u|} \sum_{i=0}^{m} \alpha_i 2^i = \frac{1}{|S_u|} \left(m \sum_{i=0}^{m} \alpha_i i 2^i - \sum_{i=0}^{m} \alpha_i 2^i (m - i) \right)$$

$$= m - \left(2^m \sum_{k=0}^{m} k \alpha_{m-k} 2^{-k} \right) > m - 2^{m+1}/|S_u|$$

$$= m - 2/\phi = \log |S_u| - \log \phi - 2/\phi.$$

One may check by directly finding the maximum that

$$\log \phi + 2/\phi \leq 2, \quad \text{if } \phi \in [1, 2].$$

From here we get that

$$L(S_u) > \log |S_u| - 2.$$

From here and from identity

$$|S_u| = \frac{n!}{\prod_{a \in A} \nu_u(a)!}$$

we obtain the second statement of the theorem.

The last statement follows from the widely known fact in probability theory that, with probability tending to 1, the inequality

$$h(\mu) - \delta < \log |S_u|/n < h(\mu) + \delta$$

is valid under any $\delta > 0$, see, e.g. [Gallager (1968); Csiszar (1998)]. $\quad\square$

In many real stegosystems the alphabet A is huge (e.g. it consists of all possible digital images of a specified format, or all possible electronic letters). In this case, the asymptotic behavior of L_n under a fixed n and $|A| \to \infty$ is of interest. For strict consideration of this case we shall use the notion of minentropy (or minimum entropy) which is defined by the identity

$$H_\infty(\mu) = \min_{a \in A} \{ -\log \mu(a) \}.$$

Corollary 11.1. *If the conditions of Theorem 11.4 are fulfilled, the block length n is finite and the alphabet size $|A|$ infinitely grows so that $H_\infty(\mu) \to \infty$ then the value of L_n satisfies the inequalities*

$$\log(n!)/n \geq L_n \geq (\log(n!) - 2)/n,$$

which is equivalent for large n to the asymptotic identity

$$L_n = \log n(1 + o(n)).$$

This proposition can be easily derived from the fact that the number of permutations of n different elements is equal to $n!$ and from the second statement of Theorem 11.4.

Let us briefly consider the complexity of the stegosystem $\text{St}_n(A)$. To store all the words of the set S_u it would have required an order of $2^n \log |A|$ bits of memory which is infeasible for large n. In [Ryabko (1998)] an algorithm of fast enumeration was suggested that allows the computation of the ordinal number of any word u in S_u and, vice versa, in order to find a word given its ordinal in $O(\log^{\text{const}} n)$ time and $O(n \log^3 n)$ bits of memory.

It is worth noting that the main idea used in constructing the stegosystem $\text{St}_n(A)$ can be applied also to more general covertext sources rather than the sources generating independent identically distributed letters. Indeed, the only property of such sources that we exploit is that all message blocks obtained by permuting the letters have equal probabilities. If a source of covertexts has a property that, at some step, some messages have equal *conditional* probabilities, then in the case that one of these messages is generated, the secret data may be embedded by replacing it with another message of the same probability. The messages that do not belong to any group of equiprobable messages are not used for secret data encoding. The sources generating independent identically distributed letters are just simple but informative examples of this kind of encoding.

Answers to Problems and Exercises

1.1 (a) $k = 17$. (b) $k = 23$.

1.2 (a) PINEAPPLE ($k = 5$). (b) MANGO ($k = 20$).

2.1 (a) $5 = 5$, $16 = 6$, $27 = 7$, $-4 = 6$, $-13 = -3 = 7$, $3+8 = 1$, $3-8 = 5$, $3 \cdot 8 = 4$, $3 \cdot 8 \cdot 5 = 4 \cdot 5 = 0$ (mod 10). (b) $5 = 5$, $16 = 5$, $27 = 5$, $-4 = 7$, $-13 = -2 = 9$, $3+8 = 0$, $3-8 = 6$, $3 \cdot 8 = 2$, $3 \cdot 8 \cdot 5 = 2 \cdot 5 = 10$ (mod 11).

2.2 2^8 mod $10 = 6$, 3^7 mod $10 = 7$, 7^{19} mod $100 = 43$, 7^{57} mod $100 = 7$.

2.3 $108 = 2 \cdot 2 \cdot 3 \cdot 3 \cdot 3$, $77 = 7 \cdot 11$, $65 = 5 \cdot 13$, $30 = 3 \cdot 3 \cdot 5$, $159 = 3 \cdot 53$.

2.4 Pairs $(25, 12)$ and $(40, 27)$ are coprime, the others are not (numbers $(25, 15)$ are divisible by 5, $(13, 39)$ divisible by 13).

2.5 $\varphi(14) = 6$, $\varphi(20) = 8$.

2.6 $\varphi(53) = 52$, $\varphi(21) = \varphi(7) \cdot \varphi(3) = 6 \cdot 2 = 12$, $\varphi(159) = 2 \cdot 52 = 104$.

2.7 3^{13} mod $13 = 3 \cdot 3^{12}$ mod $13 = 3$, 5^{22} mod $11 = 5^2 \cdot 5^{10} \cdot 5^{10}$ mod $11 = 25$ mod $11 = 3$, 3^{17} mod $5 = 3$.

2.8 3^9 mod $20 = 3 \cdot 3^8$ mod $20 = 3$, 2^{14} mod $21 = 2^2 \cdot 2^{12}$ mod $21 = 4$, 2^{107} mod $159 = 2^3 \cdot 2^{104}$ mod $159 = 8$.

2.9 $\gcd(21, 12) = 3$, $\gcd(30, 12) = 6$, $\gcd(24, 40) = \gcd(40, 24) = 8$, $\gcd(33, 16) = 1$.

2.10 (a) $x = -1, y = 2$. (b) $x = 1, y = -2$. (c) $x = 2, y = -1$. (d) $x = 1, y = -2$.

2.11 3^{-1} mod $7 = 5$, 5^{-1} mod $8 = 5$, $3^{-1} = 18$, $10^{-1} = 16$ (mod 53).

2.12 The primes less than 100 are: 2, 3, 5, 7, 11, 13, 17, 19, 23, 29, 31, 37, 41, 43, 47, 53, 59, 61, 67, 73, 79, 83, 89, 97. Among them, the numbers 5, 7, 11, 23, 47, 59, and 83 correspond to the form $p = 2q + 1$.

2.13 If $p = 11$ then generator g may be either 2, 6, 7, or 8.

2.14 (a) $Y_A = 20$, $Y_B = 17$, $Z_{AB} = 21$. (b) $Y_A = 13$, $Y_B = 14$, $Z_{AB} = 10$. (c) $Y_A = 21$, $Y_B = 9$, $Z_{AB} = 16$. (d) $Y_A = 8$, $Y_B = 5$, $Z_{AB} = 9$. (e) $Y_A = 6$, $Y_B = 17$, $Z_{AB} = 16$.

2.15 (a) $d_A = 11$, $d_B = 13$, $x_1 = 17$, $x_2 = 5$, $x_3 = 6$, $x_4 = 4$. (b) $d_A = 3$, $d_B = 19$, $x_1 = 8$, $x_2 = 12$, $x_3 = 3$, $x_4 = 6$. (c) $d_A = 5$, $d_B = 11$, $x_1 = 14$, $x_2 = 10$, $x_3 = 3$, $x_4 = 10$. (d) $d_A = 5$, $d_B = 15$, $x_1 = 7$, $x_2 = 21$, $x_3 = 14$, $x_4 = 17$. (e) $d_A = 11$, $d_B = 5$, $x_1 = 15$, $x_2 = 2$, $x_3 = 8$, $x_4 = 9$.

2.16 (a) $d_B = 13$, $r = 14$, $e = 12$, $m' = 5$. (b) $d_B = 16$, $r = 9$, $e = 15$, $m' = 10$. (c) $d_B = 15$, $r = 16$, $e = 14$, $m' = 10$. (d) $d_B = 21$, $r = 14$, $e = 12$, $m' = 5$. (e) $d_B = 8$, $r = 5$, $e = 5$, $m' = 10$.

2.17 (a) $N_A = 55$, $\varphi(N_A) = 40$, $c_A = 27$, $e = 23$, $m' = 12$. (b) $N_A = 65$, $\varphi(N_A) = 48$, $c_A = 29$, $e = 50$, $m' = 20$. (c) $N_A = 77$, $\varphi(N_A) = 60$, $c_A = 43$, $e = 52$, $m' = 17$. (d) $N_A = 91$, $\varphi(N_A) = 72$, $c_A = 29$, $e = 88$, $m' = 30$. (e) $N_A = 33$, $\varphi(N_A) = 20$, $c_A = 7$, $e = 9$, $m' = 15$.

2.18 $m = 111$.

3.1 (a) $x = 17$. (b) $x = 10$. (c) $x = 28$. (d) $x = 14$. (e) $x = 30$.

3.2 (a) $x = 20$. (b) $x = 45$. (c) $x = 34$. (d) $x = 53$. (e) $x = 25$.

3.3 (a) $x = 10000$. (b) $x = 20000$. (c) $x = 1000$. (d) $x = 12345$. (e) $x = 25000$.

4.1 (a) $s = 28$. (b) $s = 30$. (c) $s = 26$. (d) $s = 71$. (e) $s = 18$.

4.2 (a) $\langle 7, 28 \rangle$ is authentic, $\langle 22, 15 \rangle$ is not, $\langle 16, 36 \rangle$ is authentic. (b) $\langle 6, 42 \rangle$ no, $\langle 10, 30 \rangle$ yes, $\langle 6, 41 \rangle$ yes. (c) $\langle 13, 41 \rangle$ yes, $\langle 11, 28 \rangle$ no, $\langle 5, 26 \rangle$ yes. (d) $\langle 15, 71 \rangle$ yes, $\langle 11, 46 \rangle$ no, $\langle 16, 74 \rangle$ yes. (e) $\langle 10, 14 \rangle$ no, $\langle 24, 18 \rangle$ yes, $\langle 17, 8 \rangle$ yes.

4.3 (a) $y = 22$, $r = 10$, $u = 15$, $k^{-1} = 15$, $s = 5$. (b) $y = 9$, $r = 19$, $u = 13$, $k^{-1} = 3$, $s = 17$. (c) $y = 10$, $r = 21$, $u = 11$, $k^{-1} = 17$, $s = 11$. (d) $y = 6$, $r = 17$, $u = 7$, $k^{-1} = 19$, $s = 1$. (e) $y = 11$, $r = 7$, $u = 18$, $k^{-1} = 7$, $s = 16$.

4.4 **(a)** $\langle 15; 20, 3\rangle$ yes ($y^r = 1$, $r^s = 19$, $g^h = 19$), $\langle 15; 10, 5\rangle$ yes ($y^r = 1$, $r^s = 19$, $g^h = 19$), $\langle 15; 19, 3\rangle$ no ($y^r = 22$, $r^s = 5$, $g^h = 19 \neq 18$). **(b)** $\langle 5; 19, 17\rangle$ yes ($y^r = 13$, $r^s = 21$, $g^h = 20$), $\langle 7; 17, 8\rangle$ no ($y^r = 3$, $r^s = 18$, $g^h = 17 \neq 8$), $\langle 6; 17, 8\rangle$ yes ($y^r = 3$, $r^s = 18$, $g^h = 8$). **(c)** $\langle 3; 17, 12\rangle$ yes ($y^r = 17$, $r^s = 6$, $g^h = 10$), $\langle 2; 17, 12\rangle$ no ($y^r = 17$, $r^s = 6$, $g^h = 2 \neq 10$), $\langle 8; 21, 11\rangle$ yes ($y^r = 7$, $r^s = 22$, $g^h = 16$). **(d)** $\langle 5; 17, 1\rangle$ yes ($y^r = 12$, $r^s = 17$, $g^h = 20$), $\langle 5; 11, 3\rangle$ yes ($y^r = 1$, $r^s = 20$, $g^h = 20$), $\langle 5; 17, 10\rangle$ no ($y^r = 12$, $r^s = 4$, $g^h = 20 \neq 2$). **(e)** $\langle 15; 7, 1\rangle$ no ($y^r = 7$, $r^s = 7$, $g^h = 19 \neq 3$), $\langle 10; 15, 3\rangle$ yes ($y^r = 10$, $r^s = 17$, $g^h = 9$), $\langle 15; 7, 16\rangle$ yes ($y^r = 7$, $r^s = 6$, $g^h = 19$).

4.5 **(a)** $y = 14$, $r = 3$, $s = 8$. **(b)** $y = 24$, $r = 3$, $s = 1$. **(c)** $y = 40$, $r = 9$, $s = 8$. **(d)** $y = 22$, $r = 9$, $s = 5$. **(e)** $y = 64$, $r = 7$, $s = 3$.

4.6 **(a)** $\langle 10; 4, 5\rangle$ no ($s^{-1} = 9$, $u_1 = 2$, $u_2 = 3$, $a^{u_1} = 40$, $y^{u_2} = 64$, $v = 3 \neq 4$), $\langle 10; 7, 4\rangle$ yes ($s^{-1} = 3$, $u_1 = 8$, $u_2 = 10$, $a^{u_1} = 24$, $y^{u_2} = 24$, $v = 7$), $\langle 10; 3, 8\rangle$ yes ($s^{-1} = 7$, $u_1 = 4$, $u_2 = 10$, $a^{u_1} = 15$, $y^{u_2} = 24$, $v = 3$). **(b)** $\langle 1; 3, 1\rangle$ yes ($s^{-1} = 1$, $u_1 = 1$, $u_2 = 3$, $a^{u_1} = 25$, $y^{u_2} = 22$, $v = 3$), $\langle 1; 9, 1\rangle$ yes ($s^{-1} = 1$, $u_1 = 1$, $u_2 = 9$, $a^{u_1} = 25$, $y^{u_2} = 62$, $v = 9$), $\langle 1; 4, 5\rangle$ no ($s^{-1} = 9$, $u_1 = 9$, $u_2 = 3$, $a^{u_1} = 64$, $y^{u_2} = 22$, $v = 1 \neq 4$). **(c)** $\langle 7; 7, 4\rangle$ yes ($s^{-1} = 3$, $u_1 = 10$, $u_2 = 10$, $a^{u_1} = 59$, $y^{u_2} = 62$, $v = 7$), $\langle 7; 9, 2\rangle$ no ($s^{-1} = 6$, $u_1 = 9$, $u_2 = 10$, $a^{u_1} = 64$, $y^{u_2} = 62$, $v = 4 \neq 9$), $\langle 5; 9, 8\rangle$ yes ($s^{-1} = 7$, $u_1 = 2$, $u_2 = 8$, $a^{u_1} = 22$, $y^{u_2} = 9$, $v = 9$). **(d)** $\langle 6; 9, 5\rangle$ yes ($s^{-1} = 9$, $u_1 = 10$, $u_2 = 4$, $a^{u_1} = 59$, $y^{u_2} = 24$, $v = 9$), $\langle 8; 8, 3\rangle$ no ($s^{-1} = 4$, $u_1 = 10$, $u_2 = 10$, $a^{u_1} = 59$, $y^{u_2} = 64$, $v = 2 \neq 8$), $\langle 7; 4, 7\rangle$ yes ($s^{-1} = 8$, $u_1 = 1$, $u_2 = 10$, $a^{u_1} = 25$, $y^{u_2} = 64$, $v = 4$). **(e)** $\langle 10; 7, 8\rangle$ yes ($s^{-1} = 7$, $u_1 = 4$, $u_2 = 5$, $a^{u_1} = 15$, $y^{u_2} = 25$, $v = 7$), $\langle 7; 7, 3\rangle$ yes ($s^{-1} = 4$, $u_1 = 6$, $u_2 = 6$, $a^{u_1} = 62$, $y^{u_2} = 59$, $v = 7$), $\langle 8; 7, 5\rangle$ no ($s^{-1} = 9$, $u_1 = 6$, $u_2 = 8$, $a^{u_1} = 62$, $y^{u_2} = 62$, $v = 3 \neq 7$).

5.1 **(a)** $d_A = 17$, $d_B = 9$, Alice's hand is γ, Bob's is β; transmitted over the channel are the numbers $(11, 20, 21)$, (11), $(14, 10)$, (17). **(b)** $d_A = 19$, $d_B = 3$, Alice's hand is γ, Bob's is α; transmitted over the channel are the numbers $(17, 19, 5)$, (19), $(15, 19)$, (19). **(c)** $d_A = 7$, $d_B = 15$, Alice's hand is α, Bob's is β; transmitted over the channel are the numbers $(11, 7, 10)$, (7), $(11, 20)$, (21). **(d)** $d_A = 5$, $d_B = 19$, Alice's hand is α, Bob's is β; transmitted over the channel are the numbers $(21, 15, 11)$, (11), $(10, 11)$, (5). **(e)** $d_A = 3$, $d_B = 9$, Alice's hand is α, Bob's is γ; transmitted over the channel are the numbers $(19, 14, 17)$, (19), $(21, 15)$, (15).

5.2 **(a)** $\hat{n} = 103$, $\hat{s} = 52$, $r^{-1} = 24$, bank note is $\langle 11, 58 \rangle$. **(b)** $\hat{n} = 13$, $\hat{s} = 13$, $r^{-1} = 20$, bank note is $\langle 99, 22 \rangle$. **(c)** $\hat{n} = 58$, $\hat{s} = 74$, $r^{-1} = 12$, bank note is $\langle 55, 55 \rangle$. **(d)** $\hat{n} = 37$, $\hat{s} = 46$, $r^{-1} = 8$, bank note is $\langle 44, 11 \rangle$. **(e)** $\hat{n} = 49$, $\hat{s} = 70$, $r^{-1} = 4$, bank note is $\langle 77, 42 \rangle$.

6.1 Only the following points from the list are on the curve: (1,1), (2,1), and (5,8).
6.2 $[2](2,2) = (3,5)$, $[2](4,6) = (1,3)$, $(1,3) + (1,4) = \mathcal{O}$, $(2,2) + (3,2) = (2,5)$, $(3,5) + (5,1) = (3,2)$.

7.1 **(a)** $\bar{e} = 1111001110$. **(b)** $\bar{e} = 1111110101$. **(c)** $\bar{e} = 0001000110$. **(d)** $\bar{e} = 0101011011$. **(e)** $\bar{e} = 0001010001$.

7.2 **(a)** $P_1 \approx 0.002$, $P_2 \approx 0.006$, $P_3 \approx 0.623$, $P_4 \approx 0.051$, $P_5 \approx 0.311$, $P_6 \approx 0.007$. **(b)** $P_1 \approx 0.000$, $P_2 \approx 0.009$, $P_3 \approx 0.000$, $P_4 \approx 0.000$, $P_5 \approx 0.892$, $P_6 \approx 0.099$. **(c)** $P_1 \approx 0.000$, $P_2 \approx 0.697$, $P_3 \approx 0.000$, $P_4 \approx 0.004$, $P_5 \approx 0.299$, $P_6 \approx 0.000$. **(d)** $P_1 \approx 0.003$, $P_2 \approx 0.000$, $P_3 \approx 0.036$, $P_4 \approx 0.000$, $P_5 \approx 0.801$, $P_6 \approx 0.160$. **(e)** $P_1 \approx 0.196$, $P_2 \approx 0.000$, $P_3 \approx 0.001$, $P_4 \approx 0.000$, $P_5 \approx 0.018$, $P_6 \approx 0.785$.

7.3 **(a)** $H \approx 1.16$, $n \approx 6.04$. **(b)** $H \approx 0.52$, $n \approx 2.42$. **(c)** $H \approx 0.9$, $n \approx 3.76$. **(d)** $H \approx 1.08$, $n \approx 5.08$. **(e)** $H \approx 1.16$, $n \approx 6.04$.

7.4 **(a)** $P_1 \approx 0.7$ ($\bar{m} = bcacbcacc$), $P_2 = 0$, $P_3 \approx 0.3$ ($\bar{m} = acbcacbcc$), $P_4 = 0$, $P_5 = 0$, $P_6 = 0$. **(b)** $P_1 = 0$, $P_2 = 0$, $P_3 = 0$, $P_4 \approx 0.21$ ($\bar{m} = bcccaccac$), $P_5 \approx 0.20$ ($\bar{m} = abbbcbbcb$), $P_6 \approx 0.59$ ($\bar{m} = acccbccbc$). **(c)** $P_1 = 0$, $P_2 = 0$, $P_3 = 0$, $P_4 = 1$ ($\bar{m} = ccbcabccb$), $P_5 = 0$, $P_6 = 0$. **(d)** $P_1 = 0$, $P_2 = 0$, $P_3 \approx 0.000$ ($\bar{m} = acbbbbcbb$), $P_4 \approx 1.000$ ($\bar{m} = abccccbcc$), $P_5 = 0$, $P_6 = 0$. **(e)** $P_1 = 0$, $P_2 = 0$, $P_3 \approx 0.009$ ($\bar{m} = bbbcbbbcb$), $P_4 \approx 0.970$ ($\bar{m} = cccbcccbc$), $P_5 = 0$, $P_6 \approx 0.021$ ($\bar{m} = cccacccac$).

Bibliography

Adleman, L. M. (1979). A subexponential algorithm for the discrete logarithm problem with applications to cryptography, in *Proc. IEEE 20th Ann. Symp. on Foundations of Comput. Sci.*, pp. 55–60.

Agrawal, M., Kayal, N., and Saxena, N. (2002). *PRIMES is in P*, http://www.cse.iitk.ac.in/users/manindra.

Aho, A. V., Hopcroft, J. E., and Ulman, J. D. (1974). *The Design and Analysis of Computer Algorithms* (Addison–Wesley, Reading MA).

Alexi, W., Chor, B., Goldreich, O., and Schnorr, C. P. (1988). RSA and Rabin functions: Certain parts are as hard as the whole, *SIAM J. on Comput.*, **17**, pp. 194–209.

Anckaert, B., De Sutter, B., Chanet, D., and De Bosschere, K. (2005). Steganography for executables and code transformation signatures, in *ICISC 2004* (Springer-Verlag, Berlin, Heidelberg), LNCS, **3506**, pp. 431–445.

Anderson, R. J. and Peticolas, F. A. (1998). On the limits of steganography, *Journal of Selected Areas in Communications*, **16**, 4, pp. 474–481.

Aumasson, J.-Ph., Henzen, L., Meier, W., and Phan, R. C.-W. (2010). *SHA-3 Proposal BLAKE*, https://131002.net/blake/.

Aumasson, J.-Ph., Neves, S., Wilcox-O'Hearn, Z., and Winnerlein, Ch. (2019). *BLAKE2 — Fast Secure Hashing*, https://blake2.net/.

Back, A. (2002). *Hashcash — a Denial of Service Counter-Measure*, ftp://sunsite.icm.edu.pl/site/replay.old/programs/hashcash/hashcash.pdf.

Barreto, P. S. L. M. and Rijmen, V. (2008). The Whirlpool Hash Function, https://www.veracrypt.fr/en/Whirlpool.html.

Bayer, D., Haber, S., and Stornetta, W. S. (1993). Improving the efficiency and reliability of digital time-stamping, *Sequences II* (Springer, New York), pp. 329–334.

Beaulieu, R., Shors, D., Smith, J., Treatman-Clark, S., Weeks, B., and Wingers, L. (2013). The SIMON and SPECK families of lightweight block ciphers, *Cryptology ePrint Archive*, 404.

Bellovin, S. M. (2011). Frank Miller: inventor of the one-time pad, *Cryptologia*, **35**, 3, pp. 203–222.

Bently, J. L., Sleator, D. D., Tarjan, R. E., and Wei, V. K. (1986). A locally adaptive data compression scheme, *Comm. ACM*, **29**, pp. 320–330.

Bernstein, D. J. (2008). *ChaCha, a Variant of Salsa20*, https://cr.yp.to/chacha/chacha-20080128.pdf.

Bertoni, G., Daemen, J., Peeters, M., and van Assche, G. (2007). Sponge functions, in *Ecrypt Hash Workshop*, https://keccak.team/files/SpongeFuncti ons.pdf.

Bertoni, G., Daemen, J., Peeters, M., and van Assche, G. (2011). *The Keccak Reference — SHA-3 Competition (Round 3)*, https://keccak.team/files/Keccak-reference-3.0.pdf.

Bierbrauer, J. and Fridrich, J. (2008). Constructing good covering codes for applications in steganography, *Trans. on Data Hiding and Multimedia Security III*, LNCS, **4920** (Springer, Berlin, Heidelberg), pp. 1–22.

Biham, E. and Dunkelman, O. (2007). A framework for iterative hash functions — HAIFA, *Cryptology ePrint Archive*, 278, https://eprint.iacr.org/2007/278.pdf.

Billingsley, P. (1965). *Ergodic Theory and Information* (John Wiley & Sons, New York).

Biryukov, A., Perrin, L., and Udovenko, A. (2016). Reverseengineering the S-box of Streebog, Kuznyechik and STRIBOBr1, *Cryptology ePrint Archive*, 071, https://eprint.iacr.org/2016/071.pdf.

Blahut, R. E. (1987). *Principles and Practice of Information Theory* (Addison–Wesley, Reading, MA).

Blake, I., Seroussi, G., and Smart, N. (1999). *Elliptic Curves in Cryptography* (Cambridge University Press).

Blum, M. (1986). How to prove a theorem so no one else can claim it, in *Proc. Int. Congress of Mathematicians* (Berkeley, CA), pp. 1444–1451.

Borodin, M., Rybkin, A., and Urivskiy, A. (2014). High-speed software implementation of the prospective 128-bit block cipher and Streebog hash-function, in *3rd Workshop on Current Trends in Cryptology (CTCrypt 2014)* (June 5–6, 2014, Moscow, Russia).

Cachin, C. (1998). An information-theoretic model for steganography, in *2nd Information Hiding Workshop*, (Springer-Verlag), LNCS, **1525**, pp. 306–318.

Chaum, D. (1983). Blind signatures for untraceable payments, in *Advances in Cryptology — Proc. Crypto 82*, pp. 199–203.

Chaum, D. (1985). Security without identification: transaction systems to make big brother obsolete, *Comm ACM*, **28**, pp. 1030–1044.

Cormen, T. H., Leiserson, C. E., and Rivest, R. L. (1990). *Introduction to Algorithms* (MIT Press, Cambridge, MA).

Cover, T. M. and Thomas, J. A. (2006). *Elements of Information Theory* (Wiley-Interscience, New York, NY, USA).

Cox, I., Miller, M., Bloom, J., Fridrich, J., and Kalker, T. (2007). *Digital Watermarking and Steganography*, 2nd edn., The Morgan Kaufmann Series in Multimedia Information and Systems (Elsevier).

Crandall, R. (1998). *Some Notes on Steganography*, http://dde.binghamton.edu /download/Crandall_matrix.pdf.

Crowley, P. (2003). *Small Bias in RC4 Experimentally Verified*, http://www.cip hergoth.org/crypto/rc4/.

Csiszar, I. (1998). The method of types, *IEEE Trans. Inform. Theory*, **44**, 6, pp. 2505–2523.

Dabeer, O., Sullivan, K., Madhow, U., Chandrasekaran, S., and Manjunath, B. S. (2004). Detection of hiding in the least significant bit, *IEEE Trans. Signal Processing*, **52**, pp. 346–358.

Daemen, J. and Rijmen, V. (2002) *The Design of Rijndael* (Berlin, Heidelberg: Springer).

Daemen, J. and Rijmen, V. (2003). *The Rijndael Block Cipher*, https://csrc. nist.gov/csrc/media/projects/cryptographic-standards-and-guidelines/doc uments/aes-development/rijndael-ammended.pdf.

Diffie, W. and Hellman, M. E. (1976). New directions in cryptography, *IEEE Trans. Inform. Theory*, **22**, pp. 644–654.

Dobbertin, H., Bosselaers, A., and Preneel, B. (1996). RIPEMD-160: a strength-ened version of RIPEMD, *Proceedings of FSE* (Springer), LNCS, **1039**, pp. 71–82.

Doroshenko, S., Fionov, A., Lubkin, A., Monarev, V., Ryabko, B., and Shokin, Yu. I. (2007). Experimental statistical attacks on block and stream ciphers, in *3nd Russian-German Advanced Research Work-shop on Computational Science and High Performance Computing* (July 23–27, 2007, Novosibirsk, Russia), (Springer), NNFM, **101**, pp. 155–164.

Dwork, C. and Naor, M. (1993). Pricing via processing or combatting junk mail, in *Advances in Cryptology — CRYPTO'92* (Springer-Verlag), LNCS, **740**, pp. 139–147.

ElGamal, T. (1985). A public key cryptosystem and a signature scheme based on discrete logarithms, *IEEE Trans. Inform. Theory*, **31**, pp. 469–472.

Elias, P. (1972). The efficient construction of an unbiased random sequence, *The Annals of Math. Statistics*, **43**, 3, pp. 864–870.

Elias, P. (1987). Interval and recency rank source coding: two on-line adaptive variable-length schemes, *IEEE Trans. Inform. Theory*, **33**, 1, pp. 3–10.

eSTREAM: the ECRYPT Stream Cipher Project, http://www.ecrypt.eu.org/ stream/.

Feistel, H. (1973). Cryptography and computer privacy, *Scientific American*, **228**, pp. 15–23.

Feller, W. (1968). *An Introduction to Probability Theory and its Applications*, 3rd edn. (John Wiley & Sons, New York).

Filler, T., Judas, J., and Fridrich, J. (2011). Minimizing additive distortion in steganography using syndrome-trellis codes, *IEEE Trans. on Info. Forensics and Security*, **6**, 1, pp. 920–935.

FIPS PUB 180-1. (1995). *Secure Hash Standard*, http://csrc.nist.gov/publicati ons/.

FIPS PUB 180-4. (2015). *Secure Hash Standard (SHS)*, http://nvlpubs.nist.gov/nistpubs/FIPS/NIST.FIPS.180-4.pdf.

FIPS PUB 186-1. (1998). *Digital Signature Standard*, http://csrc.nist.gov/publications/.

FIPS PUB 186-4. (2013). *Digital Signature Standard*, https://csrc.nist.gov/publications/detail/fips/186/4/final.

FIPS PUB 197. (2001). *Advanced Encryption Standard*, http://csrc.nist.gov/publications/.

Förster, E. and Rönz, B. (1979). *Methoden der Korrelations und Regressionsanalyse: ein Leitfaden für Ökonomen* (Verlag Die Wirtschaft).

Fridrich, J. and Goljan, M. (2000). Robust hash functions for digital watermarking, in *Proc. of Int. Conf. on Information Technology: Coding and Computing* (IEEE), pp. 173–178.

Fridrich, J. and Goljan, M. (2002). Practical steganalysis — state of the art, *Proc. SPIE*, **4675**, Security and Watermarking of Multimedia Contents, pp. 11–13.

Galand, F. and Kabatiansky, G. (2003). Information hiding by coverings, in *Proc. IEEE Information Theory Workshop*, pp. 151–154.

Gallager, R. G. (1968). *Information Theory and Reliable Communication* (John Wiley & Sons, New York).

Goldreich, O., Micali, S., and Wigderson A. (1987). How to prove all NP statements in zero knowledge and a methodology of cryptographic protocol design, in *Advances in Cryptology — CRYPTO–86* (Springer–Verlag), pp. 171–185.

Goldwasser, S. and Bellare, M. (2008). *Lecture Notes on Cryptography*, http://cseweb.ucsd.edu/~mihir/papers/gb.html.

Guo, J., Jean, J., Leurent, G., Peyrin, Th., and Wang, L. (2014). The usage of counter revisited: second-preimage attack on new Russian standardized hash function, *Cryptology ePrint Archive*, 675, https://eprint.iacr.org/2014/675.pdf.

Haber, S. and Stornetta, W. S. (1991). How to time-stamp a digital document, *Journal of Cryptology*, **3**, 2, pp. 99–111.

Hankerson, D., Menezes, A. J., and Vanstone, S. (2004). *Guide to Elliptic Curve Cryptography*, Springer Professional Computing (New York, NY: Springer).

Holub, V., Fridrich, J., and Denemark, T. (2014). Universal distortion function for steganography in an arbitrary domain, *EURASIP Journal on Information Security*, **1**.

Kahn, D. (1967). *The Codebreakers* (Macmillan Publishing Company, New York).

Katz, J. and Lindell, Y. (2014). *Introduction to Modern Cryptography*, 2nd edn., Cryptography and Network Security (Chapman and Hall / CRC).

Katzenbeisser, S. and Petitcolas, F. A. P. (eds.) (1999). *Information Hiding Techniques for Steganography and Digital Watermarking* (Artech House Print on Demand).

Kendall, M. G. and Stuart, A. (1961) *The Advanced Theory of Statistics*, **2** — *Inference and Relationship* (Charles Griffin & Co., London).

Ker, A. D. and Lubenko, I. (2009). Feature reduction and payload location with WAM steganalysis, *Proc. SPIE*, **7254**, Media Forensics and Security, 72540A, 13 p.

Kerckhoffs, A. (1883). La cryptographie militaire, *J. des Sciences Militaires*, **9**, pp. 161–191.

Kharrazi, M., Sencar, H. T., and Memon, N. (2004). Image steganography: concepts and practice, Lecture Notes Series, Institute for Mathematical Sciences, National University of Singapore.

Kipper, G. (2003). *Investigator's Guide to Steganography* (Auerbach Publications).

Knuth, D. E. (1973). *The Art of Computer Programming, 3 — Sorting and Searching* (Addison–Wesley, Reading, MA).

Knuth, D. E. (1981). *The Art of Computer Programming, 2 — Semi-numerical Algorithms*, 2nd edn. (Addison–Wesley, Reading, MA).

Koblitz, N. (1987). Elliptic curve cryptosystems, *Math. of Comp.*, **48**, pp. 203–209.

Kolchin, V. F., Sevastyanov, B. A., and Chistyakov, V. P. (1978). *Random Allocations* (V. H. Winston, Washington, New York, distributed solely by Halsted Press).

Koo, B., Roh, D., Kim, H., Jung, Y., Lee, D.-G., and Kwon, D. (2017). CHAM: A family of lightweight block ciphers for resource-constrained devices, in *Proc. Int. Conf. on Information Security and Cryptology*, pp. 3–25.

Krichevsky, R. (1993). *Universal Compression and Retrival* (Kluver Academic Publishers).

Lenstra, A. K. and Lenstra, H. W. (eds.) (1993). *The Development of the Number Field Sieve*, LNM, **1554** (Springer-Verlag).

Lysyak, A. (2012). Analysis of gradient statistical attack at block ciphers RC6, MARS, CAST-128, in *Proc. XIII Int. Symposium on Problems of Redundancy in Information and Control Systems*, pp. 44–47.

Lyu, S. and Farid H. (2006). Steganalysis using higher-order image statistics, *IEEE Trans. Inform. Forensics and Security*, **1**, 1, pp. 111–119.

McEliece, R. J. (1984). *The Theory of Information and Coding: A Mathematical Framework for Communication* (Cambridge University Press).

McKay, K. A., Bassham, L., Turan, M. S., and Mouha, N. (2016). Report on lightweight cryptography, *NIST DRAFT NISTIR*.

Menezes, A. (1993) *Elliptic Curve Public Key Cryptosystems* (Kluwer Academic Publishers).

Menezes, A., van Oorschot, P., and Vanstone, S. (1996) *Handbook of Applied Cryptography* (Boca Raton, FL: CRC Press), http://www.cacr.math.uwaterloo.ca/hac/.

Mercle, R. C. (1979). *Secrecy, Authentication, and Public Key Systems*, (UMI Research Press, Ann Arbor, Michigan).

Miller, V. S. (1986). Use of elliptic curves in cryptography, in *Advances in cryptology — CRYPTO'85*, LNCS, **218**, pp. 417–426.

Montgomery, P. L. (1985). Modular multiplication without trial division, *Math. Comp.*, **44**, pp. 519–521.

Moulin, P. and o'Sullivan, J. A. (2003). Information-theoretic analysis of information hiding, *IEEE Trans. Inform. Theory*, **49**, 3, pp. 563–593.

Nakamoto, S. (2008). *Bitcoin: a Peer-to-Peer Electronic Cash System*, https://bitcoin.org/bitcoin.pdf.

Narayanan, A., Bonneau, J., Felten, E., Miller, A., and Goldfeder, S. (2016). *Bitcoin and Cryptocurrency Technologies: a Comprehensive Introduction* (Princeton University Press).

Nechaev, V. I. (1994). Complexity of a determinate algorithm for the discrete logarithm, *Mathematical Notes*, **55**, 2, pp. 165–172.

Nechta, I., Ryabko, B., and Fionov A. (2009). Stealthy steganographic methods for executable files in *XII International Symposium on Problems of Redundancy* (May 26–30, 2009, St.-Petersburg), pp. 191–195.

Needham, R. M. and Schroeder, M. D. (1978). Using encryption for authentication in large networks of computers, *Comm. ACM*, **21**, pp. 993–999.

von Neumann, J. (1951). Various techniques used in connection with random digits, *Monte Carlo Method, Applied Mathematics Series*. 12, pp. 36–38.

Nisan, N. and Ta-Shma, A. (1999). Extracting randomness: a survey and new constructions, *J. Comp. and System Sci.*, **58**, 1, pp. 148–173.

Nisan, N. and Zuckerman, D. (1996). Randomness is linear in space, *J. Comp. and System Sci.*, **52**, 1, pp. 43–52.

Papadimitriou, C. H. (1994). *Computational Complexity* (Addison–Wesley, Reading, MA).

Petitcolas, F. A. P., Anderson, R. J., and Kuhn, M. G. (1999). Information hiding — a survey, *Proceedings of the IEEE*, **7**, 7, pp. 1062–1078.

Plumstead, J. B. (1982). Inferring a sequence produced by a linear congruence, in *Advances in Cryptology — Proc. Crypto 82*, pp. 317–319.

Pohlig, S. C. and Hellman, M. E. (1978). An improved algorithm for computing logarithms over $GF(p)$ and its cryptographic significance, *IEEE Trans. Inform. Theory*, **24**, pp. 106–110.

Preneel, B., Chaum, D., Fumy, W., Jansen, C. J. A., Landrock, P., and Roelofsen, G. (1991). Race integrity primitives evaluation (RIPE): a status report, in *Advances in Cryptology — EUROCRYPT'91*, LNCS, **547** (Springer).

RFC 4491. (2006). *Using the GOST R 34.10-94, GOST R 34.10-2001, and GOST R 34.11-94 Algorithms with the Internet X.509 Public Key Infrastructure Certificate and CRL Profile*, https://tools.ietf.org/html/rfc4491.

RFC 5830. (2010). *GOST 28147-89: Encryption, Decryption, and Message Authentication Code (MAC) Algorithms*, https://tools.ietf.org/html/rfc5830.

RFC 6986. (2013). *GOST R 34.11-2012: Hash Function*, https://tools.ietf.org/html/rfc6986.

RFC 7091. (2013). *GOST R 34.10-2012: Digital Signature Algorithm*, https://tools.ietf.org/html/rfc7091.

RFC 7801. (2016). *GOST R 34.12-2015: Block Cipher "Kuznyechik"*, https://tools.ietf.org/html/rfc7801.

Rivest, R. (1992). *The MD5 Message-Digest Algorithm*, RFC 1321, https://tools .ietf.org/html/rfc1321.

Rivest, R. L., Shamir, A., and Adleman, L. M. (1978). A method for obtaining digital signatures and public-key cryptosystems, *Comm. ACM*, **21**, pp. 120– 126.

Rivest, R. L., Robshaw, M. J. B., Sidney, R., and Yin, Y. L. (1998) *The RC6 Block Cipher*, https://people.csail.mit.edu/rivest/pubs/RRSY98.pdf.

Rivest, R. L. *et al.* (2008). *The MD6 Hash Algorithm*, http://groups.csail.mit.ed u/cis/md6/.

Rosen, K. H. (1992). *Elementary Number Theory and its Applications* (Addison– Wesley, Reading, MA).

Rukhin, A. *et al.* (2001). *A Statistical Test Suite for Random and Pseudorandom Number Generators for Cryptographic Applications*, NIST Special Publication 800-22 Rev 1a, https://tsapps.nist.gov/publication/get_pdf.cfm?pub_ id=906762.

Ryabko, B. Ya. (1980). Information compression by a book stack, *Probl. Inform. Transmission*, **16**, 4, pp. 16–21.

Ryabko, B. Ya. (1998). The fast enumeration of combinatorial objects, *Discrete Math. and Applications*, **10**, 2, pp. 101–119.

Ryabko, B. Ya. (2000). Simply realizable ideal cryptographic system, *Probl. Inform. Transmission*, **36**, 1, pp. 90–95.

Ryabko, B. (2015). The Vernam cipher is robust to small deviations from randomness, *Probl. Inform. Transmission*, **51**, 1, pp. 82–86.

Ryabko, B. (2017). Properties of two Shannon's ciphers, *Designs, Codes and Cryptography*, pp. 1–7.

Ryabko, B. and Fionov, A. (1997). The fast method of randomization, *Probl. Inform. Transmission*, **33**, 3, pp. 3–14.

Ryabko, B. Ya. and Fionov, A. N. (1999a). An efficient method for adaptive arithmetic coding of sources with large alphabets, *Probl. Inform. Transmission*, **35**, 4, pp. 95–108.

Ryabko, B. and Fionov, A. (1999b). Efficient homophonic coding, *IEEE Trans. Inform. Theory*, **45**, 6, pp. 2083–2091.

Ryabko, B. and Fionov, A. (1999c) Fast and space-efficient adaptive arithmetic coding, *Cryptography and Coding*, Springer, LNCS, **1746**, pp. 270–279.

Ryabko, B. and Fionov, A. (2019). Linear hash functions as a means of distortion — rate optimization in data embedding, in *Proc. of the ACM Workshop on Information Hiding and Multimedia Security — IH& MMSec'19* (July 03–05, 2019, Paris, France), pp. 235–238.

Ryabko, B., Fionov, A., Monarev, V., and Shokin, Yu. (2005). Using information theory approach to randomness testing, in *2nd Russian–German Advanced Research Workshop on Computational Science and High Performance Computing* (March 14–16, 2005, Stuttgart, Germany), NNFM, **91** (Springer), pp. 261–272.

Ryabko, B. and Matchikina, E. (2000). Fast and efficient construction of an unbiased random sequence, *IEEE Trans. Inform. Theory*, **46**, 3, pp. 1090–1093.

Ryabko, B. Ya. and Monarev, V. A. (2004). Using information theory approach to randomness testing, *J. Statistical Planning and Inference*, **133**, 1, pp. 95–110.

Ryabko, B. and Pestunov, A. (2004). "Book stack" as a new statistical test for random numbers, *Probl. Inform. Transmission*, **40**, 1, pp. 66–71.

Ryabko, B. and Ryabko, D. (2007). Information-theoretic approach to steganographic systems, in *Proc. IEEE Int. Symposium on Inform. Theory*, (Nice, France), pp. 2461–2464.

Ryabko, B. and Ryabko, D. (2009). Asymptotically optimal perfect steganographic systems, *Probl. Inform. Transmission*, **45**, 2, pp. 184–190.

Ryabko, B. and Ryabko, D. (2011a). Confidence sets in time-series filtering, in *Proc. IEEE Int. Symposium on Inform. Theory* (Saint-Petersburg, Russia).

Ryabko, B. and Ryabko, D. (2011b). Constructing perfect steganographic systems, *Information and Computation*, **209**, pp. 1223–1230.

Ryabko, B. Ya., Stognienko, V. S., and Shokin, Yu. I. (2004). A new test for randomness and its application to some cryptographic problems, *J. Statistical Planning and Inference*, **123**, 2, pp. 365–376.

Schneier, B. (1996). *Applied Cryptography, Second Edition: Protocols, Algorthms, and Source Code in C* (John Wiley & Sons, New York).

Schneier, B. (2000). Self-study course in block cipher cryptanalysis, *Cryptologia*, **24**, 1, pp. 18–34, https://www.schneier.com/academic/paperfiles/paper-self-study.pdf.

Schoof, R. (1995). Counting points on elliptic curves over finite fields, *J. Théorie des Nombres de Bordeaux*, **7**, pp. 219–254.

Shannon, C. E. (1948). A mathematical theory of communication, *Bell System Technical J.*, **27**, pp. 379–423, 623–656.

Shannon, C. E. (1949). Communication theory of secrecy systems, *Bell System Technical J.*, **28**, pp. 656–715.

Shannon, C. E. (1951). Prediction and entropy of printed English, *Bell System Technical J.*, **30**, 1, pp. 50–64.

Sedighi, V., Cogranne, R., and Fridrich, J. (2016). Content-adaptive steganography by minimizing statistical detectability, *IEEE Trans. Inform. Forensics and Security*, **11**, 2, pp. 221–234.

Shih, F. Y. (2017). *Digital Watermarking and Steganography: Fundamentals and Techniques*, 2nd edn. (CRC Press).

Shishkin, V., Dygin, D., Lavrikov, I., Marshalko, G., Rudskoy, V., and Trifonov, D. (2014). Low-weight and hi-end: draft Russian encryption standard, in *Proc. 3rd Workshop on Current Trends in Cryptology (CTCrypt 2014)* (June 5–6, 2014. Moscow, Russia).

Silverman, J., H. (1986). *The Arithmetic of Elliptic Curves*, GTM 106 (Springer-Verlag).

Takahira, R., Tanaka-Ishii, K., and Debowski, L. (2016). Entropy rate estimates for natural language — a new extrapolation of compressed large-scale corpora, *Entropy*, **18**, 10, p. 364.

Thai, T. H., Cogranne, R., and Retraint, F. (2014). Statistical model of quantized DCT coefficients: application in the steganalysis of Jsteg algorithm, *IEEE Trans. Image Processing*, **23**, 5, pp. 1980–1993.

Vernam, G. S. (1926). Cipher printing telegraph systems for secret wire and radio telegraphic communications, *J. American Inst. Electrical Eng.*, **55**, pp. 109–115.

Wang, X., Feng, D., Lai, X., and Yu, H. (2004). Collisions for Hash Functions MD4, MD5, HAVAL-128 and RIPEMD, *Cryptology ePrint Archive*, https://eprint.iacr.org/2004/199.pdf.

Washington, L. C. (2008). *Elliptic Curves: Number Theory and Cryptography*, 2nd edn., Discrete Mathematics and Its Applications (Chapman and Hall / CRC).

Welsh, D. (1988). *Codes and Cryptography* (Claredon Press, Oxford).

Westfeld, A. (2001). High capacity despite better steganalysis (F5-A steganographic algorithm), in *Proc. 4th Int. Workshop on Information Hiding*, LNCS, **2137** (Springer-Verlag, Berlin, Heidelberg), pp. 289–302.

Wu, H. (2004). *The Stream Cipher HC-128*, http://www.ecrypt.eu.org/stream/p3ciphers/hc/hc128_p3.pdf.

Yahya, A. (2018). *Steganography Techniques for Digital Images* (Springer).

Index

Printed in the United States
by Baker & Taylor Publisher Services